The Trouble Is Not In Your Set

A World of Television and a World of Characters
from the 40-year Journal of a Writer

by

Mary Ann Kelly

D1114937

iii

First Edition

Copyright ©1990 by Mary Ann Kelly

The C.J. Krehbiel Company,
3962 Virginia Ave., Cincinnati, Ohio 45227

Library of Congress Catalog Card Number: 90-93268
ISBN 0-9627159-0-5

Printed in the United States of America

Second Printing 1991

"We have all lived through this together,
Excalibur." *Camelot*

The names in this book
have not been changed
to protect the innocent.
Because nobody's innocent!

Acknowledgments

Grateful acknowledgment is made to the following for their contribution of photographs to this book.

NBC — National Broadcasting Company, New York
CBS — Columbia Broadcasting System, New York
ABC — American Broadcasting Company, New York
PBS — Public Broadcast System, Washington, D.C.
WLW-T — Multimedia, Inc., Cincinnati
WCPO-TV — Scripps-Howard, Inc., Cincinnati
WKRC-TV — Great American Broadcasting Company, Cincinnati
WCET — PBS — Cincinnati
John H. Bruning, Vice President Curator - Historian
Gray History of Wireless Museum
Crosley Telecommunications Center, Cincinnati
Cincinnati Post
Kentucky Post
Cincinnati Enquirer
Cincinnati Historical Society
Cincinnati Public Library
Kenton County Public Library
Museum of Broadcasting, New York
Elder Photographics, Cincinnati
Madison Photoworks, Covington
Jack's Camera Center, Cincinnati

Grateful acknowledgment also is made to the individuals and groups listed by the pictures.

Additional acknowledgment is made to the following for research in this book:
The NAB — National Association of Broadcasters
The 4A's — American Association of Advertising Agencies
The National Academy of Television Arts & Sciences
ASCAP — American Society of Composers, Authors & Publishers
AFTRA — American Federation of Television and Radio Artists
Directors Guild of America, Los Angeles
Writers Guild of America, West, Los Angeles

Contents   Page

Chapter 1

Just a Little "Momentum" of the Occasion

We interrupt this book to bring you an important announcement. It was over forty years ago when the army of TV antennas advanced like regiments of rooftop scarecrows across the horizon, a new weather-blown shape on the American skyline. The war of the channel worlds had come! The invasion of the Mars candybar commercials was here! And flying saucer dishwashing products. With reinforcements of situation comedies, quiz shows, cops and robbers, and that spectacular of spectaculars, the weather report with award-winning weather map.

I couldn't decide what to call this enterprise. *Looking Back in Retrospect at What Had Gone Before in Former Days*, or *Just a Little "Momentum" of the Occasion*.

Anyway, I had just finished college with a major in a glorious mixture of journalism, creative writing and broadcasting, which was then only radio. Television had been invented and reinvented for the last hundred years, but it was still just a hazy word which nobody outside New York was sure of. Was it spelled with an "s" or a "z?" And it was just as hazy a picture which somebody remembered viewing at the 1939 World's Fair. Didn't Aunt Clara say she had seen President Roosevelt on a TV monitor at the Fair? Or had President Roosevelt seen Aunt Clara on the monitor? Well, she couldn't remember. But it didn't matter. When television did come, the American people would be ready for it. Or so they thought. Little did they dream what lay ahead, including TV snack tables, folding, at that. TV dinners, frozen, at that. TV rooms, rumpus, at that. TV repairmen, in pairs, at that. VCRs, that didn't work right, at that. Remote controls, not remote and out of control, at that. Antennas, dishpans, cable and satellites, at that.

1

After all, many families had floor-model push-button radios. And didn't one button have the word "TELEVISION" on it? Sure it did! That was all we needed. But nobody stopped to ask where on that floor-model radio would a television picture come in. The fellow who thought of putting the word "TELEVISION" on a radio push-button ought to be first in the docket at a TV War Crimes Trial. But back to me. I was just out of school walking the streets looking for a job. I had decided against pursuing journalism. So had the newspapers for me in Cincinnati and northern Kentucky because of the great reputation I had made with them during my college days.

While going to school, I had been employed part-time in the Associated Press office of the *Cincinnati Enquirer*, which had been one of the early great newspapers in the U.S., dating back to 1841. One of those early publishers, John McLean, was often ranked with Pulitzer, Hearst, Dana and others in the printer's ink hall of fame. He later became publisher of the *Washington Post*. His daughter-in-law, Evelyn Walsh McLean, has been called the "most" Washington hostess of all time. She owned the fabulous forty-four carat Hope Diamond, which in itself was enough to make her famous.

My Pulitzer-prize-winning duties in the illustrious *Enquirer* building Associated Press office included filling the sticky rubber cement pots, throwing away the chewed-on pencils and keeping the starlings from flying in the windows. But my real challenge was plugging in the Associated Press teletype news machines every day. My first big plug-in job came on Sunday morning at the *Enquirer* when there wasn't another living soul in the AP office or the newsroom or anywhere else in the world, it seemed. My mind went blank and I froze at the sight of the giant switchboard of plugs for the teletypes. It was either plug the right machines in the right plugs or plug the wrong machines in the wrong plugs. Which I did. With electrifying results. So electrifying, it was the beginning of the present energy crisis.

The Cradle of the Star-lings

So I bade a tearful printer's-ink-black-eye good-bye to the world of Horace Greeley and Terry Flynn, my AP boss who had let me help him write some of the stories he had sent out on the AP wire. I went to cry on the shoulder of Robert Schulkers in the *Enquirer* office, the reporter who had written the Seckatary Hawkins books we had grown up by on the riverbank. He comforted me by saying, "Don't be discouraged. Nobody makes a smash hit in the first job. Why don't you try chasing the starlings

2

(Photo courtesy of the Author and the Chicago Historical Society)

One of the historic pictures in American business and broadcasting, when "the little giant" Majestic beat the big giants in radio sales, the leading consumer item of the day, as TV sets are today. Everybody said it was like Notre Dame beating Army! Our father's company, Majestic Radio, of which he was executive foreman and production manager of the cabinet division. It was the Majestic deep bass resonance and dynamic transmission that led the way, like stereo today. It was the roaring 20s in Chicago. The radio of radios -- the 1929 Majestic. Duplicate was presented to Edison at the 1929 celebration of the 50th anniversary of his electric light in Dearborn, Michigan, given by Henry Ford and Harvey Firestone. We still have this original radio and it still plays and with the original tubes! (That's John Kelly right top of picture on page 5.)

3

FINALE OF THE
GRIGSBY - GRUNOW COMPANY'S
1928 MAJESTIC DISTRIBUTORS
ANNUAL CONFERENCE
STEVENS - BLACKSTONE HOTELS CHICAGO, ILLINOIS
12 - 12 - 28
"LETS GO FOR 1929"

out the *Times Star* window?" But my elation at his advice didn't last long, because application at the evening paper revealed that it had no starling problem as the morning paper had.

After I literally had pulled out all the plugs in journalism, broadcasting became the victim of my undiscovered talents. Radio, I thought. I'll let radio benefit from my powerful potential. So one day I walked into the big WLW Radio building, the famous Crosley Square in Cincinnati. Known as "The Cradle of the Stars"...where once performed Doris Day, Jane Froman, Red Skelton, Andy Williams, Rosemary Clooney, the McGuire Sisters, Red Foley, Fats Waller, Curt Massey, Gordon MacRae, the Mills Brothers, the Ink Spots, Eddie Albert and many more. I would be at home...among the stars!

Crosley Broadcasting had no opening in any radio jobs occupying the six floors of the building, but would I like a job in the new television office occupying one small room? With no air? Yes, I would. And went in and sat down. A telephone man was installing the phone. After taking one look at the characters beginning to assemble in that office, he probably thought the telephone would be our only communication with the outside world. We would never get television off the ground...or out of that office. And he was almost right. There was many a "hold," at the launching pad before we could report, "Tranquility base here. TV eagle has landed. One small step for man, one large step for the Jolly Green Giant."

Try Not to Get Electrocuted

The first thing I did was call home to report the great news that I was working. "I have a job! It's in television!!" To which my mother replied, "Oh, that's wonderful. But do you think it will ever be here to stay?" To which I replied, "If the word TELEVISION is on push-buttons on radios, it's bound to be here to stay someday." Then a typical mother would have said, "I'm so proud of you!" But, typical of our mother, she said, "Try not to get electrocuted."

And wouldn't my father have been proud, I thought, recalling the days of Majestic Radio and broadcasting in Chicago twenty years before in our childhood. On my office desk I placed the photo of Edison, which the great inventor's staff had given our father as production manager of Majestic after a consultation on a radio receiver. And hung the keepsake watch given to our father by the famous owners of Majestic Radio, Grigsby-Grunow. And pasted up a picture of Lee De Forest, whom I had met as a child.

6

WLW Television was to go on the air in two days. The engineers were frantically working on the preparations for the debut of one of the first TV stations in the country. WLW TV officially was going on the air, all right. But what was going on the screen?! That, we found out, was up to us...the new, naive, know-nothing little group about to assemble in that phone booth office. While waiting for the rest of the victims to arrive, I decided to borrow a book on the history of broadcasting (so far!) and (so good!) from J. R. Duncan, one of the stalwart engineers upon whose shoulders the new TV station feat was resting.

If what was past was going to be prologue, we've got to know how this all began, I resolved. So I found that KDKA, Pittsburgh, was the first official U.S. radio station back in 1920 with the Harding-Cox presidential election returns. And the first commercial was a short credit given to a music store in Wilkinsburg, Pennsylvania, for use of its recordings by Dr. Frank Conrad in his garage experimental forerunner station of Westinghouse's KDKA. But men had been toying with broadcasting stations since KQW in San Jose, California, back in 1909. And with communications leading to radio and television ages before that:

350 B.C. — Aristotle in ancient Greece discovers matter is composed of atoms, invisible and indivisible.

1752 — Benjamin Franklin brings down the sky in a storm with his kite and key.

1818 — Baron Berzelius, Swedish scientist, discovers selenium metal that generates electrical current when light is flashed on it, the roots of TV.

1831 — Michael Faraday establishes the connection between magnetism and electricity and formulates laws of electromagnetic induction in London, leading to the invention of the telegraph and telephone.

1835 — Morse invents electromagnetic telegraph, with historic message "What hath God wrought?" from the old Supreme Court Chamber in Washington, D.C., all the way to Baltimore in 1844.

1865 — James Maxwell, Scottish physicist, establishes concept of ether waves in the atmosphere. He unifies the three – electricity, magnetism, light — into the electromagnetic spectrum.

1876 — Alexander Graham Bell in his Boston laboratory invents the telephone after discovering he could hear a clock spring over a wire. Accident in lab unintentionally produces first message by Bell over phone wire, "Come here, Mr. Watson. I want you!"

1876 — Thomas Alva Edison notes strange electrical phenomenon in atmosphere, which he called etheric force, and makes electric current pass through space from a burning filament to a metal plate.

1883 — Berlin's Paul Nipkow invents the spiral scanning disc, known as the electrical telescope, the first to separate images into transmittable

THE PIONEERS

DR. V. K. ZWORYKIN invented the iconoscope, the electronic eye for scanning pictures in 1923. Another Russian, Boris Rosing, patented the cathode-ray picture tube still used today.

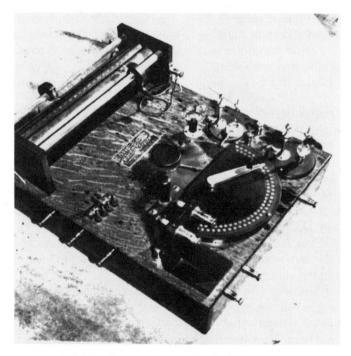

MARCONI invented the wireless in the garden of his father's Italian villa in 1895. And in 1901 sent the first trans-Atlantic message. Shown here in 1906 is the Clark Wireless Receiver designed by Thomas Clark of Detroit, which he sold mostly for Army and Navy wireless equipment. (Gray History of Wireless Museum--Crosley Telecommunications Center)

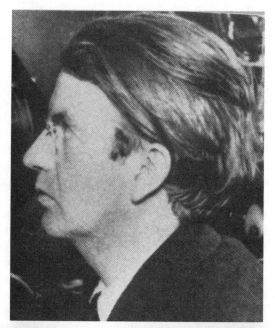

JOHN LOGIE BAIRD, British pioneer attempted trans-Atlantic television from facilities at Coulsdon, England, in 1927. American Philo Farnsworth unveiled the first practical electronic image dissector.

(Photo from Lee DeForest Laboratory, New York).
LEE DeFOREST—the father of radio, who perfected the audion tube, which permitted the transmission of voice as well as signals and sounds. In England, early TV cameramen wore white linen dusters, much like this, and looked as if they were the Jesse James gang.

9

pieces. It was descendant of this disc that transmitted Felix the Cat in 1930.

1886 — Heinrich Hertz demonstrates electromagnetic waves in Bonn, Germany.

1895 — Marconi invents the wireless telegraph in his father's Italian villa gardens. Six years later, sends first trans-Atlantic message.

1900 — Discovery that human voice can be carried over radio by attaching a telephone receiver to a wireless telegraph, perfected by Ernst Alexanderson.

1904 — Perfection of the vacuum radio tube, the soul of modern radio, by Englishman J. Ambrose Fleming; followed by the audion tube of Lee De Forest, the father of radio, permitting the transmission of voice in addition to signals and sounds.

1923 — Invention of the iconoscope, a TV camera tube simulating the human eye, by Russian Vladimar Zworykin..and the cathode ray tube in 1929 for TV sets by Russia's Boris Rosing...forming the combined nucleus of the TV operating system. A far cry from the time an ad appeared in the *London Times* seeking help on "Seeing by wireless invention"...and nobody replied!

1925 — The first actual transmission of television with the first moving silhouette pictures over wire by Charles Jenkins in Washington, D.C., showing a windmill five miles away; and at the same time by Stotchman John Baird in London with a Maltese cross, the beginning of the world's first TV station with radio shadowgraphs.

1927 — First wireless television images transmitted by Philo Farnsworth in the U.S. with the test pattern of a dollar sign (!) in San Francisco.

Other distinguished names along the way to voices and visions of TV included Reginald Fessenden, Dennis Redmond, Irving Languir, Manfred VonArdenne, Alexander Bain, Julius Plucker, William Sawyer, Alexander Popov, Karl Ferdinand Braun, A. A. Campbell-Swinton, George R. Carey, Joseph May, and a cast of thousands.

But one thing they all had in common. They did with mechanical devices what the French Impressionists did with their paintings: decompose light into small luminous dots. "Oh, to work with light!" was their dream fulfilled.

Some tidbits of information from *The Gray History of Wireless Museum* booklet which tells all!...

"The advances in electricity around 1745 led to the conviction that electricity was a fluid and could be stored in a bottle! One day while trying to pour the electric charge from the static machine into the jar, Professor Musschenbrook at Leyden University got the shock of his life, discovering the principle of the condenser.

A CAT! A DOG! A MOUSE! Felix, Nipper and Mickey! They're the ones that launched the sound and the sight of television. Felix stood on an NBC turntable back in the late 1920s and sent his image as far as Kansas. He was replaced by Mickey Mouse when his little tired papier-maché body wore out! And it was Nipper, a stray rescued from the pound, that looked into Thomas Edison's gramaphone and heard his master's voice.

11

"In 1879 Thomas Edison built a meter for measuring electric current. Called an Electro-meter, it was based on Faraday's discovery that the transfer of metal from one place to another in an electrolytic bath was proportional to the current.

"Lee De Forest noticed in 1900 a phenomenon in which the light in a Welsbach gas burner was affected by the operation of an induction coil nearby. This led to an interest in the influence of electromagnetic waves, wireless signals, on heated gas, and eventually led to the discovery of the three element vacuum tube.

"The J. J. Duck Company catalog was the last word in early radio and electrical supplies. They used as their symbol a duck dipping his head into water, which actually was the equivalent of Ben Franklin going out in a storm with a kite and a key attached! He could have gotten electrocuted! Both Ben and the ugly duckling. And turned into a beautiful swan with wings in the swan lake in the sky! But a wireless operator on a ship lying at the dock in Port Arthur, Texas, reported that he copied spark signals from New York, 1056 miles away.

"Nathaniel Baldwin, a devout Mormon, designed and built the first Baldwin headphones on his kitchen table in Salt Lake City. He sent a sample pair packed in a large baking powder can to the U. S. Navy for testing, which proved them to be twice as sensitive as any other make.

"The Paragon regenerative receiver was designed by 'Paragon Paul' Godley. It became historic when it was used by Godley in Ardrossan, Scotland, to copy the first short trans-Atlantic signals from amateur station IBCG in Connecticut on December 12, 1921. Marconi had received his famous England-to-Newfoundland letter "s" signals years before on December 12, 1901. Tom Birch used the receiver to copy IBCG's historic signals in Cincinnati. But the first regenerative receiver manufactured was a Paragon in 1915. A Paragon transmitter was used on the first transcontinental contact.

"In 1877, Emile Berliner applied for a patent on a hard carbon, loose contact telephone transmitter. An adaptation of this crude telephone microphone was used in early radio telephone. Powel Crosley bought a 500-watt broadcast transmitter in 1923 to obtain this type of microphone, which had been perfected by them.

"Early radio broadcasting had to use crude, insensitive, poor quality telephone dispatcher's microphones. To make up for low sensitivity, someone mounted a telephone microphone on the small end of a phonograph horn. In the early 1920s it was a common sight to see a broadcast performer with his head partway in the bell of a large phonograph horn!

"The electric waves of Maxwell and Hertz have carried

AWA-ANTIQUE WIRELESS ASSOCIATION OF NEW YORK at Holcomb with Bruce Kelly, early curator of the museum. "What hath God wrought?" remains to be seen...on TV! (Gray History of Wireless Museum-Crosley Telecommunications Center)

GRAY MATTER in abundance, putting their heads together, Crosley's brilliant master engineer, R.J.Rockwell (r) and wireless expert, Jack Gray, custodian of the Gray History of Wireless Museum, formerly at Mason, Ohio, now at the WCET-TV studios, 2333 Central Parkway, Cincinnati. (Gray History of Wireless Museum-Crosley Telecommunications Center)

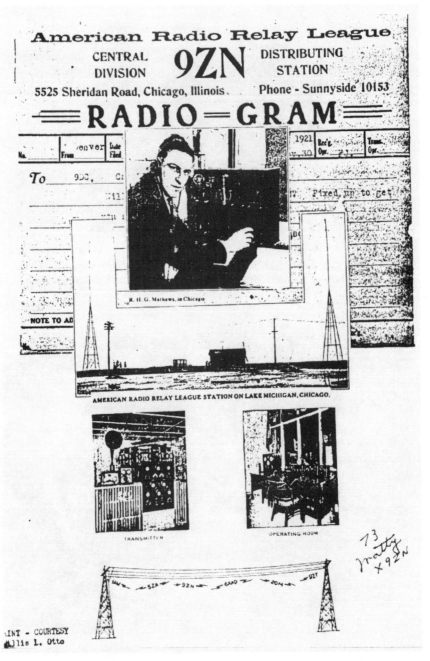

THEY NEVER GOT THEIR WIRES CROSSED - Everything was the new wireless and transmitting. Here in Chicago in 1921, bringing in the sounds out of the blue, across Lake Michigan. (Gray History of Wireless Museum-Crosley Telecommunications Center)

communications to the moon and back. Impulses from space ships circling the moon, over 200,000 miles distant, have been transmitted to earth and translated into pictures. Cloud pictures of the earth predicting weather are sent back daily from weather satellites. Perfect color pictures of astronauts returning to the Pacific or a Peace Conference in Paris are bounced off a communications satellite high above the world. Technological communication has made tremendous advances in the years since Marconi sent and received his first wireless signals from his father's estate near Bologna, Italy."

So says *The Gray History of Wireless Museum* at the Crosley Telecommunications Center, Cincinnati. And they surely ought to know!

"You've come a long way, Baby..."

So television had come a long way, Baby, from the lone Londoner transmitting pictures in his attic to a crystal ball sending out a picture the size of a postage stamp...to a diabolical object that would be the ruination of the nation...to what to do 'til the TV repairman comes....to Jackie Gleason breaking his leg before 20 million people and crawling off the stage.

But, alas, a few more statistics for your viewing pleasure...radio firsts and television firsts:

1909 — KQW, San Jose, California, experimental broadcasts, with schedule begun in 1912.

1916 — A station in New Rochelle, New York, with music broadcasts.

1919 — KQV, Pittsburgh, among first commercial stations.

1920 — WWJ, Detroit, miscellaneous broadcasting, two months before KDKA.

1920 — KDKA with Cox-Harding election returns for the presidency; the first licensed station in the U.S., in Pittsburgh; Westinghouse under Dr. Frank Conrad. First broadcast commercial was the credit given by Conrad to a Hamilton Music Store in Wilkinsburg, Pennsylvania, for use of their records on his broadcast in his garage before KDKA was officially established.

1920 — WRR, Dallas; WKY, Oklahoma City; KRKO, Everett, Washington; KTW, Seattle; KNX, Los Angeles; KLZ, Denver.

1921 — The Dempsey-Carpenter fight, the first fight broadcast, July 2, in Jersey City.

1921 — First world series on KDKA, which established other stations where Westinghouse had plants in East Springfield, Massachusetts, KBZ; KYW, Chicago; WJZ, Newark.

1922 — One of first commercially sponsored programs, WEAF, New York, by AT&T.

1921 — Powel Crosley, Jr., builds "radiophone" in his attic, the beginning of WLW Radio, Cincinnati, and the famous Crosley radio-TV empire.

1922 — WCPO; 1923 — WKRC; 1929 — WCKY — all in Cincinnati.

1924 — General Electric engineers played first baseball game under lights at Lynn, Mass., but game not broadcast.

1923 — First "network" consisting of WEAF, New York; WCAP, Washington, D.C.; WJAR, Providence, Rhode Island.

1926 — First official network, NBC, with 19 stations, with WEAF, New York, as key station purchased from AT&T by RCA, under David Sarnoff.

1927 — First coast-to-coast broadcast, Rose Bowl football game, from Pasadena. The Rose bowl was also the first coast-to-coast color telecast twenty-five years later in 1952, also by NBC.

1929 — CBS founded by William S. Paley with 47 stations, with WABC (now WCBS) as key station. Founded 1934, the Mutual Broadcasting system; 1942, the ABC Network from the old Blue Network of NBC. Then along came television as we know it today.

1936 — TV officially launched by NBC in the U.S. and the BBC in England, with a hymn to the "telly:" "A mighty maze of mystic magic rays is all about us in the blue..." Although Germany did try to televise the 1936 Olympics, with France and Russia close behind in the early TV channel swim with only a few hundred sets in these countries. The BBC threw out the early Baird mechanical system and replaced it with the electronic system, televising the coronation of George VI, which they believed their "crowning" achievement!

1939 — Franklin Roosevelt and the New York World's Fair televised by NBC, best remembered in the early days, and launched the first regularly scheduled TV even though still only a few hundred sets in New York.

1939 — British abruptly stop television for the war effort and cut it off right in the middle of a Mickey Mouse cartoon!

1939 — First televised sports event in the United States, a 10-inning Princeton-Columbia baseball game, May 17, on NBC from Baker Field, New York.

He Had the Idea for Broadcasting

Among the unsung heroes of who began it all, there remains the man who died poor in 1928 down in Calloway County, Kentucky. He is Nathan Stubblefield. One day he came up with the idea of broadcasting while sitting on his front porch looking at the stump of a tree in his front

THE CONCEPT OF BROADCASTING goes way back to this man, Nathan Stubblefield, down in Murray, Kentucky. He conceived the idea when transmitting his voice to a stump in his front yard. Nobody would listen to the idea of talking to more than one person at a time, as on the telephone. Now the world listens and looks to his idea around the world and the universe and beyond the stars in the great galaxy of communications.

yard. That was back in 1885, twenty years before Marconi invented wireless telegraphy. He thought of broadcasting as far as the tree stump, and called it the "wireless telephone," inventing his own batteries, transmitter, antenna, etc.

Everybody thought he was nuts! They laughed and said, "Who in the world would want to talk and have people listen in?" They preferred the telephone with private person-to-person conversation.

Now a museum is set up to his memory at Murray State College in Murray, Kentucky. The man who invented broadcasting, and only a tree stump would listen, now is acknowledged in the record books as the true inventor of the idea of broadcasting.

In the 1920s in Chicago, my father got his job as production manager and executive foreman of the cabinet division of Majestic Radio because he knew of Stubblefield and the idea of broadcasting was born in Kentucky!

His Greatest Invention Was Invention

Thomas Alva Edison was known as the man who invented inventing.

He was responsible for the electric light, the phonograph, the motion picture camera, the stock market ticker...and over one thousand other ideas for patents. He either came up with the idea himself or made other people's ideas work with his own ideas. The mother of the humorist-writer James Thurber worried that electricity was leaking from all the outlets in their early 1900s Ohio home, and was doing strange things to her family! And strange things Edison's inventions did to the rest of the world, like turning night into day, like preserving a voice for all time, like making a picture move on film, like making each image of each person, place or thing it captured — immortal.

Edison began as a telegrapher, a lightning slinger. And that he was. He could send messages so fast that the receivers on the other end of the line complained they couldn't pick them up. From a poor telegrapher in Louisville in 1869, who couldn't afford a pair of socks, to the man who was received triumphantly in Paris by Eiffel, Gounod, Pasteur, Edison had arrived. The doctors back in his hometown of Milan, Ohio, wouldn't know him now. He was once the little boy who was brought to them by his parents because he couldn't talk until he was five years old, and he had such a big head they thought surely something was wrong with him. The neighbors wondered what would become of him. "Sure feel sorry for the Edisons," they would say. "Having a child like that. Probably grow up to be retarded. Might have to put him away."

18

19

After taking him as a child to doctor after doctor, who all declared in mile-long medical terms, each with a second opinion, what was wrong with him, they finally agreed with one old country doctor who declared, "The only reason he has such a big head is because he has too many brains!" And, sure enough, he was right. Crammed in that big head on that little body were his thousand inventions, including the one which his head mysteriously, magnificently was shaped like, the light bulb!

So much for the first working incandescent lamp, for which the British also claimed credit. They said their arch of light was the first electric light. But it didn't work! Well, anyway, now the man who perfected the telegraph, really invented the electric light, and was a telegrapher in Cincinnati the night LIncoln was shot, turned his attention to the movies. Hooray for Hollywood!

The history of the movies and photography goes 'way back to the 1830s in France when a Frenchman took a photo of his backyard. This simple photograph required an all-day exposure. In 1833 Fox-Talbot, an Englishman, took a picture of a window inside his house in an exposure of one hour. Then came Louis Daguerre and the daguerreotype in 1840. But the French claim they invented moving pictures when Marey showed a bird in flight, while the Englishman in Wilshire showed a bullet in flight. Meanwhile, back at the ranch in California, an Englishman, Muybridge, showed a horse with a rider. Whatever happened to Freise-Greene, rarely given credit for photographing a man walking down the street? He devoted his life to the search for the motion picture in England.

Then along came Edison. Inventor Muybridge had come up with the forerunner of the movies and took his invention to Edison, who perfected it with George Eastman, and the use of celluloid film. Edison's first movie was "The Sneeze." No more and no less. He used his assistant as the actor for this Cecil B. De Mille spectacular. He charged 1¢ to see it in a kinetoscope arcade, which he had also invented. This was in 1889. Meanwhile the French brothers Lumiere thought they, too, had invented the motion picture, showing people leaving a factory. Then, in 1903, along came *The Great Train Robbery*, and Edison was in business and so was everybody else, trying to copy it.

Rounding out the threesome which made TV possible, the motion picture camera, the electric light, the phonograph recording, Edison invents your hit parade! The father of General Electric started out with a recording of "Mary had a little lamb." That was way back in 1877 in his Menlo Park, New Jersey, laboratory. Now over 100 years later, from tinfoil wrapped around a brass cylinder to elaborate electronic sound systems, Edison would never recognize his original invention of a talking machine.

(Photos from National Archives, Washington, D.C. and the U.S. Department of the Interior, National Park Service, Edison National Historic Site, West Orange, New Jersey)

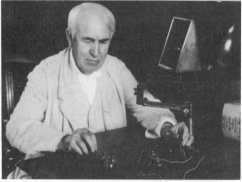

THOMAS EDISON - All he did was give the world the electric light, the phonograph, the motion picture camera, the perfected telegraph and 1200 other inventions.

1878 - With his tinfoil phonograph invention at Matthew Brady's Photo Studio, Washington, D.C. Could he ever have dreamed that Bing Crosby's recording of "White Christmas" alone would sell 40 million copies?

Early 1900s - With his perfected light invention, the incandescent lamp, and his motion picture camera invention in his laboratory at West Orange, New Jersey. And could he ever have dreamed that 80 million people would be watching one movie on TV?

1920 - With his first love and life-long interest, the telegraph, which he perfected, in his library at West Orange, New Jersey.

He had achieved what alchemists had tried for centuries, to turn metal into gold. But as Sullivan of Gilbert and Sullivan fame said, "I am astonished and somewhat terrified at the result, astonished at the wonderful power you have developed and terrified at the thought that so much hideous and bad music may be put on record forever!" On record forever...on record forever...on record...

From his Black Maria movie studio, the first one in the United States, to a machine by which he could communicate with the dead, Edison attempted it all. And mostly with great success, except of course that machine to contact the great beyond. It was greatly beyond even him.

Edison based all his inventions on the belief that "For every problem the Lord has made, He has also made a solution. And it's up to us to find it."

When he died in 1931, he still believed that great-distance TV operation was impossible because of the curvature of the earth's surface. This was before the ionized layer above the earth's atmosphere was discovered.

After he died, his chair was nailed to the floor and everything else left undisturbed in his laboratory at West Orange, New Jersey. And the clock had mysteriously stopped at the moment of his death — 3:24, October 18, 1931.

The Message Heard Was "S" for Sarnoff

Then the legendary Brig. Gen. David Sarnoff came along to RCA and NBC (formed in 1926) and really put the show on the road, beginning with none other than Felix the Cat on a moving turntable. The Russian boy immigrant who went to work in this strange new country when he was thirteen and wound up with over two dozen honorary degrees, Sarnoff was truly the father of television. The lone lad in one of the most dramatic episodes in communications who picked up the message of the sinking of the *Titanic* on his crude radio-set atop Wanamaker's department store. President Taft ordered all other wireless stations along the East Coast off the air so the young man of twenty-one could get the information on the sinking and the survivors over a grueling seventy-hour stretch at the radio receiver. The information included the fact that John Jacob Astor was among the 1500 who perished.

"The real purpose in life is to be able to express the forces within you," Sarnoff said. And what forces they were for this one man. He

BRIG. GEN. DAVID SARNOFF, the one man more than anybody else responsible for television in this country through NBC and RCA.

received citations from two presidents, the Legion of Merit from President Roosevelt and Medal of Merit from President Truman. Born in a village in rural Russia, Sarnoff never graduated from high school, yet he received twenty-four honorary Ph.D.'s among his awards. He also was made a Commander of the French Legion of Honor and praised for his assistance to the French resistance during the War. He served under General Eisenhower at SHAEF headquarters in Europe. He also received decorations from France, Israel, Italy, Japan, Luxembourg, Poland and the United Nations, to name a few.

Then, in 1956, he passed the torch on to his son, Robert, who also ranked at the top with his list of awards and accomplishments. "When Gugielmo Marconi plucked three barely audible dots out of the electric air with a wind-tossed box-kite holding a thin wire antenna aloft in a stormy sky at St. John's, Newfoundland, that December morning in 1901, it might have been prophetic that the signal flashed across the sea from England's coast of Cornwall was the letter "S". Yes, "S" for Sarnoff, as NBC put it so eloquently.

Other presidents of NBC with whom we worked were the indomitable Pat Weaver and Julian Goodman. Pat believed that shows, like *Today* which he pioneered, should be an extension of the news, not the book-plugging, song-plugging, movie-plugging, program-plugging which it is today. Julian Goodman was quite a storyteller and told us that when he was named president of NBC, he called his father in Tennessee to tell him the news. He invited his father to New York for the installation ceremony, but his father declined, saying, "I can't come up there on that day because there's going to be a mule sale here."

Some TV firsts of NBC were:

1930 — NBC took over TV experimental station W2XBS which was begun in 1928 by RCA.

1930 — NBC began experimental telecasts from transmitter atop the Empire State Building.

1931 — Introduction of the iconoscope, invented earlier by Dr. V. K. Zworykin, for RCA through NBC, one of the all-time great TV inventions.

1939 — NBC inaugurated first regular TV program service in the U.S. at the World's Fair with speech by President Franklin D. Roosevelt.

1939 — First major boxing match on TV, Nova-Baer, from Yankee Stadium, televised by NBC.

1939 — First scenes from a Broadway play, *Susan and God*, from NBC Studio.

1939 — First pro baseball game on TV, Brooklyn vs. Cincinnati, from Ebbets Field on NBC.

1939 — First tennis championship matches on TV, Eastern Grass Court

DAVID SARNOFF, as a boy atop Wanamaker's Department Store in New York, sits at his receiving set where he picked up the radio message that the *Titanic* was sinking in 1912. Young Sarnoff stayed at his post an uninterrupted seventy-two hours, while the President of the United States ordered all other stations off the air so Sarnoff could maintain the contact with the sinking ship.

(Photos courtesy NBC, New York).
NBC AND SARNOFF officially launched television in the United States at the opening of the New York World's Fair in 1939. It wasn't until 1948 that TV really got going. 19 TV stations in early 1948 and about 186,000 sets. By the end of that year there were twice as many stations and 1,000,000 sets.

Tourney, Rye, N.Y., on NBC.

1939 — First movie premier, *Gone with the Wind*, at Capitol Theatre, N.Y., on NBC.

1940 — First pro hockey game on TV, Canadians vs. Rangers, from Madison Square Garden on NBC.

1940 — First national political convention on TV (Republican), from Philadelphia, on NBC.

1948 — Interrupted by World War II, TV got its next big splurge with the beginning of its first stations, including WLW-T, Cincinnati.

Paley and CBS

Columbia Broadcasting System, formed in 1929, led the way in experimental television with young tobacco fortune heir, William S. Paley. And Dr. Allen DuMont was the jack of all TV trades with sets, shows and service.

And now a brief message from the sponsor. The first TV commercial was the Bulova Watch time signal on New York's WNBT, July 1, 1941.

The early days of radio are described in Bill Paley's book and CBS' association with Majestic, Grigsby-Grunow Company, of which my father was production manager and executive foreman of the cabinet division.

"...finding the advertisers who would pay for it all. All were equally important and they had to mesh at the same time and the same place. There were more ways than one, I learned, to put a show together and to get it on the air.

"The best way, of course, was to have sponsors come to CBS with plenty of money and willingness to accept every proposal I put to them. We even had a few like that. Foremost among them was the Grigsby-Grunow Company, the largest manufacturer of radio sets in America. With about a quarter of the whole market, they sold about one million Majestic radio sets in1929 and they loved CBS because they hated RCA. The Radio Corporation of America was their chief competitor, with whom they were continually battling in the courts over patent rights. They first sponsored *Majestic's Two Black Crows,* a very popular blackface comedy much like *Amos 'n' Andy* of later years. And they sponsored the *Majestic Theater of the Air*, a fine program which introduced to radio listeners such outstanding personalities as Ruth Ettig, Fanny Brice, Edgar Guest, Dolores Del Rio, Helen Morgan and several

(Photo courtesy CBS, New York)
WM. S. PALEY—Chief Executive Officer of CBS for over half a century. The life story
of the Columbia Broadcasting System is the life story of Bill Paley. The eye of CBS
was the eye of radio and television..

contemporary American composers, including one named George Gershwin at the piano. And the Majestic people were enthusiastic enough to sponsor the *American School of the Air*, a half-hour educational program that went out on the air twice a week and later five times a week. It was designed to be used in classrooms across the country as an educational vehicle and an aid to teachers. Majestic Radio was our first big sponsor, buying just about everything I proposed, with three or four shows running at the same time. They were very important to CBS in the beginning, a lifesaver, and there were other radio manufacturers who came to CBS because they were in competition with RCA."'

Paley had some great stories to tell, like the time he hired Caruso's Italian chef to cook for Toscanini's party, not knowing that Toscanini had sworn off Italian food.

The performers he discovered or gave their big break to were later the superstars. He heard Bing Crosby on a recording singing "I Surrender Dear" while jogging around the deck of a ship on the way to Europe. He also brought Kate Smith, Will Rogers, Frank Sinatra, Paul Whiteman to radio. And lured Major Bowes, Lux Radio Theatre, and Jack Benny away from NBC. The Mills Brothers wandered into CBS after hitchhiking from Cincinnati to New York.

WKRC Cincinnati was one of the CBS sixteen affiliated in 1928. WCAU-TV, Philadelphia, was the first in CBS TV network in 1948. And the first Ed Sullivan Show went on the air June 20, 1948.

One of the other powerhouses in broadcasting who helped get all this accomplished as the president of CBS from 1946 to 1972 was Frank Stanton.

As E. B. White first said, "I think television should be a visual counterpart to the literary essay, should arouse our dreams, satisfy our hunger for beauty, take us on journeys, enable us to participate in events, present great drama and music, be our Lyceum, our Chautauqua, our Minsky's, and our Camelot."

He must have been envisioning PBS!

But "This is London" said it best. Edward R. Murrow: "This instrument can teach; it can illuminate; yes, it can even inspire. But it can do so only to the extent that humans are determined to use it to those ends. Otherwise, it is merely wires and lights in a box."

And No Air?

But all this was taking place in New York in the 1930s. TV hadn't come cross-country by the late 1940s. There we were in an empty office with a TV station ready to go on the air commercially in two days...and no network shows through yet from either coast, no coaxial cable, no films, no air, no nothing. It had to be all live origination from Cincinnati! So the play began to take shape. The TV players began to assemble to start WLW Television on the air, one of the first TV stations in the U.S. and the beginning of the Crosley/AVCO television group. Of all the Jules Verne predictions and elaborate electronic preparations for television, nobody could have visualized the cast of characters that would strut their hour upon the 21-inch TV stage...and even more so, the characters that would appear behind the scenes.

Bill McCluskey was the first to walk in the empty TV office. One of the finest people in the business. VP and Director of Client Services. He had been with the *National Barn Dance* in Chicago and was a specialist in hillbilly talent, who have now taken over the music field with country and western songs and style, including Johnny Cash, Loretta Lynn, Ernie Ford, Charlie Pride, Roy Clark, Glen Campbell, Eddie Arnold, and the rest. Bill is truly a bonnie man with his slight Scotch brogue. He said, "Hi, kid! Guess we're in television!" But I kept screaming, "I was hired to be the first TV writer, not the contact with the hillbillies!" Some of whom could hardly read or write. And I had to pin a note on them and head them towards Nashville!

"Guess we are in TV," I replied. "But what is it?" I asked, afraid of my first full-time job, especially in a brand new industry.

"I don't know what it is!" Bill laughed. "I've never seen it!"

"Neither have I, so that makes two of us, anyway," I laughed too.

"What are you reading there?" Bill asked.

"The history of broadcasting...radio and television so far."

"Are we in there?" he joked.

"Not yet, but...but.."

"But if we don't get this station on the air, we're going to be in San Quentin," Bill proclaimed. "However, as Henry Ford said, he sings tenor who sings tenor!"

TV or Not TV - That Was the Question

Being a former professional singer, Bill then started to sing a song about the glories of television to come, making up his Scotch version as he went along. "By yon bonnie banks..and by yon bonnie..."

But somebody interrupted in the middle of the Loch Ness Monster. It was Milton F. (Chick) Allison. A two-fisted fireball of a sales executive from Philadelphia, who could sell Whistler's mother a front view

BILL McCLUSKEY - The Scotch-Irishman with a brogue and a twinkle in his eye. One I met over 40 years ago at WLW-T, as we crowded in that one office labeled "television," like the scene from the Marx Brothers movie of a jam of people in a ship's stateroom. One of the finest and most respected vice-presidents in the business. Recent Grand Marshall of Cincinnati's St. Patrick's Day Parade, with his wife Millie, former Girl of the Golden West, at his side. He "led the parade" at WLW-T and saw that it marched to a different drummer.

8 x 10 head-shot glossy picture. Of herself. He later went with CBS in New York.

"Okay, knock it off, Caruso. And let's get this television station on the air," Chick ordered.

"But," Bill replied, "I'm not Caruso. I'm Bobbie Burns, bringing a breath of heather to this..."

"I don't care who the hell you are!" Chick shouted. "Just stop singing and start...start...start...I don't know..where do we start?"

Cue for the entrance of Rikel Kent. A former Shakespearean actor with Falstaff white hair and Elsinore lordly manner. The noble thespian of our group. And pioneer radio producer. He had helped create and produce the first soap operas in the United States, which originated at WLW Radio in Cincinnati for Procter & Gamble. *Ma Perkins* and many others. But his great love was the stage. So as Bill McCluskey sang...and Chick raved...Rikel recited the Bard. He stood in the doorway of our two-by-four office, with telephone and no air, making his grand entrance.

"TV or not TV, that is the question. Whether 'tis nobler in the mind to suffer the arrows and slings of outrageous radio...or to sleep...perchance to dream...and in that sleep...ah, there's the rub...Minitrub..."

"Oh, shut up!" yelled Chick. "Who the devil are you?"

"I, my good man," Rikel gallantly replied, "am Lord Hamlet. Remember: 'To thine own self be true...and it must follow, as the night the day, thou canst not then be false to any man...'"

"Then I would thank thee to come in and shut thouself up," recited Chick.

Next to cross the television threshold was easy-going Red Thornburg, a fine sports announcer. He merely stuck his head in the door and said, "I have only one thing to say to all you characters. If you want me, I'll be over at the Music Hall wrestling arena. There's less pounding over there!"

"Not so fast, fella," Chick hollared. "Come in here and identify yourself as a member of this new foreign legion."

Good-naturedly protesting, Red cautiously came in. "What are you reading?" he asked me.

"The history of television so far. See, it says here that..."

Red interrupted me, "All I want to know is the sports part. Spare me the electronics."

"Well, let's see. It says here that the first football game covered by television was Fordham-Waynesburg, in New York, in 1939. And the first baseball game ever televised was Princeton-Columbia at Baker field, New

York, that same year. And the first Big League game was the Cincinnati Reds playing the Brooklyn Dodgers at Ebbets Field that summer."

"Horray!" Red shouted. "That's all I wanted to know. Three cheers for the Reds! Good-bye!" And he left for the "quiet" of the wrestling arena.

Then...enter...the master. Jim Hill. Who became known as the Alfred Hitchcock of the business. A brilliant writer, producer, actor. From tragedy to comedy in one scene. That was Jim. A slight-built man with sharp black eyes and slick black hair. He wore a drooping trenchcoat with the belt eternally trailing and one epaulet eternally missing. His favorite tie was a shabby red one, in the knot of which he tied his tongue. So the first day he walked into the office, it looked as if his tongue hung all the way down to his belt. And that was just the way he wanted it to look!

Jim had worked on the *Jack Armstrong* radio show in a Detroit advertising agency. So he would often sing the old familiar Wheaties jingle and school song. "Wave the flag for Hudson HIgh, boys!" ... "Won't you try Wheaties...the best breakfast food in the land...Jack Armstrong never tires of them and neither will you..."

"Not another character!" screamed Chick. "How could so many be assigned to one office? *MY* office!?"

"Watch your tone there, young man. You're speaking to Jack Armstrong, the All-American boy. Wave the flag for..."

We'll all be waving from the flagstaff if we don't get this TV station on the air," Chick huffed and puffed.

32

TOYS IN THE ATTIC - It all began there and eventually moved here to Powel Crosley's Arlington Street Studio. Among all his "toys" this genius of a man also produced a motorcar, 1939. And the most powerful radio station in the world. Over 500,000 watts that could be heard by Eskimos and men in the jungles of Australia when President Franklin D. Roosevelt threw the increased-power switch in 1934. This high power continued untill 1939 for WLW Radio.
(Gray History of Wireless Museum—Crosley Telecommunications Center)

Chapter 2

Right in the Middle of Her High C

So these were part of the cast of characters behind the scenes to help start WLW Television in February, 1948, a year or two or three or more ahead of the other TV stations in the country, and the second NBC affiliate. It was ready to follow in the famous footsteps of WLW Radio, which had been one of the first radio stations back in 1922. The Crosley/AVCO empire dated back to that day in the early 20s when Powel Crosley, Jr., stopped into a Cincinnati store to buy his young son a radio, one of those new toys, a radiophone as they were then called. The clerk said the price was $130. Crosley thought this was too expensive for a boy's gadget, so he bought the parts and built him a radio set at a fraction of the price.

With wires and an oatmeal box, rather than an expensive crystal, Crosley tried to pick up and transmit for a distance of seven miles across town, but suddenly was picking up seven hundred miles! Not even realizing how the cereal box contraption he had rigged up worked. Intrigued with the new toy, he started making more and more of them for only $20, revolutionizing the industry in a year with 500 sets a day. This naturally led to an interest in the broadcasting side of the radiophone. So he started broadcasting from his living room, swathed in draperies like a maharajah's tent, for acoustical effect. And very appropriately played "The Song of India" over and over again on a recording; soon adding live talent, which had to be interrupted periodically for passing locomotives and distress signals form ships at sea...plus the replacement of delicate tubes blown out in those early transmissions by eager sopranos and their high notes! The first mike looked like a giant megaphone, eight feet long and three feet wide, so the announcer had to put his head into it to be heard...and the soprano, her high C. From a little 50-watter in 1922, Powel Crosley took WLW Radio up to 500,000 - watts in 1934, the most powerful radio station in the world. It could be heard coast to coast and so was called "The Nation's Station." Crosley certainly had brought radio

500,000 WATTS! The only station in the world ever to broadcast with such power, 1934-1939. That's why it was called "The Nation's Station." This is the WLW Radio installation that blew the world away! With its power and its programs and its performers and its producers...and its writers. (Gray History of Wireless Museum—Crosley Telecommunications Center)

out of the garage, the attic, the storeroom, the closet, the dark ages. WLW, along with KDKA, Pittsburgh; WJZ, New York; WWJ, Detroit; and a few others were really the cat's whiskers among the cats-whisker-wire-and-crystal sets.

There was something intriguing about those old crystal sets, as if each listener were a Marconi or a Morse, responsible for bringing in his own personal messages and being a part of the new communications magic. Then, when the box and cabinet radios came along, there was something intriguing, too, about them. Its appearance, its mystery, its marvel that the world could be coming out of that talking box. The faceless voices, the instrumentless musicians, the objectless sounds, that all let the imagination translate the features of the faces, the kinds of instruments, the objects making the noises, each to the own individual ear of the listener.

Who could ever forget the hoofbeats of *The Lone Ranger*, the sound of *The Green Hornet*, the voice of Eddie Cantor singing "I love to spend each Sunday with you," the trains of *The Railroad Hour*, *This Is London* of Ed Murrow, the rattle of Jack Benny's Maxwell car, the earthquake of Fibber McGee's closet, the accents in Allen's Alley, the squeaking door in *Inner Sanctum?*

Crosley gave to the world the first real soap opera with *Ma Perkins* sponsored by P&G, the first quiz shows, like *Dr. I.Q.,* the first mystery programs in *Dr. Kenrad's Unsolved Mysteries*, the first symphony, and a long line of firsts. WLW became known as "The Cradle of the Stars" with such names as the Clooney Sisters from Maysville, Kentucky; Red Barber, the old redhead; Doris Day; Jay Jostyn, who later became Mr. District Attorney; Bill Nimmo of CBS Wednesday night fights' fame; the Mills Brothers; Red Skelton in his early days; Jane Froman; Singing' Sam; Little Jack Little; the Charioteers; musical director Burt Farber; the Ink Spots; the McGuire Sisters; the Modernaires; Andy Williams and his brothers; Smilin' Ed McConnell; Gordon McCrae; Ralph Moody; Anita Ellis; Billy Williams Quartet; sports announcer Al Helfer; Floyd Mack; announcer Durward Kirby; Eddie Albert; Bill McCord and Ann Ryan. And from the country music field: Lulu Belle and Scotty, Kenny Price, Red Foley, Bradley Kincaid, Curt Massey, the Lucky Pennies, Ernie Lee, Merl Travis, Chet Atkins and many more.

And the stories they could tell, like the piano that wouldn't play until a cleaning lady discovered what was wrong with it. Fats Waller had used it for gin bottle empties!

Then there was *Moon River*, the original one. "A lazy stream of dreams...Twined in the hair of night..Float on, drift on, Moon River, to the sea." Written by Ed Byron, who later created *Mr. District Attorney,*

37

I'VE GOT RHYTHM swings this black group, early performers on WLW Radio, another example of why WLW was called "The cradle of the stars."

The Mills Brothers from Columbus

Ma Perkins (Virginia Payne)   Al Helfer   The Mills Brothers   Andy Williams   Rod Serling, writer

Red Skelton   Jane Froman   Dick Noel   Fats Waller   Durward Kirby

Rosemary Clooney   Ralph Moody   Bill Nimmo   McGuire Sisters   Frank Lovejoy

Janette Davis   Eddie Albert   Doris Day   Ink Spots   Red Barber

"THE CRADLE OF THE STARS" — that's what WLW Radio and TV are known as. And no wonder! Just some of the talent who performed here.

Moon River carried WLW in broadcasting history, "Down the valley of a thousand yesterdays."

WLW Farm and the Corn Cob Mike

In the booklet *The Gray History of Wireless Museum*, the story goes that Lewis Crosley (brother of Powel) purchased a 500-acre farm near the WLW transmitter in Mason, Ohio, in 1941, to set up a working farm operated by farm people who talked on farm programs. Called "Everybody's Farm" it served as the center of WLW rural programming.

When the need for a distinctive mike arose, R. J. Rockwell, then technical director, asked Earl Neal, the tenant at "Everybody's Farm," to bring him the largest ear of corn that he could find. An aluminum casting was molded and machined out to hold an RCA salt-shaker type mike. After painting it to look like an ear of corn, it was put in service.

This special microphone became famous part of the WLW Farm activities, which hosted thousands of programs and visitors over the years at "Everybody's Farm." As a result, WLW Radio was voted the number one outstanding farm station in the nation. Roy Battles, Bob Miller and the gang, take a bow! And all those chickens who layed all those eggs we used to get delivered fresh on our desks every week.

Meanwhile over at WCPO, Dorothy Frye recalls the hillbilly talent there. "WCPO used to be in the Keith Theater Building on Walnut Street. That is where we did Colonel Andre Carlton's *Six-to-Niner Show* with Montana Fay and Ray, the Kentucky Colonels, Pappy Jess Gaddis, the world's champion yodeler, Tex Edwards, the Tuma Cowboy, the Kentucky Briar Hoppers, later on *The Midwestern Hayride*, and not to be forgotten on the marquee, "Lady Known as Lou," also one of the southern Sisters. On WCKY the famous L. B. Wilson Station, John Lair had a program with the Coon Creek Girls and later founded the famous Renfro Valley down in Kentucky. Lily May Ledford was the leader of the Coon Creek Girls and was the first all-woman string band on radio.

With all this talent and these station facilities in Cincinnati, it's a wonder they let them get away. But Nashville stole them with their recording facilities and *Grand Ole Opry* and the rest it had to offer.

Crosley Broadcasting
Firstest with the Mostest!

The Crosley Broadcasting Corporation was responsible for many a first in the broadcasting and telecasting business:

(Photo courtesy Cincinnati Historical Society)

SOAP OPERA WAS BORN at WLW Radio, with the sponsorship of Procter & Gamble, headquartered in Cincinnati, hence the name soap opera. In 1952 the star of the first soap opera, Virginia Payne (Ma Perkins), was welcomed back to WLW by (l to r) newsman Peter Grant, Charles Egelston, Virginia Payne, violinist Virgillio Marucci, writer Jack Maish. In 1933 WLW started *Ma Perkins* in Cincinnati and it continued from New York for twenty-eight years.

DR. CONRAD'S garage in Wilkensburg, Pa., in which his station 8xk was later to become the first Westinghouse station.

VOICE OF AMERICA - Crosley's early installation of the first 10,000 watt international transmitter, in 1933, beaming to Europe and South America at Mason, Ohio, now taken over by the State Department transmitting programs in many languages to many countries. Joyeux Noel! Feliz Navidad! Frohliche Weihnachten! Buon Natale! (Cincinnati Historical Society)

One of the first radio stations in the United States, WLW, 1922.

First 10,000-watt international transmitter to Europe and South America, 1933.

One of the first television stations in the United States, 1948.

One of the first and largest domestic installations of "Voice of America", in 37 languages, 1942.

First to bring COLOR TV programs to Midwest, NBC Colorcast of Rose Bowl Parade, Jan. 1, 1954.

First NBC COLOR affiliate, Jan. 1, 1954.

First licensed PBS Station in United States, WCET, Cincinnati, 1954.

First independent telecaster to originate own live COLOR Programs, August, 1957.

First to COLORCAST day baseball on a local and regional level, Cincinnati REDS 1959 season, May 2.

First to COLORCAST night baseball, Cincinnati Reds 1960 season, May 16, under normal lighting.

First to COLORCAST indoor sports remotes, Cincinnati Royals and University of Cincinnati basketball games 1959-60 season, with new low-light tube. All this was going on, yet there was only a scattered paragraph or two in the papers in 1948 about the beginning of it all. Everybody thought Powel Crosley was over there at 9th & Elm Streets in Cincinnati fooling with another toy. Little did everybody know it would sweep the world, the most powerful yet known to man.

He Opened His Mouth and Got the Weather Report

"Now listen, everybody," I announced. "Did you all know that WLW Radio was once so powerful that a lady turned on her washing machine five hundred miles away and got Peter Grant and the News? And a man in a dentist's office with a lot of new fillings in his teeth picked up the WLW weather report way out in Iowa?"

Chick Allison, continuing in his state of supersonic seizure, but trying to control himself, remarked, "We don't care what happened on radio or even experimental television yesterday. All we have to care about is when this station stops being experimental and goes on the air officially and commercially in two days! None of you can seem to get that through your thick heads!"

"Speaking of thick heads," Bill McCluskey added, "did you see that new hillbilly performer who applied for a job here this morning? He had a head..."

"Never mind!" screamed Chick.

"That's right. Now let's be serious," I agreed. "Let's all cooperate with Chick. But first, listen to this want ad that ran in the *London Times* back in 1923. It says: 'Seeing-by-wireless inventor wishes to hear from someone who will assist in making a model.' And guess what?"

"What?" weakly whimpered Chick.

"Nobody answered the ad of this Scottish inventor of television, in his attic, John Baird, tinkering with cardboard discs, lenses made from bicycle lamps, and radio tubes from World War I surplus stocks. What do you think of that?"

"I think nobody but screwballs like the ones right in this office were reading the *London Times* that morning!"

"That was even before the days of Jack Armstrong, the All American boy," commented Jim Hill.

"I give up!" moaned Chick...and laid his head on his desk. "Revive me back to consciousness in two days after the station has gone on the air."

We Threw the Overalls in Mr. Murphy's Chowder

The word had gone out, like "The British are coming!" Any questions, call John T. Murphy at NBC in New York. So we did. Every hour on the hour. With headline questions on the half-hour. Our lead-in sounded like a song from a musical comedy. "Oh, Mr. Murphy, won't you tell us please.." Of course, the first question was how do you spell television? Is there really an "s" or a "z" in it? He informatively answered, "There's an "s" as in stupid, not a "z" as in zany!"

We tried to pacify him by saying that we fully sympathized with his plight...and that the only other fellow we felt as sorry for was St. Anthony, also the patron of hopeless cases. John T. Murphy, of course, became head man of all the AVCO stations. He probably thought it would save on the phone to New York that way. And no doubt we were the ones who drove him to putting gin in his swimming pool.

At least we knew how to pronounce the word television. Imagine what would have happened if some of the other original ideas for the medium had been used. Visual telegraphy...radio cinema...radio vision...distant seeing...electrical telescope. But the Greeks had a word for it, so somebody wisely chose it. "Tele" meaning at a distance, added to the Latin "video" to see. To simplify it all, I scholarly read to the no-air, one-office gang that: "Television is merely a mechanical device that does

WHEN THE FLOWER POT SPOKE, everybody listened. "This is WLW, the Nation's Station." And it was to be the only station ever in the world with 500,000 watts. FDR threw the switch to this power, which caused a sensational reaction from people everywhere. One man said he went to the dentist and upon leaving the office with his new fillings, picked up Peter Grant and the News! Another woman reported she turned on her washing machine and got *Moon River!* The Nation's Station was everywhere, and everything, and everybody. WLW—the most famous call letters in the world, even broadcast over one man's lawnmower.

When the flowerpot spoke...

CROSLEY BROADCASTING CORPORATION, *a subsidiary of* **Avco**

WLW-T, Television, Cincinnati / WLW-D, Television, Dayton / WLW-C, Television Columbia/WLW-I, Television Indianapolis/ WLW RADIO

(Photos originally from the files of WLW and WLW-T, Cincinnati)

CHARLES BUTLER, representing years of engineering dedication at Crosley, shown here with an early Master Control Panel and later with the master engineer himself, R. J. Rockwell, who was responsible for many engineering developments and communications inventions at Crosley, including the Rockwell Cathanode Modulation System.

what the French Impressionists did through their paintings. Decompose light into small luminous dots."

"I'm going to decompose you all into small luminous dots if you don't get to work!" ordered Chick.

"Right!" agreed Bill McCluskey. "I'm leaving right now to get my paint-by-number set." And disappeared out the door heading for the Cuvier Press Club, the Valhalla of the communications world Norsemen...and escape from what ails TV, radio, and newspapers, curable or not.

Then I went into a meeting to see how the whole thing worked. Rockwell, they said, was going to explain television to us. The first thing he did was whisper to me, "You have to turn it on." I apologized, "I thought it came on like a movie." "You have to turn the ON knob," he continued. "Of course!" I thought. "Why didn't I think of that...the ON Knob."

WLW-TV had been on the air experimentally since 1937 as W8XCT. The engineers thought if we were going to work in television that we'd better watch some of the shows the experimental station was now putting on. They were mostly remotes, like races, fashion shows, etc. So we had all gathered in the office of R. J. Rockwell, Crosley VP and magnificent chief engineer, to view them on the very large model set he had helped put together himself. We lined up in straight-back chairs, in rows, like the Ladies Altar Society and peered out around each other's heads for a view of the new altar cloth. People in old photos sitting on a radio bench with their heads into the first radios looked no more ridiculous than we did. Nobody ever dreamed in the late 40s that television viewing would ever become an easy-chair affair with slippers and snacks and Stroh's. We thought our stiff positions the upright thing to do justice to the awesome new venture and debenture and denture of television.

There Was Ease in Casey's Manner as He Stepped Up to the Mike...

Well, the big day finally arrived that February 1948. WLW-T was going on the air, one of the first television stations on the face of the earth. Everybody was delirious. Some with excitement. Our truly great leaders, Jim Shouse and Bob Dunville, two of broadcasting's masterminds, would make speeches in a very impressive ceremony. Like driving the gold spike on the first transcontinental railroad or welcoming Lindy and the *Spirit of St. Louis*. No greater preparations had been made in those last two frantic days than for the sailing of the Nina, the Pinta and the

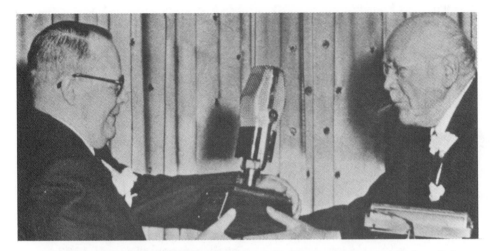

FIRST MIKE AWARD was presented to James D. Shouse, chairman of the board of the Crosley Broadcasting Corporation, by H. V. Kaltenborn, formerly of WLW, at the Latin Quarter, New York, from the Broadcast Pioneers in 1961.

REDS BASEBALL was presented to Brig. General David Sarnoff, chairman of the board of RCA, by Robert Dunville (r) president and general manager of Crosley, and John T. Murphy (1), vice president for Television and general manager of WLW-T, Cincinnati. It was the first baseball ever used in the first night game to be broadcast in color, May 16, 1960.

Santa Maria. Ours, too, would be a great day in history. With a great ceremony. And what happened on that great day? At that great ceremony? The TV picture was perfect like an engineer's dream. But the sound..the glorious sound..which had been perfected for twenty-eight years since the birth of radio...FAILED. There was no joy in Mudville. Had we struck out?

Only for seventeen minutes and forty-five seconds! The rest was a grand slam! We were off and running!! And I do mean running...three jumps ahead of the sheriff. Television was operating in the red in our little office, while the rest of the building with five floors of radio was flourishing in the black. We had no budget, no money. We had to beg, borrow or steal all the props, people and places we put on the air. In fact, we just plain stole them all. Clothes almost off each other's backs. We let Bill McCluskey go home in a storm one night and get drenched because we had stolen his raincoat for use on a program. Of course, he recognized it on the TV screen that night and threatened to call down the curse of the banshees on us if we didn't stop lifting costumes.

So we finally talked a costume shop into letting us use some of their things in exchange for advertising. We would go over to the shop, put on all the costumes we wanted, then run through downtown Cincinnati back to the WLW Television studios. One day I dropped a spear and helmet crossing at a busy intersection. As I stooped over to pick them up, I set down a music stand in the middle of the street and forgot to pick it up again. When I got to the other side, I saw the traffic cop turn around and start directing traffic with the music stand in front of him like Toscanini at 42nd and Broadway. I wonder whatever happened to that music stand or that cop?

Yes, it was really wild those early days in television. One good reason was because nobody had ever worked in TV before. Some of us hadn't even seen it. The whole thing could best be summed up in the question asked in a program meeting one day. We were all working on the proposed TV schedule for the week when Jim Hill asked, "Is this Mad Monster show live or on film?" And to add to the confusion, anybody who had a TV set in those early days kept calling our office for repairs. We couldn't even keep the pencil sharpener working right. There were not TV repairmen yet. That breed of species with antennas sticking out of their heads had yet to be developed...who arrive in station wagon UFO's...and speak in vertical/horizontal jabberwocky.

I'll never forget the day we were discussing the early baseball games to be televised. I voted to put one camera on the pitcher's mound just like Charlie Brown! And later Snoopy as shortstop! And night-blooming cereus in the infield!

49

The Library Went Public

Our biggest problem remained what to put on the television screen, now that the engineers had invented the medium. Television was going on the air, but what was going on the screen? There were no network programs yet, no coaxial cable through to inland cities, no syndicated shows, no programs, no films, no nothing, and still no air...in our office. So we put everybody we could find locally on the screen. Neighbors talking about their blooming begonias. And neighbors not talking about their blooming begonias. Anybody who could hum or hymn. Or whistle a happy tune. Or unhappy tune. Barbershop quartets that weren't worth a shave-and-a-haircut-two-bits. Kids from dancing schools that should sure have gotten the gong. And didn't. Unfortunately. Anybody who could shuffle off to Buffalo we tapped for in front of the camera. They were so bad, we really did have to shuffle them off to Buffalo. For fear of their lives..and ours.

Then we had doctors talking about health and lawyers talking about the law and firemen talking about fires and police talking about policing and teachers talking about teaching. But the ones I'll never forget were the rubber band manufacturers talking about rubber bands. That was really a television first. Probably still is.

Finally, we decided film was the answer. But what film? Where do we get film? There was no film yet made for TV or cleared for TV. Ahhhhh...the public library was the answer. The unsuspecting public library. The innocent public library. The pure public library. So we started borrowing their films and putting them on the air...without clearance...and without even screening them! One was called *Little Friends Around the House*, or something like that. It turned out to be a two-hour close-up of termites! Almost every bar in town called (that's about the only place that had TV sets in those days) and said to get those bugs off the air! All their customers thought they were having the DT's...or were being terrorized by Otto the Orkin Man. Either way, it was tough to be mugged by a termite.

Alka-Seltzer and Percy B. Shelley

After we decided this wasn't such a good idea, we thought we'd better go back to anybody who could warble or wobble. Our battle cry, like "Remember the Maine," became "Contact Bill Lassiter at International Harvester." This had absolutely nothing to do with anything. It was put by the talent department on all notices sent to the hillbilly performers on radio, and now on TV, for personal appearances at State Fairs. Bill Lassiter became our Kilroy. There was something so resonant-sounding about our new motto. So restfully rousing. So onomatopoeia-etic.

Things began to pick up. Sponsors began to come in. The best sign in the business that you are in business. The ups began to outnumber the downs, including the time the woman called and said that her Alka-Seltzer wouldn't fizz. She saw it advertised on one of our shows, but theirs wouldn't fizz like the commercial on television. After cautious interrogation, we found that she had used the white paper disc that sits on top of the first Alka-Seltzer disc in the bottle...and sat waiting for it to fizz. So we told her to try the second disc and it would fizz! She thanked us warmly...and said that from then on she would always start with the second Alka-Seltzer rather than the first tablet.

Then there was the day a viewer wrote and told us how much she liked a poem read on one of our TV shows and asked us to forward her letter to the author, Mr. Percy B. Shelley.

With such sterling audience as this, we began to get curious about just how many television sets there were in the area. So we made a survey, calling up a cross-section of people to find out, mostly the saloons. Nine out of ten of these suds shops answered that they did have television. Then we asked, "What make is it?" Most replied with an answer like this: "Cherry 1-1892." Those were the strangest results on a survey since somebody asked the old ranger what laundromat he goes to...and Carmen Miranda what was her favorite fruit...and the Lead Balloon Company why it went under...or didn't go over.

Imagine The Waltons in The Twilight Zone

On the Crosley Broadcasting staff in that early period was Rod Serling, who later created *The Twilight Zone*, *Night Gallery* and *Requiem for a Heavyweight*, plus a host of other award-winning TV and movie productions, and became president of the Academy of Motion Picture Arts and Sciences. Never will I forget one day going into another writer's office and asking him what he thought of my first TV script. I happened to be the only TV writer then, the other four wrote only radio. This particular radio writer just looked up, smiled, and said, "You're the TV expert! Not us!" They good-naturedly enjoyed dumping the unknown element of television writing on me as they remained secure behind the familiar medium of radio. That script was a commercial for Shillito's department store. A toy mechanical cow. Not knowing how to write

51

THE OLD WALTON'S HOUSE overgrown with memories on the Warner Brothers lot in Burbank. "Good-night, John-Boy."

LORIMAR

TO: THE KELLY AND.
FROM: FARRELL FAMILY

EARL HAMNER

WITH MUCH LOVE

AND AFFECTION

HOLLYWOOD - 1982

To MARY ANN
HUG AND KISSES

(Photo courtesy Warner Bros. Pictures, Burbank, California)

JOHN BOY AND THE WALTONS, one of the most memorable programs ever on TV, seen in about sixty countries around the world. Autograph of Earl Hamner, the creator and narrator of the autobiographical series, given to me on a visit to the Warner Brothers lot in Burbank, California, in memory of the early days when we worked together at WLW-T. I wound up the Shillito toys and marched them by his door, driving him and other radio writers up the wall. His Blue Ridge Mountains of Virginia were ever so peaceful!

53

video instructions yet, I simply typed the word "cow" on that side of the paper. "How do you like my video instruction?" I asked the radio writer.

"Inspired! Simply inspired!" he laughed. "That should win you the first TV writer's award."

Frustrated that none of the radio writers would help me put together the television scripts, I gathered up all the toys Shillito's had sent over for their commercials, wound them up and let them march down the hall past the radio writers' doors to annoy them. When they couldn't stand it anymore...the mechanical cows, toy soldiers, fire engines, army tanks, spinning tops, musical clowns, choo-choos, and Willie the worm...one of them came out of his office and ushered me and the toys out of sight...and sound. It was the one who told me my commercials were inspired. A young fellow who had grown up in the Blue Ridge Mountains of Virginia...with seven brothers and sisters...grandparents and parents he could never forget...a white mule...two neighbor ladies who made Papa's recipe...the grocer Ike Godsey...a dog named Reckless...and a host of other memorable characters who would become television immortals. Yes, it was Earl Hamner, creator, narrator and supervisor of *The Waltons*. John-Boy.

"Now stay out of sight," he laughed, "until television has come and gone."

Other stalwarts who kept the Crosley/AVCO stations on the air then were Dave Partridge, who went on to Westinghouse; Ed Fienthel, who made the printers and promotion people happy; Charlie Butler, who made the engineers happy; Milt Wiener, who made AFRA and the Musicians Union happy; Howard Chamberlain, the classy moderator who made the news happy; Bernie Matteson, who made the scripts and punctuation marks happy; Rudy Prihoda, who made the art department happy; Chet Herman, who made the producers happy; Jim Cassidy, the public relations expert who made the performers happy, and later joined Hill & Knowlton in New York; and I. W. Harper, who made everybody happy. Especially across the street at Jack Abrams Emporium, better known in non-missionary circles as "The Mission."

Let's not forget Sid Ten-Eyck among the illustrious bunch in broadcasting. He is walking encyclopedia of who's who, what's what, when's when, where's where, and how's how in the history of broadcasting. The Waite Hoyt on the other side of field...who can field one with the best of them.

And there's Bill Myers, the forever-young-looking, like Dick Clark. Bill can recall when Channel 5 was Channel 4! That goes way back to the beginning. And you still hear him with those unflinching traffic reports and PBS helper. And whatever else is going on, Bill is on the screen and

Rod Serling—Writer, who left WLW-T because they wouldn't give him a $5- a-week raise! Or so the story goes! Went to Hollywood and became president of the National Academy of Television Arts & Sciences. Famous for his *Requiem for a Heavy-Weight, The Twilight Zone* and others, setting a standard of excellence for the rest to follow. (Photos courtesy of WLW and WLW-T files)

Singer, Ann Ryan McCord, Bill McCord, announcer.

HOWARD LEPPLE, WLW-T's chief engineer (l), and Crosley president Robert E. Dunville accept a General Electric award from G.E.'s Frank Miller (r) for Crosley's contribution to the development of the 1960 "Emmy" award-winning supersensitive color camera tube, which permitted colorcasting with the same light used in black-and-white telecasts.

on the radio. Always the kindly soft-spoken gentleman like Nick Clooney.

They Committed the Perfect "Crim"

It was great cast of characters in the scenes and behind the scenes. But there was one person who wasn't tops on the popularity list. He gave everybody a hard time. So a few of the guys put on their thinking caps to get even with him. They came up with the Cal Crim Perfect Crime, as they called it. But they wouldn't tell anybody else what it was. One of their wives, however, thought it too good to keep, so she let us in on the secret..the day the plot was executed. And them almost with it! The reason they called it what they did was because the sign about Cal Crim's detective agency was in all the restrooms, testifying to the fact that they were under such protection for safety. So they wired the men's room for sound and had it secretly connected to the man's office whom they didn't like! The next time he had a big meeting going on in there, they turned on the loud speaker hidden behind the draperies and leading from the men's room. The result was indescribable! To this day, everybody swears everybody was completely innocent of the famous Cal Crim Crime! But when the moon is full, strange spectres rise out of the night and point accusing knarls in the direction of the WLW-T television tower, where the phantom echoes of such memories still linger in laughter and innocence. But as the dedication to this reads, "None of the names in this book have been changed to protect the innocent. Because nobody's innocent!"

We Found Walt Disney on Mount Olympus

At this point, there was only one thing we knew for sure. Sure as radio, television was here to stay. So we decided to start giving things names as if they were going to be around for awhile. The ideal place to start was the towering WLW-T tower, high on a point overlooking the Queen City of Cincinnati and the Kentucky hills beyond. Everybody agreed we should call the transmitter site Mount Olympus. Silhouetted high against the sky and rushing clouds, it truly looked like the home of the gods, drawing down from the heights of the heavens a mighty new thunderbolt power of Zeus, called television. Yes, Zeus, the cloud-gatherer, controlling the heavens and their phenomenon, sending out new eagles of communication from lofty peak of power, that would prove to be the greatest man had ever known.

One night I arrived at the transmitter and started to walk around its breathtaking site, just taking in the beauty of it all in the brilliant night air. Suddenly I noticed someone else alone on the other side doing the same thing. He was looking out at the Fantasia sky...maybe dreaming what happens "When You Wish Upon a Star"...and really believing that the Milky Way is the pathway to the palace of Zeus. He said not a word, but was lost in thought. What was he thinking? What was he envisioning, imagining at that moment? I recognized in the fleeting shadows and flickering starlight who he was, but wouldn't have disturbed him for the whole world. Because he was the whole world...of imagination...and adventureland...and tomorrowland. Then, finally, he slowly turned away from it all, as if not wanting to leave this welcome reveries, and walked into the studio to be interviewed on a program. It was Walt Disney. But before he left, he turned to me and said, "Makes you want to wish upon a star, doesn't it?"

What a thrill it was for my mother and me to go to Steinberg's on a rainy night and buy our first TV set back in 1948! It was an RCA table model, a very large, heavy object. And we signed enough papers on it to buy the Taj Mahal. We didn't know what we were doing and neither did the salesman. When we got it home, we watched every live program until the WLW TV station went off the air, programs I had worked on all day. We sat in straight chairs right in front of the set! Like the radio bench of the old radio days. No couch potatoes!

Bill Nimmo Just Couldn't Breakaway

But suddenly the quietude of the home of the gods was shattered with yelling from around the back of the studio as if Zeus were after somebody with one of his thunderbolts. Willie Thall, like an Olympus lightning flash, came running out with Bill Nimmo after him. Thall was emcee on the *Midwestern Hayride* program and Nimmo was the announcer. He later became a well-known New York TV announcer on the Wednesday Night Fights, sidekick of Johnny Carson, Jack Lemmon, Robert Montgomery, Jackie Gleason, Garry Moore and others, and was later with the University of Cincinnati.

"Now cut that out!" Thall was shouting, as Nimmo was laughing hysterically, holding a fiddle in his hand, trying to hit Thall over the head with it. I had written this fiddle, which was supposed to be a trick breakaway fiddle, into a skit for them on the Hayride program. When I tried the fiddle earlier in the day, it broke away as it should. The handle automatically collapsed to make it appear as if it were actually breaking when someone was hit on the head with it. But it failed to break away just now on the television show. Nimmo almost knocked Thall out on the

UP IN CENTRAL PARK with Bill Nimmo, Joyce Renée and Sam Messer, originally from Cincinnati, better known as Bob Middleton who played in *Give the Little Lady a Big Hand, Friendly Persuasion, The Desperate Hours,* etc. Is that a real horse?!

BON VOYAGE TO THE BIG APPLE - Announcer-emcee Bill Nimmo receives a little going-away present from the WLW-T gang as he leaves for New York. (l to r) guitarist Clarence Neone, director Honore Nichols, performer Bob Shreve, performer Willie Thall, announcer Bob Merryman, singer Dick Noel, singer Margo Good, director Gene Walz, floor manager Bob Gilbert.

THE PURPLE HEART - Received by Bill Nimmo, from Major General James Gavin, head of the famous 82nd Airborne Division, at the American headquarters in Berlin during World War II.

(Photos courtesy Bill Nimmo)

REMEMBER DAGMAR!? The gorgeous big blond on Jerry Lester's *Broadway Open House*, the first late night show, the first *Saturday Night Live!*

air...and was continuing to chase him for fun all over the home of the gods.

The joke was on Thall this time. But the previous week it had been on Nimmo. In that skit, I had included a bicycle-built-for-two. The bike was supposed to remain stationary on the TV set; but when they started to pedal it, the thing went flying with them right off the stage and crashed into some scenery. Nimmo wound up with a bloody nose, still singing, "Daisy, Daisy, give me your answer do..." as Thall concluded, "You'll look sweet upon the seat of a bicycle-built-for-two." And both crawled out of the debris. And the studio audience, thinking it was part of the act, wildly applauded for an encore. And when I took the bike back to the rental shop, the proprietor wanted to know what happened to it. Rather than the Gay 90s, it looked as if it had been in the scene of Hannibal crossing the Alps with a round-trip ticket.

She Was Just a Yodelin' Girl Cow

On working with the *Midwestern Hayride* show, things were always happening like this. But the one that took the cake was the cake. I had a very special cake made for presentation on the show celebrating its anniversary on the air. I specifically ordered cowboys and cowgirls to be put as decoration on the big cake. But when it was presented that night on the show, there...grazing through the snowdrift icing...were instead boy cows and girl cows! Nobody in the Hayride cast, including Willie Thall, could figure out what in tarnation those cows were doing on the cake. Thall laughed so hard he could hardly continue emceeing the program. And Bonnie Lou, the well-known singer and personality, was in convulsions on close-up camera over the cow-cow-boogie cake. And watching it at home, I had an instant coronary occlusion.

Everything I had worked on all day at the station, I went home and watched all night on the air..followed by nightmares of how it all turned out. A big help to me in getting WLW-T on the air and keeping it there in those early days was a black fellow who worked for our family for forty years. He was the master and we were the slaves around the old family Kentucky home built by my great-grandfather at the end of the Civil War. He'd often help me round up hard-to-find props, ransacking everybody's attic, basement and garage in town. Then he'd deliver them to the lobby desk at Crosley Square across the Ohio River in Cincinnati. And go back and tell everybody that he'd just been over to that "Crosby" place again. I constantly corrected him, "It has nothing to do with anybody named Crosby. It is Crosley...Crosley."

61

WILLIE THALL - A pork-pie hat, a plaid flannel shirt, a pair of blue jeans - that's how Willie Thall will best be remembered, as driver of *The Midwestern Hayride* wagon. It was the show that was carried live out of Cincinnati from 1948 to 1972, the Midwest's answer to the WLS *Barndance*, Chicago; the *Grand Ole Opry*, Nashville; the *Louisiana Hayride* of the South; and Renfro Valley, Kentucky. Thall grew up in Chicago and started with WLS there. Later, when he came to Cincinnati, he formed "The Buccaneers" group, singing and playing the clarinet and bass fiddle. He soon became Ruth Lyons' right-hand man on her popular show. Bonnie Lou was the singing and yodelling cowgirl on the Hayride, which was a summertime NBC and ABC show in addition to Cincinnati...and the tri-state.

THE HOMETOWNERS on the Hayride show.

(Photo courtesy WLW-T, Multimedia Broadcasting)
THE LUCKY PENNIES - They played and sang on *The Midwestern Hayride* show. The group was named for Penny Richards, wife of Dean Richards, also on the Hayride, along with the Turner Brothers, Ernie Lee, Bobby Bobo, Wally Procter, Lee Jones, Buddy Ross, the Boyer Sisters, Wally Moore, Chick Rich, Carlie Gore, Martha Danforth and her Square Dancers, the Kentucky Briarhoppers, and, of course, Kenny Price, big-hearted and big-talented, "walkin' on new grass."

BOB SHREVE—Watch out for that tie! It has a spring in it! Here as the beloved character of the country bumpkin opposite Willie Thall in *The Country Store*. The classic checker player. Shreve wore many hats. An Irish tenor; a children's show host; creator of various characters at WCPO-TV; night-time movie crazy emcee, later WKRC-TV. Shreve did it all, mostly ad lib, attracting the big daddy of 'em all, none other than the number one man himself, Bill Cosby, to *Past Prime Playhouse*, 1980. Shreve with his multiple personalities, Irish tenor wit, rubber face, bags of tricks had no equal even on the networks. It's an honor to have known him. "They just don't make them like that anymore." (Photo with Bill Cosby by James Cunningham. Photos courtesy Bob Shreve, WLW-T, WCPO-TV, WKRC-TV, Cincinnati)

"You mean," he'd constantly ask, "that don't belong to that fella they call Bing Crosby?!"

"No, it doesn't belong to Bing Crosby. It was named for Powel Crosley, who started WLW Radio back in 1922 and who owns the Cincinnati Reds."

"Then you say he don't sing," Jim would reply.

"No, he don't sing," I'd reply.

"Then he don't do nothin'," Jim would mumble.

Just in Case Truman Got Elected

One of our biggest program challenges came when we were faced with televising the first presidential elections returns...the Truman-Dewey contest, November, 1948. I had to write the script for the three-hour special, our first real documentary. Wow! What a job...for somebody who knew what he was doing...much less for somebody who didn't know what she was doing! My best buddies, Jim Hill and Rikel Kent and I, produced the show. And what a show. We really got off a flag-waving documentary, aging ourselves and the United States of America several centuries in those few hours. Uncle Sam turned gray, yes, that was when it happened, that night at the WLW-T transmitter. We all lost about ten pounds and ten years of our lives that night. Everybody, but Harry Truman, that is. He refused to get excited about the whole thing.

We started the big show off with a rousing patriotic "This is America...This is a profile of a land and this land's possessors...And it consists of many things...men making their way over miles of prairies and hills with crude wagons rumbling behind them and illusive dreams beckoning before them...For this land, its possessors, everything lay ahead..." We were sure Jesse Stuart was quaking in his shoes.

The entire program was put together with the idea that Dewey was going to be elected. We had based this conclusion, of course, on the major national polls which showed a clearcut Dewey victory. The nation went to bed that night thinking Dewey had won...everybody, that is, except Harry Truman. Fortunately, we had prepared a hurried alternate script just in case of an upset. "In the event of a Truman victory, you will find herewith some Truman material." But just so everybody would be happy, Democrats and Republicans, we wound up the John Philip Sousa special with a bang for the whole shebang. Whittier's lines about the American voter being king for a day on Election Day:

"The proudest now is by my peer,
The highest not more high;
Today, of all the weary year,
A king of men am I.
Today, alike are great and small,
The nameless and the known;
My palace is the people's hall,
The Ballot Box My Throne!"

But somebody in the typing department had left off the last line. So the verse made absolutely no sense as the grand finale of our great three-hour, first documentary special of a presidential election. Then after the announcer read his last word "hall," we all shouted off-camera the conclusion, "The Ballot Box My Throne!" Which sounded as if it were coming from the masses. Very appropriate. But what masses? What messes! I still have script with my name on it as the writer, which I keep hidden in a dark closet! And to think that we sent out TV schedules from the station "warning" everybody who had a TV set what was coming each week. The schedule wasn't in the daily paper yet and no *TV Guide*. They probably didn't want anybody to know about it!

Incidentally, Gene Walz was the floor director of the big election show and Rudy Prihoda was the art director. I doubled as the assistant to them all. In those days we all doubled as everything and everybody because there weren't any distinct lines drawn as to who was doing what. You just did anything that had to be done and without fancy or definite titles for the responsibility. Writer or producer or director or assistant or assassin!

WALTER BARTLETT—president of Multimedia with headquarters in Cincinnati, now the parent company of the WLW Television operations and other TV and radio stations around the country, and producer of many programs and specials including the Phil Donahue Show. The big chief, the top banana, super-duper CEO.

Chapter 3

POWIE! ZAM! BANG!

It Was Here to Stay

After this strenuous channel swim of putting a television station on the air when there were hardly any television stations on the air (!)...I bade a TV red-eyed farewell to my Crosley comrades in camaraderie and went out to look for greener pastures with less work and easier hours. So I joined an advertising agency, which turned out to be the Pepto Bismol detour of the Fourth Estate.

But it was a great thrill the first day I sat down at my desk and opened the drawer. There were carved the names of all the writers who had used that old wooden desk before me. The last one was Damon Runyon, Jr.

In my new agency job, I thought how quiet and serene it will be far from the sparks of a TV station. But suddenly..POWIE! ZAM! BANG!...The agency said it would be starting to advertise on television and I would be assigned to work on the commercials and programs with WLW-T. Furthermore, since I had Crosley Broadcasting experience, I was being assigned to write the Crosley account! My reaction was the same as the little old Italian's exclamation when he saw the white signal coming out of the Vatican chimney heralding the election of a new pope. "Holy smoke!"

The Ralph H. Jones Advertising Agency in the Carew Tower in downtown Cincinnati was legend in the business. If WLW was known as "The Cradle of the Stars," its advertising agency was known as the hand that rocked the cradle. An assemblage of characters, creativity and craftsmanship, the like of which will probably not be seen again. Like the "old days" of Crosley itself. It was the master...and "his master's voice" all over again. "The Nation's Station" unequalled in its time or space.

Pink Pills for Pale People

The advertising agency. Just the title conjures up a consummation devoutly to be wished. Or all hell broke loose.

Didn't Churchill say that Americans have an effervescence for life unequalled by any other people in the world? That effervescence must be Coca-Cola. And wasn't that Ronald Reagan in a Van Huesen shirt ad? Wasn't Day's Soap advertised as "The greatest invention aside from the electric light?" And didn't N. W. Ayer say in their ads, which was their motto, "Keep everlastingly at it?' And didn't Bret Harte write for Sapolio Soap? And Lord Byron for Warren's Shoe Blacking? And then there was Kennedy's Ivory Tooth Cement, which "makes everyone his own dentist!" And tobacco was originally advertised as "A wonder drug!" It was a wonder anybody ever survived it.

There was always a cure for everything from cancer to the can-can. "A gradual increase of flesh and nervous vigor until she could walk, without unusual fatigue, several miles over surrounding hills," advertised Buffalo Lithia Spring. And Egyptians were a pushover for dried mummy. The master showman himself advertised one of his freak shows, "What is it? The most singular creature ever known, evidently connecting link between the human and brute creation, bearing alike the characteristics of each. What is it no one pretends to tell." He must have been exhibiting an advertising account executive.

The cure for what ails you could surely be found in Old Sachem Bitters, Wigwam Tonic, Dr. Thatcher's Electric Belt, Dyke's Beard Elixir, or the Improved Home Turkish-Russian Folding Bath Cabinet.

And now a word about Ivory Soap. It floated because a workman went to lunch and forgot to shut off the valve that whipped air into the mixture. It got its name from the Forty-fifth Psalm: "All thy garments smell of myrrh, and aloes, and cassia, out of ivory palaces."

It was all a long way from the invention of Coca-Cola in 1886 by Dr. John Styth Pemberton in Atlanta...a long way from the poem on a tombstone, "Here lies Lester Moore/Four slugs from a Forty-four/No less/No more!"...a long way from the rhyme, "Once there was a big canary/Far away in Timbucktu/And it ate a missionary/Skin and bones and hymn book, too!"

All of which brings us to the same conclusion as Dr. Samuel Johnson, "I cannot but propose to these masters of the public ear whether they do not sometimes play too wantonly with our passions."

But, Oh, to dream of it! "The cure for creeping numbness."..."Pink Pills for Pale People." "They make pale folks pink and

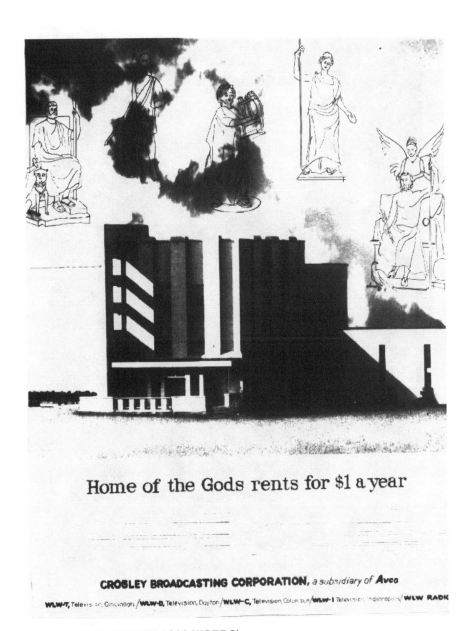

Home of the Gods rents for $1 a year

THE PICTURE WORTH 1000 WORDS!

THAT'S CHEAP RENT! - Early ad we prepared for WCET, Cincinnati, the first licensed PBS Station in the United States. Their building and facilities were donated by Crosley to begin this outstanding television service to the community. And the rent was only $1 a year!

71

(Photos courtesy WCET, Cincinnati).

WCET-PBS - Charles Vaughn - president and general manager. The big boss who kept the station ongoing almost since the beginning for 30 years, following the death of Uberto Nealy. He has an extensive record of experience and awards covering the whole gambit of television.

RONALD WILSON - Vice president of telecommunications, in charge of WCET programming, production, engineering and instructional television. Formerly a director and producer for WLW-T and Stockton, West, Burkhardt Advertising Agency in Cincinnati. We pay this tribute to Ron Wilson.

(Photos courtesy of PBS, Washington, D.C.)

THE PROGRAMS ON PBS

SESAME STREET - With Big Bird, and Oscar and his garbage can, and Bert and Ernie, and the Cookie Monster, and all the gang. And where's Jim Henson and the other Muppets? Gone off to invade Manhattan with Kermit and Miss Piggy and Fozzie. When NBC in New York was tearing out a wall, they found faces like Muppets even on the plumbing pipe joints where Jim had made them. And what a congregation gathered that day in the New York cathedral for his memorial service. Never before had the legions of angels in the sanctuary looked down on legions of muppets in the pews, lovingly clutched by children from all over New York city.

THE JEWEL IN THE CROWN salute was a festive postscript to Masterpiece Theatre's critically acclaimed production of the original Jewel. Susan Wooldridge and Art Malik in the tragic romance, one of the program's many series.

thin folks plump and weak folks well and despairing folks happy.".

For the trivia buffs: the word slogan is derived from the Gaelic sluagh-ghaiurm meaning battle cry. The camel on the cigarette pack was named Old Joe, with the Barnum and Bailey Circus. His Master's Voice was a dog named Nipper in London, who accidentally peered into an old Gramophone one day, listening to the voice.

So they had come a long way, Baby, from "They Laughed When I Sat Down at the Piano," to "I Was a 97-Pound Weakling," to Barnum's early claims "brought to you at great expense from beyond the sea . . . a mighty mirror of departed ages." But the greatest ads of all time and the greatest slogans will remain a part of the American scene forever. "The Pepsi Generation"..."Quick, Henry, the Flit"..."Somewhere West of Laramie"..."The Penalty of 'Leadership'"..."Good to the Last Drop"..."The Pause that Refreshes"..."The Skin You Love to Touch"..."See the U.S.A. in Your Chevrolet"..."There's a Ford in Your Future"..."The Golden Arches of McDonalds".

The great names in advertising that will always be a part of the history of American Business are: J. Walter Thompson, McCann-Erickson, N. W. Ayer, Young & Rubicam, Ogilvy & Mather, Ted Bates, BBDO, :Leo Burnett, Foote Cone & Belding, Grey, Doyle Dane Bernbach, Benton & Bowles, Compton, Campwell-Ewald, D'Arcy, and the list goes on.

But still Fred Allen described an advertising agency as 85% confusion and 15% commission!

When not working on a booklet of table manners, I was writing a television storyboard, ideas for new television programs, or a Nashville jingle, or a news story for an election, or a film on the history of paper, or a speech for a councilman, or a booklet on the dawn of aviation. What a cross-section of experience an advertising agency gives. But my favorite of all was the Crosley Broadcasting Network. The ads, the promotions, the programs, the presentations like the ones for the Golden Mike and Medal of Freedom. And then there were those for the first public TV station, WCET. I'll never forget that night I went to the library to look up Mt. Olympus. I still have my notes on it years later. Crosley was going to lease (donate) some of their facilities to get WCET started. So I wrote. "Home of the Gods Rents for $1 a Year." That was cheap rent, especially for the home of the gods!

Jack Armstrong Arrived in a Helicopter

There was no escape. Television was here to stay. I was doubly sure of it one day when something went by my window. A toy helicopter. Handmade with paper clips and rubber bands. I reached out and grabbed it. Inside was a note. Help! I'm a prisoner in an advertising agency! I knew in a minute it must be one of my former WLW-T comrades, another attempted TV escapee. Sure enough. It was Jim Hill in the next office leaning out the thirty-first floor window ready to launch another helicopter. Jack Armstrong, the All-American Boy!

"Okay, Jim Hill, the jig's up! Get off that launching pad," I admonished. He turned around...wearing the falseface of a baboon. "My! You're looking well!" I commented. "Better than I've ever seen you!"

Jim laughed, took off the face, and threw it on the desk with a half-dozen others. "Why the Halloween in July?" I asked. "Can't you wait 'til the frost is on the pumpkin and the fodder's in the shock?"

"Nope!" he smiled. Then explained, "I was commuting between Cincinnati and Chicago on weekends while working up there on some special TV. So I bought these to break the monotony of the long drive. Every once in a while I would put on one face for a few miles. I told Burr Tillstrom about it and he said he'd give me one of Kukla or Ollie for my next trip. But I decided to stop it because last time I caused a woman to run into a mud hole with her baby carriage, scared a horse out of his feed bucket, and sent a policeman the wrong way up a right way street!"

Jim already had made a great reputation for himself in television. He had produced and written, among his many credits, one of the funniest shows ever on TV. It was with Bob Shreve and Bill Thall as two country bumpkins in a country store. The program in those days was on live for fifteen minutes every night like a serial. The planned storyline plus the ad-libbing was so funny that the cameramen couldn't stop laughing. The TV screen always looked as if it were shaking because of the convulsed cameramen. Thall and Shreve often couldn't control their laughter at themselves and had to stop right in the middle of the performance on WLW-T.

The funniest night was the skit in which Shreve was supposed to have gone on a trip to the moon, when all the time he was merely hiding on the roof of the country store. Periodically, he would send Thall a message, supposedly tied to a meteorite, which was just a big rock. One time Shreve threw the message in the window tied to the meteorite rock and almost knocked Thall dead live on the show. But Thall, being a master performer, struggled to his feet and exclaimed, "That Elmer! Wish he'd stop sending those messages from the moon tied to that stale green cheese!" There was no studio audience for the show, but those of us there working it with the cameramen and engineers burst out in applause for one of the most masterful ad-lib performances we had ever seen.

The Rise of Byron Keating

Three months ago, advertising trade papers carried stories that Byron Keating had opened an advertising agency. When he landed his first account—the Little Tot Food Products Co.—such trade papers as *Broadcasting* carried the news. Then *Advertising Age* bulletined that Byron Keating Co. ("Cincinnati's fastest growing agency") was planning a new campaign for Soyscuits, a soybean biscuit mix.

But Keating made his biggest splash in the report of his talk before the Cincin-

A month ago, advertising trade papers carried news of the death of "Byron Keating, 59, after a heart attack attributed to overwork." Actually, Byron Keating was killed by his own parents—the two Cincinnati copywriters from whose lively imaginations he had sprung to hoax the advertising world.

Keating's creators were small, witty James B. Hill and big, sandy-haired John L. Eckels, advertising-agency copywriters. They dreamed up Keating to win an argument that political bigwigs are built by publicity, that they could create a tycoon in their own business out of thin air. They

Eugene Smith

HOAXERS HILL & ECKELS
They buried Mr. Keating in a desk drawer.

nati Businessmen's League. Said Keating: "Agencies are doomed unless they establish totalitarian principles . . . with clients. Businessmen should keep their fingers out of advertising. Many agencies are producing inferior advertising, against their better judgment, for fear of losing lucrative accounts and because account executives 'butter-up' the client."

From frustrated copywriters all over the country, this speech brought Keating high praise, along with requests for jobs. Commented *Advertising Age:* "It's things like this that reaffirm our occasionally wavering faith that it's fun to be in the advertising business." Worldly-wise *Variety* headlined the talk "Just Let 'em Pay the Tab—Keating."

spent $4 on letterheads, sent publicity releases to newspapers and magazines, invented companies and clubs for Keating to address. When the American Newspaper Publishers Association and Dun & Bradstreet Inc. requested financial statements, Authors Hill and Eckels decided the hoax had gone far enough.

Last week the remains of Byron Keating—piles of news clips—were decently interred in Keating's "office," the middle drawer of Hill's desk. Hill and Eckels have only one regret: "We had a corker planned. We were going to phony up a foundation-garment account for Byron Keating. We were going to have the phony company pick a Miss Uplift from clerks behind brassière counters."

TIME Caught Up with Them

Jim Hill had previously worked at this advertising agency. One day when things had gotten dull, he and a fellow writer, John Eckels, decided to liven things up around the shop. They concocted the idea of creating an imaginary advertising agency. They made up a fictitious name, fictitious owners, fictitious accounts...and then sent our fictitious publicity releases to all the magazines and newspapers. Never did they dream in their wildest imagination, and it was wild, what would happen. They thought the little joke would end there with the publication of the publicity. But instantly they began getting inquiries from prospective clients, requests for appointments, even demands for meetings. The whole thing snowballed so fast that they frantically had to start sending out excuses why they couldn't take on more clients, and come up with all kinds of side-stepping means to avoid divulging what they had done. Finally *TIME* magazine got wind of what was going on and ran a story on it, but not until after Jim and John had killed off the phony agency with the phony death of the phony headman from a phony heart attack caused by phony overwork!

Not long after Jim told us this story of his earlier escapade, we planned a small celebration for his birthday. That morning all of our cards were on his desk in the mail. We waited with little birthday surprises for him to come in, as was the tradition in the department. But he never came. He had died suddenly of a heart attack. Just like the fictitious character he had created in the *TIME* story. On his desk calendar was his scribbled note, "Start writing book with gang about TV." This we were going to do with him, each contributing our favorite anecdotes. But the title then we planned to be: *What To Do 'Til the TV Repairman Comes.* Nobody, however, had the heart to do it without him.

Somebody Lowered the Boomlay!

I shared an office with John Healy, head of the writers. John was a magnificent writer himself. Serious or humorous. His special talent was a masterful trait and touch of subtle Irish/English wit, which resembled Alec Guinness in a classic cobblestone scene by London lamplight.

One day John said he had something he'd been wanting to tell me. When I detected the expression on his face, that imaginative whimsical look, I knew John was delving again into the realms of creativity. He spoke in a whisper.

'I just wanted to let you know I'm a prince."

Dumbfounded, I waited for him to continue. But he was waiting for me to say something.

"You're a what?" I mumbled.

"I'm a prince," he continued to whisper.

"Oh, my soul!" I began to whisper, too.

"Yes, my ancestors in Ireland were royalty. Irish kings. Which makes me a prince."

"Oh, my heavens!"

"Our ancestral estate was called Kuhnflush."

"Oh, my gracious!"

"So I'm really a prince, you see. An aristocrat. In fact, I used to wear a monocle and spats."

"Oh, my goodness!"

"I'll never forgive Lady Catherine for bringing the bad teeth into the family."

"Oh, my gums! But please do forgive her, John," I begged.

"All right. If you say so. But begrudgingly."

Then we both broke down and laughed. "What do you think of my routine?" he asked, still laughing.

"It scared me!" I confessed.

John was really great putting on an act like that, especially this, his own special formula for his theory of relativity. He truly was a prince..of a writer. He wrote a gem of a little book about his childhood attending an almost all-girls' school in Price Hill, a suburb of Cincinnati, entitled, *With Sunshiny Faces.** And he wrote some brilliant ads, like the old Roman soothsayer arriving home from work, "Had a hard day with the omens, dear" And the ad for which the famous cartoonist Charles Addams did the illustration. A typical Addams spooky setting with spooky characters sitting in a seance scene and the headline, "Aunt Bertha is coming in clear now." But his masterpiece was a classic Christmas message for General Electric, "When the lights go on next door..."

*J. B. Lippincott Company, Philadelphia, 1963.

The Man Was a Little Cuckoo

One morning John arrived at the office in a downpour, soaking wet, yet carrying an umbrella. "How in the world did you get so wet with an umbrella?" I asked.

"You'll never believe me," he replied. "I used my umbrella to keep a cuckoo dry!"

JOHN HEALY—the writer of writers, a superb Irish wit, "prince John." Said he used to wear a monacle, spats and a cravat. But somebody mistook him for an Englishman. We remember him best the day he arrived with the cuckoo clock and the day he put up the wall!

DICK PERRY - A superb writer in all media, he turned his talents from the DuMont Network and ABC-TV to other writing. The author of many short stories, magazine articles and plays, his greatest claims to fame are his books - *Raymond and Me That Summer; The Roundhouse, Paradise and Mr. Pickering; Vas You Ever in Zinzinnati; Not Just a Sound.* He used to write for George Gobel, whom he looked like, with the same dry wit. One morning he came into the writing department muttering, "I wouldn't say the air in here is bad, but the canary just died." (See story page 111)

"Who was he," I joked. "Anybody we know?"

"No, never saw him before," John seriously continued. "He was some old man walking down the street and he stopped me to ask if he could share my umbrella. Generously, I obliged. As we were walking, I noticed he was holding something under his coat."

"Oh, that was the cuckoo!" I concluded, greatly relieved.

"Yes, that was the cuckoo. When we arrived here at the building he confessed he just wanted to keep his clock dry, as I stood there half dripping from sharing my umbrella. I hope that clock never cuckoos again!"

Then he started on a soliloquy on umbrellas.

"Umbrellas used to be a gentile part of a person...a trademark of character...a sign of the times...a friendly weather warning...an intimate companion. But today everybody just takes his umbrella for granted. Or doesn't even bother to take it at all..."

A beginning like this was all we needed in the writing department to start us chiming in and scurring to the books to add to the umbrella philosophy.

"And listen to this from *The Elf and the Door Mouse**...
Where is my toadstool, loud he lamented
And that's how umbrellas were first invented."

"Here's Jonathan Swift," somebody else added.
"The tucked-up seamstress walks with hasty strides,
While streams run down her oil'd umbrella sides."

"But wait'll you hear this!" One of the guys announced.
"Beat an empty barrel with the handle of a broom,
Hard as they were able,
Boom, boom, BOOM,
With a silk umbrella and the handle of a broom,
Boomlay, boomlay, boomlay, BOOM." **

At which inspiration we started a congo line down the hall, running right into Stan Willer, the vice president and general manager, who gave us the look everybody reserved only for the writing department. which translated meant, "The inmates are running the institution again."

* Oliver Herford, *The Greatness of Poetry*, edited by Mary Austin, Queenie Mills Allyn & Bacon, Inc., Boston 1963

** Nicholas Vachel Lindsay, *Famous Poems and Little Known Stories Behind Them*, edited by Ralph Woods, Hawthorn Books, New York, 1961.

It Seemed As If There Were a Wall Between Us

All went well sharing an office with John until we had the inevitable disagreements over some writing and advertising campaigns, especially a few television commercials. He wanted to do them his way and I wanted to do them my way. So one day when I was out of the office at an all-day business meeting, he decided the office wasn't big enough for the two of us. Somebody had to go! But since nobody could go, he arrived at another conclusion. He had a wall put up! Between our desks!

The next day I nonchalantly returned from the meeting, not realizing the wall was there. After laying my things on my desk I turned to hand him a summary of the meeting and proposed television advertising schedule. And walked right into the wall! When I felt it in front of me, I did a doubletake like a Lucille Ball skit. In a state of absolute shock, I felt my way along the wall up and down, backwards and forwards, sideways and wideways...a human fly...until I came to the doorway opening. And there sat John in his office behind the wall, laughing harder than I'd ever seen him. I didn't say a word. I couldn't. I was speechless and screechless.

But now, how to get even with him? That was the question. Whether to suffer the outrageous fortune...or to sleep on it...perchance to dream up some sweet revenge. And come in the next day with a diabolical scheme. In all the annals of history, religion, arts, sciences, yes, everything — there is never recorded a more dedicated person than a human being in the process of getting even with somebody...in thinking up a return-match dirty trick. Especially if that person is a lady licked. Hell hath no fury like a woman walled.

Recovery was quick and deadly. The next day I entered the office to the tune of the triumphant *Marseillaise* ringing in my ears. "Marchon, citoyen!" A new republic was about to be established. The Bastille would be stormed. A tale of two copywriters was being written. 'Twas a far, far worse thing that I was doing than I had ever done. Madam Lafarge was knitting and purling. I placed my weapons of war on my desk. A big bag of walnuts with a nutcracker. And I sat there and cracked nuts all day, every day, for days, which John could hear through the open doorway of the wall. He pretended not to hear them, though. And didn't speak to me for a week. Finally at 4:55 P.M. on Friday afternoon, a special delivery letter arrived on my desk. It read, "Stop cracking those nuts!"

(Photos courtesy of Ed Elfers, former V.P. secretary-treasurer, and Mary Jane Knolle, Cincinnati former librarian, The Ralph H. Jones Company)

THE KEYS TO THE KINGDOM of advertising. Ralph H. Jones turns over the company to the new owners, C. M. Robertson, Jr., and Stanley Willer in 1943, after twenty-five years in the business. Before his retirement, he saw his company grow to the largest in Cincinnati and one of the largest in the entire Midwest. Considered a genius in his field, he left a legacy to live up to only equalled by the top names in the advertising field in New York.

THE HEAD TABLE—there they are, the head men of the legendary Ralph H. Jones Advertising Agency in Cincinnati. (1 to r) Gus Lemperle, vice president of production, Stanley Willer, vice president and general manager; Paul Myers, vice president who became president; Charles M. Robertson, Jr., president; Richard Geis, vice president and senior account executive on the Ashland Oil account; Edward Elfers, secretary-treasurer, who paid all the bills!

NOW LET'S TAKE ONE STANDING and with some additions. (1 to r) head of the Columbus office; V.P. art Bob Hayes; V.P. production Gus Lemperle; V.P. and general manager Stanley Willer; V.P. who became president Paul Myers; V.P. senior account executive Dick Geis; V.P. and senior account executive Walter Krause; V.P. secretary-treasurer Ed Elfers.

Chapter 4

How Did the Dull Child Get in There?

Stanley Willer, V.P., co-owner and general manager, was, I deemed, a man of impeccable judgment because he hired me. At first meeting, I thought him to be like a stern Prussian General. He kept looking out the window with his back turned during the entire interview, making what I thought were disapproving grunting sounds. But which I later learned, after working with him, were just the opposite. When you wrote something good, he'd route it around the office with a complimentary note on it. And when it wasn't good, you'd get it back with another kind of note on it! To translate his handwriting, we always had to seek the help of his invaluable assistant, Vera Freitsch.

"Vera, does this say hold up on this assignment or order a pound of petunias?"

"It looks more like catch the next stage that comes through!" she'd laughingly reply.

I'll never forget Stan's note attached to one of my first television commercials for the *Mr. Peepers* program, starring Wally Cox and Tony Randall. I had written in the commercial: "This new soft margarine can be sliced down with a dull child's knife." Stan's reply note read, "This commercial is dull enough without putting a dull child in it." Well, at least it wasn't like that shoe polish TV commercial that said to use it on your beat-up children's shoes!

Never Look a Gifted Horse in the Mouth

But I will not divulge his reply to my commercial for the Groucho Marx *You Bet Your Life show*. Instead of spelling the word "foil," I hit the wrong key on the typewriter and wrote, "Now this margarine comes in a great new shiny fowl package." Groucho should have gotten ahold of that one. Or the starch commercial into which I accidentally slipped an extra word...an extra body. The commercial read: "This starch gives your clothes an extra body." It actually went on the air that way. The announcer broke up over it, which really took the starch out of me when I heard it. But it also took the starch out of the stores. A sell-out! Like

Betty Furness when she couldn't get the vacuum sweeper on the television commercial to work, so she kicked it, and it went like crazy. So did the sales! Probably because it struck a familiar note with sympathetic housewives who were used to struggling with octopus vacuum sweepers...and winding up kicking the tentacles out of them.

Another of the early assignments with Stan Willer was to read and judge the "Grandma Sayings" submitted in a contest. Each winner would receive $5 for an old saying and get her entry published in farm papers. By mistake, I chose the ones I thought were unintentionally funny. So the sayings in the first few installments read thusly: "Never look a gifted horse in the mouth."..."You can't milk a silk purse out of a sow's ear."..."A rose by any other name would spell as sweet."..."Don't count your bridges before they're hatched."..."When in Rome do as the Romings do."

After I got the newspaper ads with these "Grandma Sayings" all lined up, I started to write television commercials out of them. For the gifted horse, I put a horse playing a sonata...but was stopped before I continued the crime by Stan Willer's grunting intervention, "Maybe we'd better put you on another assignment instead of this margarine account."

The development of margarine was one of the most interesting in the history of products. It had been created by a Frenchman, after Napoleon III urgently issued a decree for a butter substitute during the emergency of the Franco-Prussian War in 1870. Disproving the fact that a highly unsaturated army marches on its cholesterol.

A Kosher Recipe for Corned Beef and Cabbage

Nu-Maid Margarine was always one of our favorite accounts, produced by the famous Miami Margarine Company, makers of over 400 brands, one of the largest such companies in the world. All managed by the distinguished Heidrich family, fireball Whitey Whitehurst and classy Elmer Weber. Nu-Maid's history-making table-grade slogan in the early days of margarine literally put margarine on the American table, bringing it from a second-class citizen for cooking.

My first Nu-Maid assignment was to create some Jewish cookie recipes! Why me? But they proved so successful, I was assigned to all the Jewish recipes from then on..in! If they only really knew how bum a gentile cook I was, they never would have entrusted me with this ecumenical endeavor...of the endives.

But my margarine advertising masterpiece, I thought, which nobody else did!, was the television commercial about the scientists working with their colossal invention of a giant computer as it snorts electronic beeps and peeps and flashes lights and brights. One scientist says to the other: "Herr Professor, come quick! The giant computer is about to give the answer to the secret of the universe!" The other scientist shouts, "Ach du lieber! It's a great day in the history of the world! The hope of humanity!" And the first scientist excitedly whispers, "Sh-h-h..here it comes out of the computer. Look! Look! Ahhhhhhh...ah-hahhhhhhh..." The second scientist screams, "For heavens sakes, Professor, what does it say?" And the first one exclaims, "It says 'Pass the Nu-Maid!"

However, even if this secret of the universe never saw the light of day, the moose-crossing, yolk-lovers, big-mouth campaign did. Well...

Oh, but the television campaign that would surely make me famous was the series of commercials on table manners then and now. "The history of the human race might have been recorded best by its ever-changing table manners," I gallantly read in a meeting, behind closed doors and before unbelieving ears. "The proper 'migration' to the table. The 'hieroglyphics' on tablecloths known as graffiti by modern man. The biographies of butlers. The conquest of cutlery. The exploitation of the table napkin. And the unmistakable imprint left on humanity by the waiter's thumb in the soup. Not to mention that perplexing problem which has been with us since the dawn of creation...what to do with the pits. Ladies and gentlemen, be seated.

"After all, it is true that people's fortunes are often decided by their table manners. In fact, a nation's fortunes. A century's fortunes.

"This is certainly true as proven by *The Ladies and Gentlemen's Manual of Elegance, Fashion and True Politeness* of 1853: 'If there not be any napkin, a man has no alternate but to use the table cloth.' And at the turn of the century, the napkin pin became almost as famous as m'lady's hat pin. It kept the napkin from sliding off a woman's bouffant skirt or a gentleman's slick trousers.

"It's a fact that in the days of the Borgia kings, many scheming royal hosts invited their enemies to dine in order to poison them. So it became the duty of non-poisoning hosts to partake of the food first to prove their good intentions. And, of course, a century ago it was not elegant to gnaw Indian corn. The kernels should be scraped off. And ladies should be particularly careful how they manage to handle so ticklish a dainty, lest the exhibition rub off a little desirable romance. And the old table manners books explained that some table knives have been curled to easily convey food to the mouth. And so does the book of *Good Manners and Good Morals*.

"It was also customary a century ago to serve a cup-plate on which to place a cup after pouring out the coffee into a saucer for drinking. And here's one for a gentleman from a quaint old etiquette book called, coincidentally, *A Gentleman*. It says that a person who would cut an oyster in half is a cannibal. And summing it all up...remember you cannot use your knife or fork or plate or cup or teeth too quietly."

As the client and staff sat in utterly utter disbelief, I proudly concluded, "Oh, I forgot! Pass the Nu-Maid!"

A Call for Sam Bloodshot, Private Eye

After I had been taken off the account, my next assignment was for Bavarian Beer on the *Midwestern Hayride* television program. That suited me fine because I loved going back up to the WLW-T transmitter and working with the Crosley crowd. The tremendous spirit and comradeship of most of the people who work at Crosley/AVCO, or have ever worked there, is an indescribable thing. Like days of the newspapers of the last century or the great magazines of yesterday. It's rare in broadcasting. And rare in this century...period.

I made up some humorous skits for Bill Nimmo and Willie Thall with Nimmo as Sam Bloodshot, Private Eye...Thall whipping up a brew dressed as a witch, "When the hurly-burly's done, there'll be beer for everyone. Quiet, mortal, while I talk to the spirits."...Nimmo as a famous gangster, Mugsy Bavarian...and singing "Yankee Doddle" with a fife and drum. At the end of this last skit Thall was supposed to chase Nimmo off the stage in a parody to "Yankee Doodle," singing "Willie Nimmo always sings after we have coaxed him...Then he never wants to stop 'til after we have choked him!"

As Thall did this, a man from the audience got up and chased one of the other Hayride performers off the stage. Everybody applauded wildly. As I stood behind the scene, I saw Nimmo come flying off with Thall after him, then the performer with the strange man after him! While the rest of us still had our mouths open, Thall quickly saved the day and rushed back on stage shouting a conclusion to the commercial: "Remember, Bavarian is the kind of beer that was once the toast of the barbary coast...and still the lustiest beer on the bar! Brother, I'll have another!"

But my great slogan was lost in the applause. And so, thank goodness, was the reason for the man chasing the performer off the stage. It seems he had been trying to date the man's wife. So the fellow just planted himself at the show to punch the performer on the air! It looked like an Abbott and Costello routine from their own syndicated show, which we also were on for Bavarian.

88

"Wouldn't you like to spend every night on the Riviera?"

Other accounts which Stan Willer handled were Zero Frozen Custard and TEN-B-LOW Ice Cream Concentrate from M&R Dietetic Labs in Columbus. For their advertising we lined up Joan Bennett, Penny Singleton and Rhonda Fleming. Another M&R product was Pream for coffee. We did one campaign with a series of COW-TOONS in newspapers to be adapted later to television. One showed two cows watching another at night high up in the sky. One was saying to the other, "Millie was so happy that her cream was used in Pream that she jumped over the moon!" Another was, "Pream is the best thing we have come up with since the Cow-Cow Boogie." But nobody seemed to cow-tow to our ideas so they barnstormed the account elsewhere.

DAZY Air Freshener from the Drackett company, now a part of Bristol Myers, also benefited from our fresh-air talents. Drackett made Windex and Drano. We planted DAZY on the *Don McNeill Breakfast Club* and *Today* show, then with *Dave Garroway.*

But the account for which Stan Willer had a special fondness was the small Stearns & Foster account, makers of famous mattresses and Mountain Mist Quilt Filling. I loved the simple beauty of this account, a writer's pure pleasure in McCall's Needlework: "A long time ago...like a legend...a quilt filling came into being...as lovely as a mist...as hearth-warming as mountain lore. It was called Mountain Mist. From log cabin firelight to quilt show spotlight..." And I wrote my greatest headline for this ad, "Make this quilt." That even beat my triumph to date of "Now you, too, can putty windows." Or my second-runner-up for the Liberty Cherry account: "With Liberty and cherries for all!" But truthfully I really thought my headline for the Stearns & Foster Riviera mattress ad was summa cum laude: "Wouldn't you like to spend every night on the Riviera?" But it went in file 13, known in the parlance of the great expanse of the business world as the wastebasket.

Then the executive sweet saved the day, some tasty samples of one of our accounts, Bissinger's Candies. The Bissinger family back in Europe were originally the royal candymakers, the court confectioners to Napoleon.

One of Stan Willer's favorite lines was by Lady Esther. They came out with the first powder compacted into a pressed powder. He'd repeat this line, "Now you can bite Lady Esther." The only conclusion was to do a follow-up campaign, "Now Lady Esther can bite you!"

(All photos this section by Keller Studios, Cincinnati)

"CHIP"—CMR, Jr., our leader. Mr. Robertson was president of The Ralph H. Jones Company from 1943 to 1967. Just one look and you knew he was somebody. Parts of his desk gadgets are still missing on the streets below the Carew Tower in downtown Cincinnati!

"Chip"

Our glorious leader and president was C. M. Robertson, Jr., better known as "Chip." A multi-millionaire, he was the power behind the throne, and the throne. One of those persons with a presence about him. When he walks into a room, you know he's somebody. He always reminded me of the man who broke the bank at Monte Carlo. But didn't care if he did or didn't. He'd wear an old slouch hat and wrinkled raincoat even to the most important meeting where a fortune in advertising was at stake, especially a television plum. He always spoke with great authority and had a tremendous ability for getting wandering idea or campaign or meeting or person back on the track. All the time, however, you thought he wasn't listening. Because during most meetings he would get out his miniature gold tool set and fix all the gadgets on his desk. So occasionally a spring from a lighter would fly through the air and you had to catch it if it came your way. One day the main part of something or other flew right over his shoulder and out the thirty-first floor window!

"Where the hell did that go?" he asked everybody. But nobody had the heart to tell him it was at that moment being run over by a street-cleaning truck at Fifth and Vine. No wonder everybody got so nervous when it was their turn to speak in a meeting in Chip's office. There was the ever-present fear that one of the parts of his desk gadgets would come flying at you, just as you were about to recite your great idea and script for the latest TV sponsor.

My fondest memory of him was an incident that showed his humility in spite of his wealth and position. One day, by mistake, he wore to the office his tuxedo trousers with a black satin stripe down the side.

"Now how could I have put on the wrong trousers this morning! And just when we have a big client meeting! I look like a waiter at the Netherland Hilton!"

"Then you'll just have to stay out of sight, we said. Half of you, anyway!"

We told him if he sat behind his desk and didn't get up, the client wouldn't notice his trousers from the other side of the room. He agreed. So he wouldn't try to rush home and change them. But it was just too good a ribbing opportunity for some of the characters in our office to pass up. So right in the middle of the meeting in the presence of the esteemed client, they urged Chip to stand up for some trumped-up reason.

"What ad are you referring to, Mr. Robertson?" one asked. "Would you please walk over and point to it for us?"

JEAN TELGATER - Golden girl! The statuesque, beautiful blond that married her dream man, Dick Calmer, assistant to Bill Blis, head man of the entire AVCO Corporation, the former Aviation Corporation of California. Among her many jobs, it was Jean's duty to summarize the daily soap operas for the Kroger Company, one of the advertising agency's big accounts and sponsor of the "soaps". As a result, she would be sitting at her desk with tears rolling down her face about the latest happenings on the shows, especially on *Linda's First Love* (1937-52); *Mary Foster*, the Editor's Daughter (1932-51); *Hearts in Harmony* (1941-51); all our "soaps" which the agency owned.

Then another fellow would say, "Would you please stand up and hold this flip chart for me?"

Chip's answers to these leg-pullers were classics of double meanings filled with undertones of just wait'll I get even! This went on and on until we were all just about in hysterics. Finally, he broke down and told the client what was going on. The client got such a kick out of it, we were sure it helped secure the account and a large television advertising budget.

"C.M.R., Jr.," was a broadcasting expert, grocery products authority and soap opera pioneer. His father came out of retirement from the Baldwin Piano Company at the age of sixty-seven to become president of the Kroger Company food stores and help lead it and the American supermarket to its position in the U.S. today. It all began back in 1883 when Barney Kroger, a young man with high hopes and $772, started a little grocery store near the Ohio River waterfront in Cincinnati.

The memorable soap operas which we handled for the Kroger Company were *Mary Foster, the Editor's Daughter; Hearts in Harmony;* and *Linda's First Love.* We had to write the lead-ins and lead-outs. "Can any heart have more harmony?"..."Will Linda really make this her first and final love?"..."Can an editor's daughter take this action?"..." Tune in tomorrow and see when Kroger again brings you another interesting episode. Meanwhile..."

Muzzy Parrish, Daisy Keppelmeister, Aunt Sarah Crockett

Kroger decided to cancel one of these soap operas and sent instructions that it was to be terminated on a certain date. Well, it so happened that on that particular Friday afternoon, one of the principal characters in the story was on her way to the hospital to have a baby! And Monday the show didn't return to the air. The result was chaos at the stations across the country. Listeners deluged the stations with mail and calls wanting to know how everything turned out. Was it a boy or a girl? And the stations in turn deluged Kroger, who in turn deluged us to add another episode quick. Winding up the whole thing happily ever after. Never in the history of soap operas did so much happen in one episode. We had the kid born, grow up, and grow old!

This was just another proof of how seriously listeners and viewers take broadcasting. The most unforgettable was probably the time that Ma Perkins' son was killed in the war in one episode. The stations around the country were flooded with telegrams and cards of sympathy. And the

NBC station in New York received hundreds of wreaths the next day.

Jean Telgater and Roy Madison in our department used to handle the story synopsis and publicity for the soap operas. The names and characters were quite a homey heap of creation. *Mary Foster, the Editor's Daughter*, was set in the little town of Valley Springs with Parker Fennelly playing the editor to such neighborly folk as Muzzy Parrish. And *Linda's First Love* included Daisy Kappelmeister and Aunt Sarah Crockett. As if this weren't enough, some dear little old lady off her rocker used to write into NBC telling the characters absent from a scene what the other characters were doing or had said about them that day. These letters were forwarded to Jean, who used to read them aloud to us. We decided we would use that dear little old soul in our department. She would fit right in with the basket-weaving and pot-holder-making gang at arts-and-crafts hour.

But Jean's story had a very happy ending, anyway. She married Dick Calmer, assistant to VIP Bill Blis, head man at the original AVCO Aviation Corporation in California. One of those business-world romances that makes it all worthwhile, in spite of the stray little old ladies who work themselves up in a lather over soap operas and get dissolved in a basin of blues.

J. Thadius Toad and His Crosley Car

Some of Chip Robertson's most unforgettable experiences resulted from his personal and professional associations with Powel Crosley, Jr., who owned WLW (1921-1946), the Cincinnati Reds (1936-1961), Crosley Motors (1939-1952), and so on. Our advertising agency had the Crosley Broadcasting and Crosley Motors accounts. These were the little cars that were at least twenty years ahead of their time. Before "the Bug" or the compact was a twinkle in car dealers' dashboard eyes. This was only a part of Powel's accomplishments. He had many that never saw the light of day...and many just for his own satisfaction...and amusement like the hair dryer and iceball machine.

To test these "inventions" he was always summoning Chip Robertson; Jim Coombe, head of the Powell Valve Company; and Stan Rowe, president of the First/Third Bank. It was just like Kenneth Grahame's classic story about J. Thadius Toad, an English gentleman of great renown and master of Toad Hall, who was years ahead of his time, always experimenting with contraptions like the horseless carriage, steam engine and flying machines. And best of all, always trying them out on his friends, Rabbit, Mole and Otter.

94

"TOAD'S ESCAPED!" - There he goes again! This time into the wild blue yonder, Powel Crosley up where eagles soar with the wind beneath his wings. Reminiscent of Kenneth Grahame's classic story, *The Wind in the Willows,* with the brilliant Toad years ahead of his time in the motor car and airplane and his other inventions, leaving us all behind.. the moles, weasels, otters of this world to fret yet finally to follow him. (Gray History of Wireless Museum — Crosley Telecommunications Center)

"AFTER YOU!" said the comet polite.
(Gray History of Wireless Museum—Crosley Telecommunications Center)

"I'll never forget the day he asked us," Chip recalled, "to go for a ride in his new little Crosley open car. Jim Coombe and Stan Rowe and I went flying over the countryside with him holding on for dear life. It unquestionably had great technical advancements; but Powell would put only seventy-five cents worth of upholstery in it, so it was like the buckboard bounce all the way! We were like his valet, on whom he was always testing his latest contraptions, including a boat propeller that tossed his gentleman's gentleman into the briny brink."

I fully sympathized with Chip when I had the same wild ride in the backseat of a Crosley car to write the account from a woman's point of view, which was a great milestone in woman's lib! My bones denounced the buckboard bounce as Powel proclaimed "Wait 'til you see me pass this truck!" And wail 'til you see me do this and that . . . .

Powel Crosley had made his first automobile when he was only twelve years old, with his brother, Lewis. It looked like a soap box or a jitney bus, as we used to call them. He later made even flag holders clamped on car radiators which sold "like cold drinks in an arid desert," he remarked. His early little "giants" got about fifty miles to the gallon and sold for about $350. They were advertised at the New York World's Fair in 1939 as the car of the future. Little did he dream then how true it was.

Crosley started his empire on a shoestring, a $1,500 note for which he was eventually to receive $12,000,000 in cash from Victor Emanuel, head of Aviation Corporation of California (AVCO)! This was to buy only part of his empire.

When World War II came along, his genius devised and built many operational items for the Government, including radio receivers and transmitters in the field and on the ships.

He also did early experimentations on lighting because his family once owned the famous Pike"s Opera House in Cincinnati, where he tried out his ideas. Then when TV came along, Crosley would be ready for it. He had already experimented with the intriguing new contraption on the electronics horizon back in 1929. And later in 1939. But put it away 'til after the war in 1945. His greatest fear was its cost. So he turned it over to AVCO to further develop it. On his own Crosley TV sets, he worked with DuMont and Sentinel to perfect them.

The Iceball Cometh

Everybody said he had the Midas Touch. Everything he touched turned to gold. Even the common baseball turned into a gilmmering, shining sphere under the lights in the first night game in major league

SONG OF INDIA? - Not quite! Powel Crosley had come a long way from his beginnings with radio when his first musical recordings were interrupted for passing locomotives and distress calls from ships at sea! Pictured here with cartoonist of Andy Gump. "Oh, Min, I'm at WLW." (Cincinnati Historical Society) (Blue Book of Radio by Powel Crosley himself)

history when the Cincinnati Reds played Philadelphia on May 24, 1935. It was the president of the United States, Franklin D. Roosevelt, in the White House who pressed the magic button that lit 632 lamps illuminating Crosley Field that night.

So Powel Crosley , Jr., had done it all! Created or invented or perfected the "Taylor-Tot" which he called the "Go-By-By" originally; ice machines; motorboats; hair-growing machines; car-starters; car tires never needing air; snow plows; tricycles; in addition to his radios, his TV sets, and the radio and TV stations with the most famous call letters in the World – WLW.

He did it all with the philosophy, "He who serves best, profits most." He said that nowhere but in America with its freedom would it have been possible. Our freedom and our rights of individual advancement, he explained, "will progress for the benefit not alone of ourselves, but for the less fortunate people of the world."

The Greatest Ad-Man of'em All

Jim Nelson was the VP who worked on the Kroger and other big accounts of Mr. Robertson's. And he, too, was in his glory when matched with his match, Powel Crosley. Jim handled the Crosley Motors account, with the great prospect of it going from newspaper and magazine ads to the new bonanza of advertising, television! His call reports of his visits to see Powel Crosley, even when the great man was ill at home, were classics of the business. Jim recounted that his bedroom looked like what Ben Franklin's must have looked like, with all kinds of inventive gadgets everywhere...plus hunks of cotton balls stuck in the satin bed drapes. It was like Stanley interviewing Livingston, rather than a client meeting. And Jim's call reports read like a bylined story in the old *New York Herald*.

One day Crosley asked Chip Robertson and Jim Nelson to have our agency think up some names for a new automobile brake and a new engine he had perfected. I became the happiest little cub copywriter in the block when Jim reported that the two names Powel had chosen were my ideas, the hydro-disc brake and the quick-silver engine. Jim laughed and said that Powel insisted that we secretly had an engineer consultant work on those names. The genius wouldn't believe that it was a young girl copywriter who had never even driven a car and didn't know a brake from a break.

Jim Nelson was the truly great ad-man. A first-class pro. And a magnificent person, privately and professionally. A scholar, writer, editor,

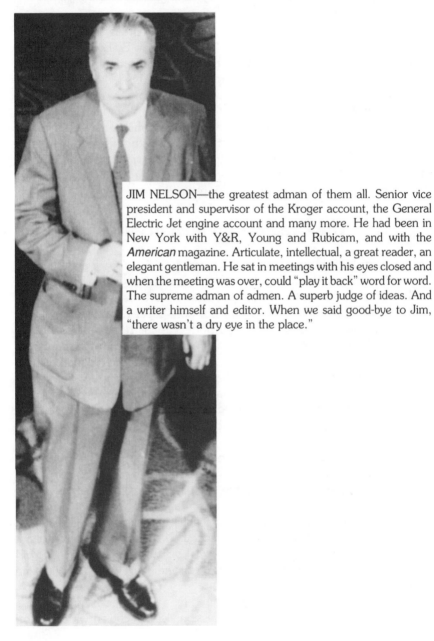

JIM NELSON—the greatest adman of them all. Senior vice president and supervisor of the Kroger account, the General Electric Jet engine account and many more. He had been in New York with Y&R, Young and Rubicam, and with the *American* magazine. Articulate, intellectual, a great reader, an elegant gentleman. He sat in meetings with his eyes closed and when the meeting was over, could "play it back" word for word. The supreme adman of admen. A superb judge of ideas. And a writer himself and editor. When we said good-bye to Jim, "there wasn't a dry eye in the place."

superb account executive. Brilliantly creative. Jim had been with the *Chicago Daily News, American Magazine* and Young & Rubicam Advertising Agency in New York. It took a big man like him to laugh at a mistake we made on the Crosley Motors account. Somebody forgot to fill in the price on the printed window cards. So they all went in dealers' showrooms reading "$00"...which caused Powel Crosley to go into a rage in Toad Hall. But Jim placated him and turned it into a clever publicity stunt about all the checks Powel received from people with the amount made out "$00."

Powel Crosley was, indeed, the Grand Sachem of business, baseball, broadcasting. "The Boss," as he was affectionately called by his men. He was interested in anything that worked, especially cars and radios and selling. He once drew up his own design for an electric car after studying engineering and law at the University of Cincinnati. He also created and/or marketed other gadgets and delved into everything from planes to refrigerators, originating the famous Shelvador, the first refrigerator that had shelves in the door. I remember when our agency was asked to come up with an idea that would get the salesmen's and dealers' wives interested in the Shelvador. So we sent them each a fine earring, stating that if they came to the next meeting with their husbands, they could have the matching earring. It worked!

One day his son, Powel Crosley III, died suddenly from an insect bite. And Powel Crosley IV was killed in Korea just a few days before the armistice was signed.

Both Jim Nelson and Powel Crosley reminded us that our lives turned out to be our favorite slogans. In their case, sadly yet sweetly, it was "When the iron man begins to rust."

Thanks for the Memories of Bob Hope

At our regular brainstorming sessions of seven artists and ten writers, Jim Nelson sat with his eyes closed listening to as many as a hundred ideas delivered in cash-register rapid fire. Often he said not a word until the meeting was over. Then with equal rapidity, like a flash, without hesitating a second, he named the best idea of the hundred he had just heard. He certainly had a way with ideas and a way with words. And surely agreed with Bill Bernbach's philosophy that every product and every company has a soul and a character. And Jim went even one step further...every human being. He helped train me as a young copywriter, an experience I'll never forget, learning from the master.

Best of all, he was the most forgiving person. He handled the large Kroger Food Stores' account. I'll never forget the day we went to the Kroger Food Foundation to get some ideas for some television advertising. This was to include a part about the history of coffee. As the coffee cans came off the assembly lines, I stupidly picked one up to examine it, which almost caused a cataclysm. And such a case of coffee nerves I never did see! The rest of the cans went flying merrily off the end of the ramp and piled up all along it like a junk car lot. Good to the last drop. Men's heads appeared in every door, window and hole in the floor...all shouting in Tower of Babel salutations. It was enough to cause Juan Valdez to fall off his mountain. But rather than get mad, too, Jim just turned to me and said, "That's okay."

We did get what we came for, however, an extensive Kroger campaign with what goes on behind the scenes in the food market. And we lined up stars, including Bob Hope, Betty Hutton, Herb Shriner, Roy Rogers and Dale Evans, and Alan Ladd, to get the whole thing going. Hope really laughed at my scripts, maybe because he thought they were funny "uh-oh" rather than funny "ha-ha." LIke the one with the meat-biting machine that actually bites the beef to check its tenderness. I had the machine say, "Make mine rare." A stroke of genius I remarked gayly on the copy, but either Hope or somebody on his staff crossed out the "of genius." Then there was the consistency testing disc for preserves and canned vegetables, which I say in the commercial, "Now let's all stick together through thick and thin." Then there was the crumb testing machine which pressure-tested the freshness of bread. I had the machine say, "Only crumbs allowed." Then I decided to do a whodunit series of TV commercials with these ideas we had gotten down at the Kroger Food Foundation. The first episode would be called "The Ghosts Who Came to Dinner." And the lead-in read, "Police Chief Bunsen Burner turned the heat on Willie the Test Tube..."

The stars were supposed to come in with a voice-over plug for Kroger. But for some strange reason, the commercials were never produced as I had written them. Because somebody else wrote across the scripts, "Whoever came up with these food commercial ideas deserves twenty lashes with a wet noodle."

Well, maybe I would have better luck working on another of Jim Nelson's accounts...Sal-Fayne cold and pain capsules. Relieve that pain with Sal-Fayne had been a well-known slogan for thirty years. So I sprightly added the thoughts of break the tablet habit...the adult pain reliever...and for relief beyond belief. And topped it all off with a limerick:

"There once was a fellow named Sam
Who took every tablet what am,
But none seemed to lick

His cold miseries quick
Then he tried Sal-Fayne capsules...and wham!"

This probably gave the client Excedrin headache number one and inspired Rosser Reeves' slogan for Anacin — "for fast, fast, fast relief." But I suppose for really fast, fast, fast relief he retired from the advertising go-round, especially far from the TV tremors...and buffered business of buffeted aches and pains...plus varicose brains. Maybe the first Maalox moment!

We Found General Electric in Martha Washington's Cookbook

Every writer's dream was the General Electric account, for its Jet Engine Division here. From its very beginning of three men to thirteen thousand employees, we worked on its public relations and advertising with our own Jim Nelson and their Dick Peake, the pro of pros. They gave us a free hand, no phantom taboos typical of the advertising business and broadcasting industry. We went to work with broadcasting subjects including everything from Lindbergh's landing in Paris...to a man who founded a tick-tock town...to Aesop's Fables...to *Martha Washington's Cook Book*...to old Valentines...to the day a scarecrow came to town and couldn't believe his button eyes. And, I suppose, this more than anything else best describes, too, the day Jim Nelson left the company.

The day he retired most of us cried. We couldn't bear to tell him good-bye. It was the end of an era in more ways than one. Jim was of the old school, if you want to call it that. A better term would be the good school. The writing, communications, broadcasting and advertising school that believed a writer had to be a writer and an artist an artist. He was not of the new breed of flip headliners who don't know how to begin, then to write, the first sentence. Who try to out-clever each other. The boy wonders. Jim believed in the Four Horsemen of the communications Apocalypse education, experience, ability, loyalty. We never saw him reading books with such titles, *How to Write for Television*...or *What to Put in Space Copy*. We once asked him what he thought were the best broadcasting and advertising books. He replied, "The Bible, Shakespeare's plays, Chesterton, and so on and so on..."

Jim himself certainly could have written his own *Confessions of an Ad-Man,** like David Ogilvy, or another *Tale of the Blue Horse and Other Million Dollar Ads****, like Stanley Arnold. Or a Calkins or Lasker or Hopkins story.

*Atheneum, New York, 1962.
**Prentice-Hall, Inc., Englewood Cliffs, New Jersey, 1968.

McCALL'S MAGAZINE AWARD for the 50th Anniversary of The Ralph H. Jones Company ad agency, presented by the magazine rep (1) to C.M. Robertson, Jr.,(r) chairman of the board, and Paul Myers, president.

ALL ABOARD! The S .S Jones, skippered by "Captain" Paul D. Myers is all set to sail from its home port, The Ralph H. Jones advertising agency, Carew Tower, Cincinnati. Surrounded by pretty crew, all members of the agency, The Ralph H. Jones Company played nautical host for representatives of national consumer magazines on the eve of their 30th Annual CINCIAMA Party. A tradition, the Jones company played host since 1949 for the get-together, long considered one of the most unique events in the world of advertising, which brings together media, the agency and the client for an evening of socializing and business discussion. A darling picture of Paul!

He Was Among the "400"

Of all the remembrances of Paul Myers, who became company president, there's one I'll never forget. The time he adopted his first child. Although he had achieved everything, top man in the national 4'A's, American Association of Advertising Agencies, and all the rest this was his finest hour. Socially, professionally, personally.

When he came to work that day, he had a different look about him. As he walked into his office, he sat down behind the desk and gazed out the window for a long time, as if contemplating the future with such awe and fulfillment. Then he slowly turned and said, "I've got me a son! I've got me a boy! I'm a father! The adoption has come through!" And we all burst out crying.

When he came back from lunch, he had another announcement to make. An announcement about announcements!

"Well, I ordered the announcements," he proudly proclaimed.

"That's good," we all joyfully agreed. "Not wasting any time!"

"No, siree," he still gleamed. "Four hundred," he happily said.

At this we all looked at each other. "Did you say four hundred? Four hundred what?"

"I ordered four hundred announcements," he boasted.

We were all dumbfounded. "You...ah...well..." we muttered in disbelief.

"That's the same reaction I got from the saleslady at Closson's. She asked me how many I wanted. And when I told her four hundred, she said, 'I beg you pardon. I misunderstood you. I thought you said four hundred.'"

"I did say four hundred announcements," I told her.

"I never heard of anybody ordering four hundred...I mean that's quite a large number...I mean are you sure...Does your wife know about this?" the saleslady continued.

"Four hundred," Paul repeated emphatically. To which, at this point, she weakly answered, "Oh, my goodness.."

DICK GEIS—carried on where Jim Nelson left off in the agency. He took over the huge Ashland Oil account. A superb account man with all the savvy of what a good account executive should be. Never saw anybody work as hard. But the most memorable day was when he was mistaken for Rudolf Valentino on the street. It was too good to let drop. So we...(read on for rest of the story!)

Chapter 5

There Was Something Sheik About Him

One day the movie about the great Rudolf Valentino was showing in town. As a promotions stunt, the theatre had a man walking the street that week who was supposed to represent Valentino. And if any women asked him if he were Rudolf Valentino, they would receive free tickets to the movie. Well, it so happened that Dick Geis, one of our vice president account executives, was not aware of this theatre promotion gimmick. So when he returned from lunch that day, he was really beside himself.

"I've come to the conclusion," he expostulated, "that women are nuts! Absolutely stark raving mad nuts! Five of them came up to me on the street today and asked me if I were Rudolf Valentino! I'm telling everybody, the world is going bananas!"

Of course, the rest of us knew what was going on, but it was too good a joke on Dick to let him in on the secret. So we pulled his leg, telling him that was probably because he so resembled the great sheik. We even hid his coat, taking it off the coat hanger in his office closet and hanging a bedsheet around it instead as the appropriate outer garb for a sheik. "You bunch of riffs and raffs," he laughed. "I know who did this!"

Dick was the super-duper, big-time, first-class-all-the-way VP in charge of the big Ashland Oil account, handling it with their first-class-all-the-way George Sisler. A book has been written about Ashland's Rex Blazer, one of the great figures in the industry. I always had a soft spot in my heart for this account, not because I knew a horn from a honk, but because my great-grandparents settled in Ashland Kentucky, when they came over from Ireland. That's why I pleaded with Dick to let me try my hand once at writing something for the account.

"Okay," he gave in. "But I don't believe in women drivers. Besides, you can't even drive."

"Maybe that's why I could come up with something different," I hopefully explained. "You know, kind of removed from the scene. Maybe I can see the trees for the forest..or is it the forest for the trees?"

"Sounds like you're off to a glorious beginning," Dick moaned. "But go ahead and give it a try. Do an Ashland gasoline television commercial on using seat belts."

Wow! My big chance, I thought. On the big Ashland account. Okay, one on seat belts. A little prayer to the patron saint of writers, William Wordsmith. And here comes the inspiration after the aspiration! Sheer genius. Finished in no time. Now to turn it in. "Are you ready for the gasser?!" I exclaimed. "A real go-go commercial!"

Breathing his last, Dick weakly whispered, "Okay, let's have it."

"Camera! Lights! Action!" I set the stage. "Here comes the great *Sunset Boulevard* scene when Gloria Swanson descends the staircase. Silence please. I am ready for my closeup, Mr. DeMille."

"I'm not even breathing," mumbled Dick.

"There once was a fellow named Selt
Who didn't have on a seat belt,
And one foggy day
He drove down a one-way
So now his head is one welt!"

"O-h-h-h-h-h..." Dick groaned.

"Wait now!" I pleaded. "Maybe you'll like the next commercial!"

"There once was a driver named Velt
Who didn't own a seat belt,
And she never did learn
To signal a turn,
So there's little left of her pelt."

"But here's the best one! You'll love it!" I raved.

"There once was a fellow named Gelt
Who didn't like a seat belt,
And he ran a red light
That dark dismal night,
When they yelt, he did go to helt!"

"Call the life squad!" Dick laughed. "There's been an accident!! I need oxygen and an octane transfusion!!!"

Needless to say, these limericks caused the beginning of the gasoline shortage, because when anybody heard them they headed for the border.

Vas You Ever in Zinzinnati? Vell, Vas You?!

(See photo page 80)

Who could efer or rather ever forget working with Dick Perry, one of the most versatile and voluminous writers? His well-known books include, *Not Just a Sound, *the Story of WLW Radio; Vas You Ever in Zinzinnati;** Raymond and Me That Summer;*** The Roundhouse, Paradise and Mr. Pickering;** a history of Ohio; and others. Dick also has been the ghost writer for the autobiographies of well-known people.

Dick Perry was the George Gobel of the copywriting department. Then, before his beard, he looked like Gobel, acted like Gobel and joked like Gobel. "I was coming around that last corner from a New Year's Eve party on that dark icy night and was making it okay until somebody stepped on my hand."

A prolific pounder-outer, he could knock out ads, TV commercials, magazine articles and stories all in one day. But his special talent was satire. He could pull anybody's leg at the Achilles' heel and that person wouldn't realize it. You'd think it was just a stretch sock that wasn't stretching or a dangling supporter. He satirized everybody and everything. No cow was sacred. Or no bull. If someone joined our department who was not such an award-winning writer, Dick would good-naturedly give him the needle.

"Haven't I seen your name someplace before, like on the Declaration of Independence?" But when the writer did come up with something good, Dick would confuse him even more by saying, "Where did you get that idea? It's the best one of mine you ever thought of!"

One afternoon somebody rushed in trying to be funny, which the remark truly was. "There's a meeting in the general office. Company's presenting a gift to a guy who's been with the firm a hundred and fifty years."

Dick didn't bat an eye. Merely looked and asked, "Why are they giving him a gift?"

Not to be topped, the bearer of the news and the joke replied, "Because he's never been late, never missed a day, never left early."

But he couldn't top Dick, who simply retorted, "That's not a man. That's a streetcar!"

When Dick confronted you alone with his special brand of happy prickly heat, that was one thing. But he usually chose to try to embarrass you in front of someone else. Like the day the office manager, Ed Elfers, was at my desk going over some report with me. Dick stuck his head in the door and remarked, "The office picnic has been called off for this afternoon." Which, of course, really threw the office manager for a

111

minute. How could there be an office picnic and he not know about it? As if that weren't enough, Dick returned a few minutes later and added, "So you can take the deviled eggs back home."

Dick rarely took a requisition seriously, even though in the end he turned out a top-flight piece of work. But he had to good-humoredly joke with it awhile. He could see humor in anything. One requisition called for a new name for a Pecan Sandy Swirl cookie. Dick turned in, "Swirl Pecan Sandies...Sandy Swirl Pecans...Sandy Pecan Swirls...Pecan Swirl Sandies...Swirl Sandy Pecans."

Another time, an account executive chastised the writing department for cutting up so much and demanded we turn in some really "pithy" ideas. So Dick replied with his list, "Pithy helmets...watermelon pithys...snake pithys." The follow-up requisition further chastised our department for taking assignments lightly and demanded ideas of "general" nature. So Dick couldn't resist it again. His list included "general nuisance...general delivery...general information...general interest...generalissimo."

At which the account executive complained in a terse note there was such general confusion in the writing department that the company couldn't accomplish anything.

To which Dick replied, "There's one I forgot. General confusion."

*Prentice-Hall, Inc., Englewood Cliffs, New Jersey, 1971.
**Doubleday & Company, Inc., Garden City, New York, 1966.
***Harcourt, Brace & World, Inc., New York, 1963.

It Was Too Much for the Canary

At that time we had ten writers all in one big office, like a city room at a newspaper, but with glass cubicle partitions. So we really shared the same office and the same air. It would get so heavy with smoke, that we started a pollution control petition to send to the United States Congress in behalf of the writing department! It got so bad one afternoon, Dick Perry came running through again yelling, "I wouldn't say the air in here is bad, but the canary just died!"

"No wonder!" I replied. "I've heard of writer's cramp, but this is ridiculous. We'll probably get the bends when we go outside!"

Another of Dick's typical comments on the department smog was one of the most famous lines in advertising history, the old stand-by of the olden days, "Have you used Pear's Soap today?" And we all assured him in a sing-song chorus that we had all done so, which didn't help the smog one bit. No pool hall smelled as bad as our department. Everybody even used to complain about us as we walked through the halls.

"Oh, well," I remarked to Dick, "They all have to admit there's a certain air about the writers, anyway."

"Yeah," he laughed, "And it's a kind of pigpen perfume."

Not to let the heady atmosphere of the writing department go unnoticed by everyone passing by, he made a sign and hung it on the door: "Hoof and mouth disease checkpoint."

Then one day a roach ran across the floor. "That does it!" I proclaimed. "We've not to clean up this department. Now we have roaches!"

"Now don't get excited," Dick comforted. "I say if they can write, let'em come."

"You've been reading Archie and Mahitabel," I replied. "I say they go...talent or no talent. How can I get any work done around here? I can't concentrate on my latest Crosley Broadcasting campaign. I'm trying to think of ways to say that the WLW group are the best salesmen on TV."

"What have you got so far?" he asked.

"Well, I've got 'How to sell a Zulu an iglu'...'How to sell King-Kong ping-pong.'"

"How about...'How to sell a fishwife a steak knife!'" he added. And further added. "Say, did you know who is mentioned most in the Bible?"

"No, who?"

"He who."

At this, Dick gave his usual farewell address to the troops of our department as he left for the day. We had our choice of, "Okay! Everybody out of the pool!" Or "I'm going to the drinking fountain and I won't be back."

A Cure for Creeping Numbness

Now a pause for station identification...with a few hundred TV commercials thrown in.

And how did television advertising come about. Certainly Lee De Forest, who helped make radio possible with his audion tube, wouldn't have liked it. In the early days of broadcasting he violently objected to commercials on radio. What he would have said about those on television, only somebody's hair dresser knows for sure. About radio advertising De Forest lamented, "What have you done with my child? You have sent him out on the street in rags to collect money from all sundry. You have made him a laughing stock of intelligence, surely a stench in the nostrils of the gods of the ionosphere."

This, of course, was an extreme of opinion. On the other extreme, as everybody knows, the history of advertising, including television, has some lofty, important moments in the business and manufacturing progress of our country. "The business of America is business." And advertising is this business of this business.

Going back to the beginning of it all, even though as I said before, the word slogan is derived from Gaelic battle cry, its usage is much more modern. It was the 19th century era of patent medicines that were good for what ails you and what didn't, which gave advertising it first big surge of power. For fast, fast, fast relief in those days, from drooping drawers, knock-knees, baggy britches, even creeping numbness...you could take just one medicine and it would do the trick...supposedly. These early wonder drugs could each get rid of a spot on the lung or a spot on your vest. For itchy itches, fungus feet, or mother-in-law-itis, just take Dr. Smith's Miracle Medicine. One such cure-all was guaranteed, remember, to make plain folks pink and thin folks plump and weak folks well and despairing folks happy. With such utopian promises of complete cure, who could resist taking Old Sachem Bitters and Wigwam Tonic and Swamp Root?! And who could bypass that certain kind of BVD's that promised a substitute, warm and clinging, for romance:

Though love grow cold
Do not despair,
There's Ypsilanti
Underwear.

In addition to this medicine sideshow, it was the sideshow of P. T. Barnum that laid the cornerstone of huckstering. Barnum was called the Shakespeare of advertising and promotion. He so believed in it that he said, "The only liquid man could safely use in excess was printer's ink." In his poster describing one of his strange sideshow attractions, he really could have been describing the modern TV commercial! Or TV ad-man. Remember, he said, "What is it? The singular creature ever known — evidently the connecting link between the human and brute creation, bearing alike the characteristics of each. What is it no one pretends to tell, and the universal inquiry is, what is it?"

Or did I say this before? Well, I'll say it again! Worth repeating. (The Cincinnati Advertiser's Club is the oldest in the world, one year even older than New York's!)

The Ivory Palaces Turned Out
to be 99-44/100% Pure

Then along came the birth of the advertising agency and the great copywriters, including Claude Hopkins, Elmo Calkins, Albert Lasker, Bruce Barton, John Powers, Bill Bernbach and the rest.

Their slogans became part of the American language: "They Laughed When I Sat Down at the Piano"..."I'd Walk a Mile for a Camel".."The Pause that Refreshes"..."Quick, Henry, the Flit!"..."For the Skin You Love to Touch"..."They Satisfy"...and the scores of others which helped make life a little better and a little happier for hundreds of thousands of people. Even the slogan, "Good to the Last Drop," supposedly came from a president of the United States, Teddy Roosevelt, when served the coffee, Maxwell House.

Trademarks became as familiar as the slogans. And the names of the products became a part not only of our language but our civilization. Coke..Frigidaire...Kodak...all contributing to give man the highest standard of living since the beginning of time. Remember, even the name of Ivory for its soap came from the forty-fifth Psalm.

And make thee glad all these products have, even though maybe some of the commercials have made thee turn down the sound button on thy set. Of all the early titles and names given to television, one of the best was the Encyclopedia Britannica's definition: "the broadcasting of faces." And years later Churchill added an amendment to that, which could be the amendment of the TV commercial. When informed that he would be on TV in the early days of the medium, he replied, "I hope the raw material is as good as the distribution."

Advertising on television had come a long way from the type of advertising associated with the characters in Dickens' stories. Like the tavern handbills reading:

If I know'd a donkey wot wouldn't go

To see Mrs. Jarley's wax-work show.

No wonder the Old Curiosity Shop did a good business.

My very own favorites of all time are Jordan Motor Cars' great classic ad of its day, "Somewhere West of Laramie...the lass whose face is brown with the sun...she loves the cross of the wild and the tame...of laughter and lilt and light...who rides lean and rangy into the red horizon..." Cadillac's "Penalty of Leadership: That which deserves to live, lives...That which is good or great makes itself known, no matter how loud the clamor or denial." Kodak's "Turn Around" TV commercial to Harry Belafonte's song depicting the life of a girl growing up and "The Pepsi generation." all of which, summed up, mean "Born Free."

Chapter 6

An Increase of Flesh and Nervous Vigor

One afternoon in reading over ads of the good old days, back to the Gay Nineties, I decided just for fun to use some of the wording in a modern medicinal commercial. This was not supposed to be seen by the client, of course. It would be only for our own amusement. When I had finished the television commercial, with a very straight face I took it into the office of another writer, Don Leshner, and proudly announced it was my most recent accomplishment. I was careful not to give away the fact that I was only joking with the outlandish wording of a bygone era and had no intention of turning this in for the assignment.

My TV commercial read, "This unusual medicinal product causes a gradual increase of flesh and nervous vigor until you can walk without help and fatigue over the surrounding hills and dales." Word for word, the old wording of the old ad.

After reading it, Don came up with one of his typical, talented asides. Not sure whether or not I was being serious about turning in this TV sixty-second catastrophe, Don looked up and with as straight a face as the one that I was trying to pretend, and mumbled, "ummmmrrrhhhhh."

"I beg your pardon," I said, "I didn't hear you."

Then he followed up with his second other typical, talented habit. The unflinching unfinished sentence. Staring blankly at the TV script he commented, "Well, from this commercial it's obvious, more than ever, that the only thing to do with you is..."

"Yes?! Yes?!" I hopefully asked.

"That's right," he concluded. "Yes, you're absolutely right."

"Right about what?" I persisted. "Right about the TV commercial or right about yes?"

"Right, you know the old saying. There's more than..."

He Could Don any Personality

Anybody could keep up this Bud-Abbott-Lou-Costello routine with Don Leshner for many a happy hour.

THE WRITERS - PRODUCERS - DIRECTORS

(Photos courtesy/Don and Jerry Leshner, Don Leshner Productions, Cincinnati)

DON LESHNER - Writer-producer-director par excellence, Don has worked with stars from the east coast to the west coast, beginning with Mickey Rooney in the Armed Forces Radio Network in Europe during World War II. The stories he can tell are priceless; about keeping Vincent Price waiting while he got a haircut; about a James Mason recording session of "The Pied Piper"; about his days with the George Burns crew in L.A. and on the serious side, here at General Electrec Jet Engine division, Cincinnati. But his greatest story was when the pressure was on and he turned into "Dracula." Stop the Pounding! Everything was a pushover for Don, including that tree!

Don was our communications expert with accent on the theatre and its relations to broadcasting. He was another Crosley Broadcasting grad from the famous WLW stations. He could write, direct, produce, announce, act. A theatre major, he excelled in writing and delivering dialect copy. Don could imitate the Jewish comedian, Myron Cohen, in superb skits. But his greatest routine was his take-off on Count Dracula from Transylvania...stop the pounding! And whenever things got pressurized in our copywriting cabin, Don would rush from his desk shouting, "Stop the pounding!"

He also had a great collection of friends — some real, some imaginary with a great collection of names — some real, some imaginary. These included his architect friend, Archie Church...and the designer, Artie Craftsman...and Yo-Yo Yogurt, the meat packer. Not to mention Tom Failure, who owned the Lead Balloon Factory. And Absorbine, Jr., named for his famous father, Absorbine, Sr.

His other speciality was his knack for dealing with, meeting with, coming up with, and accidentally running into celebrities. If a piece of paper would blow off his desk, he'd comment, "Oh, there goes my letter from Mrs. Eisenhower," And if he made out a laundry list, it would be scribbled on the back of a message from Haile Selassie. One day Don turned in some TV commercials and a letter from the President of the United States was accidentally sticking to the back of them!

When Don Leshner worked for NBC Television and for CBS out on the coast and for Frederic Ziv, he did a lot of interviewing and recordings for the stars. He unintentionally kept Vincent Price waiting for half an hour while getting a haircut. Price said, "Think nothing of it." And they proceeded to record Hamlet's soliloquy and Poe's "Telltale Heart." Don recorded many of the great stars...James Mason reading "The Pied Piper"...Steve Allen...and others. But his greatest encounters with celebrities were his accidental ones. Like reaching for the last newspaper in a Los Angeles rack along with somebody else, who turned out to be Bill Frawley, probably most famous for his role in the *I Love Lucy* series with Lucille Ball. And standing behind Jack Lemmon in a supermarket checkout line. Don couldn't resist this opportunity, so he said to Lemmon, "Say, I've got a great idea for you to make a musical comedy, based on the book, *The Organization Man*." Lemmon looked at him as if he were some kind of a checkout-counter nut. But later somebody did make a musical out of it, a smash hit, *How to Succeed in Business Without Really Trying!*

Don's other encounters with the stars at the famous Brown Derby Restaurant relate like an Art Buchwald column.

We all agree if Don Leshner ever went to the Himalayas, he

119

Mickey Rooney - Don Leshner, World War II

Don Leshner at GE

would surely stumble over the mysterious, illusive Abominable Snowman on a mountain trail and propose the ideal part in a TV commercial to him. And if Don ever ventured to the Holy Land, he would certainly run across one of the twelve apostles at some wayside well. And when Don goes to heaven, he will most assuredly accidentally sit down in the chair next to St. Peter...or Abraham...or Isaac...or Jacob.

He Proudly Held on to the Academy Award

One evening in Los Angeles, Don and his wife, who was with *TV Guide*, went to a party at the home of Hugo Friederhoffer, winner of the Academy Award for the musical score in *The Best Years of Our Lives*. Don noticed the beautiful gold Academy Award statuette in an obscure place, he thought, on a bookshelf. Impressed by its glittering appearance, Don proceeded to take it down and put it in a prominent place in the distinguished musician's household. He started wandering around in the middle of the party guests looking for just the spot, oblivious of the party going on around him. Finally, Friederhoffer noticed him, probably thinking he was walking in his sleep, and asked, "What in tarnation are you doing with that?" And Don in his superb unfinished sentence style replied, "I was just trying to...Yes, I was about to...Which is the reason for my..."

In Don's spare time he's quite a golfer. And rather than take a coffee break at the office, Don would practice his golf swing with the building cleaning equipment. So if you walked into his office, not forewarned, you might get a mop flung in your face or a broom wrapped around you neck, it having been mistaken for the 18th hole. This happened to Toby Balcom, (HTB, III), son of the chairman of the board of the Wiedemann Brewing Company, one of the super suds outfits. At the time, Toby was a junior account executive and a displaced person with his desk in the writing department smog suite. Another in the long line of DP's who used to get lost temporarily in the copywriting cataclysm. Toby, too, has never been the same since. It always did something to the soul and the psyche to be left adrift in the outer space and time of the wordsmithers. Other people, the earthlings, never fully recovered their equilibrium. Or their belongings. Or their batteries in their transistors or tape recorders.

The librarian was another person who was temporarily placed in the copywriting ward. We caused Mary Jane Knolle to age ten years by clipping things out of her magazines, circulating all her non-circulating books, constantly losing the company library card, searching in her

SWEET HARMONY or is it Adeline? Posing for an ad, this "intriguing" barbershop quartet gets off a few bars, and that's probably where they wound up or where they began. (1 to r) Writer Gene Dailey, secretary- treasurer Ed Elfers, account executive Dick Geis, writer-producer Don Leshner. The mustaches are most delicately put on with rubber cement (!) reminding one of that old familiar slogan, "You'll wonder where your gums went when you brush your teeth with rubber cement." A great group! The cream of the crop!

research files, and munching on vanilla wafers while borrowing her morning paper.

One afternoon I went to the public library to see what new films had arrived and found a life of Tolstoy. I checked it out to take back to the office to show at our lunch-hour film sessions. But it was so heavy, I could make it only halfway down the street. So I had to call Don and Toby to meet me, stranded at a busy intersection in a phone booth with Tolstoy. After we viewed the film, somehow it got mixed up with our reels of television commercials and presentations. So in a meeting the next day with a potential client, what in the whole wide world is put on the projector by mistake as an example of our years of creativity and TV award-winning commercials, but scenes from *War and Peace, Anna Karenina,* and *The Death of Ivan Ilvitch*...with a grand climax of a massive horde of Russian peasants carrying Tolstoy's casket over the Ukraine countryside! The catastrophic result was that the potential client remained potential.

The Best Lines Were by Vines

Among our other communications characters and colleagues was Ralph Vines, a fine writer. I always considered Ralph as a kind of fourth brother. Advisor, critic, sympathizer, friend. He's like the Damon Runyan of the business. Basically a newspaper man. A who-what-where-when-how champion of get the facts, man, then put them into words. A writer, reporter, editor, co-author of several textbooks, and most of all a delightful human interest entrepreneur. Ralph, too, was a Crosley Broadcasting alumnus with all the qualifications of that great WLW call letter character crowd. He had also been a columnist for the *Cincinnati Enquirer* and the *Dayton Daily News.* And later worked with National Cash Register as a speech-writer and with Mead Johnson on Metrecal.

How Ralph got his job with Mead was an episode in itself. He went on a Metrecal diet. Then walked into the Mead office at Evansville, Indiana, holding up his trousers with one hand and his belt in another. "Look!!" he exclaimed. "I'm a walking example of Metrecal! And I've had twenty years experience in the communications field." How could they resist?

It was said of Winston Churchill that he mobilized the English language and sent it off to war. And it could be said of Ralph Vines that he double-checked the gear of each word as it went. He was forever word worrying and weighing and whittling. The master word watcher. And as with all talented people, Ralph had a glorious sense of humor. He loved,

RALPH VINES - The quintessential newspaper man with all the talent and instincts of the great reporter. Get the facts, dig deep, research the material. He had been a reporter and columnist for the *Cincinnati Enquirer* and *Dayton Journal*. While writing, he always played his Mozart recordings and typed according to the tempo of the music! Every summer he and his wife "Skippy", a history professor at the University of Dayton, took off for the British Isles to peruse Oxford or where he pursued his second great love to Mozart, golf at St. Andrew's.

(Photo courtesy Burke-Dowling-Adams, Atlanta, division of BBD&O, New York)
AL BOAM - The classy New Yorker, with all the style of an actor. And forever forty, never ages, Al became a writer and account executive in Atlanta for Delta Airlines with Burke, Dowling and Adams, a division of Batten, Barton, Durstine and Osborn of New York. And New York is forever calling Al home with the "rattle of the subway train, the bustle of the taxis" and the play's the thing. Once a New Yorker, always a New Yorker. Simply superb in every way. (See story page 134)

especially, to create characters and write stories and TV skits about them. An example was Phil Dirt, his hero for a new Western. And Mr. Stump, the neighborhood garden-and-yard fanatic. Then there was also Mr. Dank, the sewer inspector. Once we were working on a television commercial series and Ralph included the character of Amelia Jenks Bloomer. Many laughed and thought it was another of his imaginary people. "But there really was a woman by that name," he insisted. "That's where bloomers came from!" he persisted. As the laughter crescendoed to a roar, somebody shouted, "But where did they go to?!"

This character-creating at the office led to many an amusing episode. When accounts did not require a maximum staff of writers, (in other words, when we had lost some business) — we would have several empty offices in the writing department. So Ralph decided we should all create imaginary writers to inhabit the empty offices. Ralph created Ses Pool...somebody created Les Miserables..and I made my neighbor Sally Forth. The head of the department we made Lydia Pinkham. We even put coats and hats in their offices and other personal belongings characteristic of the characters. And hung name signs on their desks.

Then one day a new young account executive came through the department showing a prospective client our offices. He proceeded to introduce each of us and alluded to the others by name. "Also in the writing department are Ses Pool...Les Miserables...Sally Forth...and Lydia Pink..." Suddenly it dawned on him that something was wrong. It also dawned on the prospective client. And we lost our prospective. It's a good thing he didn't see the imaginary writer we decided not to hire, but decided to send her instead as the first bug on the moon. Luna Tick.

I Apologized for Lydia Pinkham

One winter morning, I came to the office and the plumber was fixing the stopped-up sink in our department. Ralph said that the plumber had told him that marshmallows had stopped up the sink. Well, I immediately sank into guilt-stricken melancholia because I was in the habit of making hot cocoa with marshmallows every morning and pouring the remains down the sink. And whatever we were guilty of, we blamed on those make-believe colleagues we had created to fill the empty offices. Ralph added to the tale by saying that he had informed the plumber that the marshmallows were poured down the sink by Mrs. Pinkham, head of our department. I didn't realize that Ralph was putting me on. It sounded like something he might really say for fun. But he had said nothing to the plumber, nor had the plumber said anything to him about what was causing the sink to stop up. Immediately, I went in and apologized to the plumber for Lydia Pinkham's marshmallows stopping up the sink. I figured I might as well put the blame on her, too, since Ralph already had. That let me off the hook as the guilty party. At my statement, the plumber dropped his monkey wrench, slowly looked up at me, wiped his brow, shook his head, and muttered, "It takes all kinds of nuts and bolts to make a world."

A very special specialty of Ralph's was having running friendly feuds with people. Like the bus driver. It seems that Ralph did a Dagwood Bumstead act every morning, racing for the bus and barely missing it because the driver would shut the door in his face. At which point Ralph would pound on the glass of the bus door with his fist. But to no avail. The driver would drive on. Finally, one day Ralph had had enough. So he politely, invigoratingly tapped on the bus door with his umbrella and politely, invigoratingly rammed the handle through the glass. The startled driver threw open the door, with broken glass flying everywhere. And Ralph calmly boarded the bus and said, "Thank you." Then the driver slammed the door, with broken glass still flying everywhere, and drove off in a rage...as Ralph sat smilingly, silently, innocently in the front seat. When he arrived at the office that morning, he was wildly waving his umbrella in triumph. Or what was left of it. The thing looked like a TV antenna which had been struck by lightning...because of its desperate journey...through the bus' glass door. "Never again!" yelled Ralph. "Never again for the rest of my life will a bus driver shut the door in my face!"

Another friendly feud Ralph had was with a certain account executive. Everytime Ralph made a suggestion in a meeting, this fellow would veto it by sitting there and simply shaking his head...and shaking his head...and shaking his head. Finally, one day Ralph remarked, "When your spasm is over, I'll continue with the explanation of my ideas for this TV campaign."

Ralph later spent his summers at Oxford, England, with his wife who was a history professor at Dayton University. Truly a Yank at Oxford.

And Away We Go!"

Jack Keating should have been in Steve Allen's book, *The Funny Men.** A great gag writer, gag teller and master of ceremonies, Jack was a daily double of Jackie Gleason. He could do "And away we go!" imitating to a tee Gleason's special brand of "tea." Jack had been with CBS in Chicago, Paramount and David O. Selznick Studios midwest

(Photos courtesy of Mrs. Jack Keating, Cincinnati)

JACK KEATING- "And away we go!" He was a perfect double for Jackie Gleason. Looked like him, acted like him, talented like him. The emcee, always ready with a funny line or a funny face. His favorite jokes were "the little old nun" jokes. He especially liked the one about the little old nun who felt sorry for a bum begging on a street corner, so she gave him $5.00. The next day the bum turned up at the convent door dressed fit to kill. "Just came to thank you, Sister," he said. "God Speed paid 100-to-1 in the fifth."

region, the *Cincinnati Post*, and naturally Crosley Broadcasting, the WLW group.

One of his greatest talents was his retortfulness to a stupid question or remark. On a particular St. Patrick's Day, Jack was in the process of pinning a green carnation on his coat. As he looked for a pin in his desk drawer, he held the green carnation between his teeth. Somebody in passing remarked, "Hey, Jack! What are you doing with that green carnation between your teeth?" Jack retorted, "I'm doing the Irish version of Carmen tonight at the opera!"

Jacks favorite prop was an old Beattle wig, which he often wore around the office for a gag. A fellow with whom Jack was not so friendly once gave with a big guffaw and bellowed, "What are you wearing that wig around for?" Jack replied, "Because I've got a soft spot in my head for you." And when someone asked Jack if he liked his office, he answered, "Yes, but it's so small I have to go out in the hall to change my mind."

Being very Irish, Jack was really in his heyday when JFK was in office. And loved to relate the jokes and stories circulating then about the church. One of his favorites was "It used to be a mortal sin not to go to Mass on Sunday. Now it's a federal offense."

*Simon & Shuster, New York, 1958.

The Little Old Nun Never Had It So Good

And, of course, his trademark was the little old nun joke. These he could dream up by the hour. It seems a little old nun was standing outside a saloon waiting for a bus on a cold winter day. The new bartender on duty saw her and invited her to step inside the door out of the cold. But she shyly replied, "No, thank you, sir, I daresn't come in." However, after a kindly conversation he finally persuaded her to come in and wait for the bus. Then he commented, "Sister, you're shaking. Let me give you a little drink to stop that chill." Again the little old nun refused his hospitality.

"No, thank you, sir, I daresn't take it." But the bartender insisted.

"Come on now, Sister. Just a little bit in the bottom of the glass to warm you up." He finally persuaded her to take it. Then her bus came. As she was leaving, the regular bartender came on duty and, noticing the kind elderly Sister leaving, shouted to the saloon owner in the back room, "Hey, Charlie!! That little old nun was in here again!"

Glenn Ryle, a well-known personality on Taft's WKRC-TV, was listening to Jack tell this joke and bent over laughing at him. Glenn was a quiet, industrious member of the department, constantly interrupted by the

Jack Keating

AND AWAY WE GO! And he almost did! Jack Keating almost drowned when posing for a client ad, as the folding chair floating in the swimming pool collapsed in deep water.

capers of the rest of the copywriters. And just so Glenn couldn't get back to work, Jack would start on another little old nun joke. This time it would be about the one who saw a bum begging on a street corner. She felt sorry for him and gave him a $5 bill and whispered, "God Speed!" Well, a day later, the former bum turned up at the convent door, dressed fit to kill. The little old nun answered the bell. She didn't recognize the man at the door as being the bum on the street corner the day before. "Who are you, my good man?" she asked. "And what do you want?" The fellow beamed and exclaimed, "I'm the guy you gave the five bucks to yesterday. Just came to repay you, Sister. God Speed paid a hundred to one in the fifth at Santa Anita!" That was Jack. All you had to do was give him an audience, even of one person, and he was off and running just like "God Speed." I'll never forget the time I was standing in the Crosley Square lobby with him. We were waiting to go into a meeting to see a pilot film on a new television show. Another person happened to be sitting in the lobby with us. While passing the time waiting for the meeting to start, I happened to comment to Jack about the new rules on waste as advocated by some government official, the beginning of the big ecology movement. In answering, Jack included the other man sitting in the lobby in the conversation. Jack turned to him and said, "Yeah, that's what I say. Stop wasting our natural resources. Stop cleaning out your ears with the paper clips...and pull the roller towel only halfway down." The man stared at him with the most baffled look on his face. It was Al Unger, then with Frederick Ziv, producers and distributors of some of the greatest radio and TV shows. Later he was a top VIP with Warner Brothers and Universal Studios in Los Angeles, husband of an Irish family friend who used to live across the street, Suzanne Lanigan Unger, in our little Kentucky town.

And not to let a good audience get away, Jack continued, "Say, did you hear about the new asbestos olives, in case there's a fire in the bar?" Al Unger didn't say a word. Just looked at us as if there were a convention of men in white coats in town and we were the subjects of the closing-day seminar.

The 77th Trombone Led the Big Parade

What Jack Keating was with humor, Larry Gilbert was with music in our writing group.

Almost all the writers in our advertising, promotion, publicity and public relations operation had worked at Crosley/AVCO Broadcasting at one time or another. It seems you just weren't a complete communications person unless you had some background with the famous

(Photo courtesy Mrs. Larry Gilbert, Cincinnati)

LARRY GILBERT - The music man, the 77th trombone that led the big parade. He began his music career by winning the Arthur Godfrey Talent Scouts TV show. And it was music, music, music all the way from then on...to his years in Nashville...to composing "The Queen City Suite" for the Symphony Orchestra. "With 110 cornets close at hand...Horns of every shape and kind...76 trombones caught the morning sun..."

WLW stations. Included in this luminous alumni was our music man, Larry Gilbert, a brilliant musician, composer, arranger, producer and creative talent; we called him "the 77th trombone."

Larry looked like somebody right out of Tin Pan Alley. He was part of the great crowd of musicians who used to gather at Kern Aylward's old Irish pub in nearby Covington, Kentucky. Another was Haven Gillespie, who wrote "Santa Claus Is Coming to Town," "Up a Lazy River," "That Lucky Old Sun," and many, many more hits. Kern and Larry and Haven and the others plunked down their talent on the old worn-out piano. So old and so worn-out that half the white keys were black and half the black keys were white. Everybody got up and did his own thing, some good thing! Great songs, great people, great enjoyment, all presided over by old-time minstrel man and vaudevillian, Kern Aylward.

Larry Gilbert was at home enjoying the music men at Kern's saloon or joining the music men at the Cincinnati Symphony Orchestra. One of the highlights of his career was when the symphony, under Max Rudolph, performed his piece *Queen City Suite*, a beautiful musical story of the sounds of a city. Larry always credited his early music training to Sister Catherine, a Charity nun, his instructor as a boy in the Price Hill suburb of Cincinnati. "And a Protestant boy at that!" he'd smile. He had been a winner as a member of a singing quartet on the *Arthur Godfrey Talent Scouts* TV program, and had extensive experience in the broadcasting and advertising business, including McCann Erickson, New York, on the Buick account.

Larry was forever composing...everything from orchestral arrangements to commercial jingles. We would always remember the day he was working on his latest song "Never Put Your Elbow in Your Ear." We all joined in the chorus with matching gestures of trying to put our elbows in our ears, at which point the great Bill McCarthy of Eagle Picher walked in. Bill was a legend here, a man never without a smile and one of the most respected in the business world. Another client might have frowned on the elbow gymnastics during a busy working day. But Bill, typical of him, just roared. "Gee! I wish I could do that!" he laughed.

Of Larry Gilbert's many campaigns, my favorite was "The Quiet Bread"...so fresh it never makes a sound. But Larry couldn't stand any taste tests the business is famous for. Once when asked to take a taste test on a product he replied, "No thanks. It gets in my mouth."

When Larry Gilbert and Don Leshner were out on an assignment together, they'd come back with an award-winner every time. The best was the one for the Ohio Road Bond Issue campaign with Don acting the part of the henpecked husband trying to drive with his wife in the rush hour. Don should have surely gotten a Clio commercial acting award for

133

that. But, as usual, he got something even greater, the satisfaction of doing a fine job, the best award there is on this earth.

A secretary of our department once complained to the office manager that she thought everybody in the writing section was a borderline case. The word got back to us and I said, "She surely means of anemia." The rest shook their heads. Joining in the game, "You don't mean," I dramatically gasped, "anemia of the cranium?" What in the world could make her think that?! She had complained, "one of the writers constantly whistles. Another makes funny faces. And another keeps stray dogs under her desk. Another plays his own tape recordings of himself at the organ like a late-night horror movie. Another practices golf swings with a dirty mop."

Well, the general office manager, Ed Elfers, couldn't believe all this. So he came into our department that day and spent some time meandering around spying on us. And sure enough...one of our fine producers, Norman Roberts, was whistling one tune after another that would have driven even the madman, "The Whistler," nuts. Dick Best, our chief at the time, was playing his own tape recordings of himself at the organ in a rendition of the Russian work song or something like that. Jack Keating was standing in front of the mirror making faces, imitating some of the guys at the Cricket bar. Don Leshner was in the middle of a golf swing with a wet mop. And I was dishing out some lunch of Ken-L-Ration to something under my desk. The office manager just shook his head and said to himself, "I knew it was the truth without even coming in here to look!" Dear Ed Elfers, so understanding we thought. What would we have done without him. He knew us better than we knew ourselves. Now, where did that can-opener go for the dog food?

He Never Let the Peas Porridge in the Pot Get Nine Days Old

(See photo page 124)

There was no doubt about it. The copywriting department always kept things humming..or just plain kept humming, which really would drive outsiders like secretaries to distraction. Al Boam was one who was humming all the time. And what he was humming was, "Skeeters are a hummin"...adding to the madness..."on the honeysuckle vine."

Al was a classy New Yorker and looked like the actor, a Broadway actor. He was a wonderful writer with a real flair and a temper with a real flare, too. One of the most talented and spunkiest fellows we ever worked with, a graduate of Columbia U.and a World War II Air Force vet who was marched halfway across Europe as a prisoner of war. Al had been with

Fuller, Smith, & Ross in New York and went on to a division of Batten, Barton, Durstine & Osborn in Atlanta, Burke, Dowling, Adams. He really meant business. If anybody wanted a writing job done and done right and done right now, Al was the one to do it. He never wasted a minute or a word or an eraser or an idea.

On one occasion somebody suggested that we do some kind of rhyme campaign for a client. Al didn't like the idea for television, but was forced to do it anyway. He begrudgingly wrote the first TV commercial with this rhyme:

Peas porridge hot, peas porridge cold
If we don't sell these products soon
They'll be too damn old!

And he turned it in that way. The person to whom he gave it complained to the manager.

"Look at this!" she whimpered. "And on top of it, he uttered something!"

"What did he say?" inquired the manager.

"He didn't say anything. Just uttered a guttural sound."

"What kind of a sound?"

"Like...like...like..."

"Like what?"

"Like ughahahahagggghuaghaha...!"

"Like throwing up?"

"Yes, like throwing up!"

"Well! well!"

When informed that a complaint had been made to the head office about him, Al's only comment was, "Whoever suggested that TV campaign in the first place ought to be taken out and tied to the vine where skeeters are hummin.'"

"I agree," chimed in Bud Chase. "Either that or stabbed right in the middle of their vertical/horizontal!"

Bud was one of Al's best friends and a supremely talented performer, plus writer. But, early in his career, delivered one of the most famous lines in the history of broadcasting: "Paper, Mr. First Nighter?" He was the newsboy on the *First Nighter* radio program of dramatic stories in the "little theater off Times Square," but which was actually broadcast from Chicago. It came direct live, as did all the radio shows in those days, not recorded in advance. Even the standard openings and closings were all done live over and over again at each performance. So Bud got to say, "Paper, Mr. First Nighter?" and shout, "Paper, get your paper..." time after time on the show. A big dramatic event then for a young boy just starting in show business and broadcasting. Later in

"STRINGBEAN" - With the baggy pants the beloved character portrayed by Bud Chase on WCPO-TV. Pictured here reading a story to his children, Pam and Mike. He began his career at sixteen as a CBS office boy in Chicago and later appeared in bit parts on *Ma Perkins* and the old *First Nighter* theater radio show. Remember, "Paper, Mr. First Nighter?" That was Bud. At a station in Kokomo, Indiana, his closest friends were performer Jack Remington, who took his stage name from his typewriter, and Dick Hageman, later a WKRC-TV announcer, who was killed in a car crash.

Cincinnati, Bud had a daily program on television, WCPO-TV and WKRC-TV. He played Stringbean, a memorable creative character with baggy pants and funny hat.

One day Bud came back from lunch pulling a little red wagon, which he had bought as a present for his little son, Adam. He tied a requisition on it and sent it back to the art department for them to paint the little boy's name on it. We all agreed that Adam really hitched his wagon to a star, his dad. Bud went with ABC-TV, Chicago, and Leo Burnett Advertising Agency. Because Chicago was forever "calling him home." The last time I saw Bud he was pulling the little red wagon at the busy intersection of 5th & Vine and disappeared into the crowd.

This reminds me of some other little munchkins which used to pay me surprise calls at the office. One day the phone rang and the switchboard operator said, "There is an invasion of little people out here in the reception room." It turned out to be four of my nieces and nephews with a policeman. "How in the world did you get here all by yourselves?" They told me they had sneaked away from the babysitter. "But how did you find me?" Then they explained they got off the bus downtown and asked the first policeman they saw where my office was. "But you didn't know the name of it?" They related that they told the officer they were looking for their aunt "who thinks up things, especially for television."

By process of elimination, the policeman figured out it must be an advertising agency, chose the building with the most agencies in it and let the elevator starter take it from there as the children described me. With such a touching episode as this, I decided not to join the Planned Aunthood Association after all, but rather the SPCA and turn my twenty little stray nieces and nephews in all shapes and sizes and ages and breeds over to the humane society for the care and feeding of aunts.

"We came to take you to lunch," they smiled. They really had just come to "take" me. As usual. For chocolate sodas, popcorn, and all those things that little boys and girls jam down their childhood disposals...aided and abetted by their aunts, much to the concern of their parents.

Ganon the Canon

I'll always remember the day I first heard Stu Ganon coming down the hall. It sounded like a twenty-one gun salute. Stu was really a fireball. When he was around, you knew it. He made everything fly with a zoooooom! He was a powerful guy in more ways than one; a powerful temper; and powerfully in love with his native New York. There was no other city in the world like it to him. He was Madison Avenue, up and down, and down and around. Stu had all the ways of a New Yorker: the debonair disregard of traffic lights; the shortest distance between two points was to cross the street with Stu. He reverberated that never-stand-still-a-minute or sit-still-a-minute hustle and bustle of Times Square. He had an interest in everything and everybody. "What lousy sparrow really did kill that cock robin?" he once wrote.

Stu Ganon, Dick Best, and John Healy were our department heads in that order, or rather out of order. Nobody could keep order in that group of characters. How these creative directors ever put up with us is the question of the century. Especially Dick Best, an easy-going person who never gave anybody a hard time. Dick was as much a Chicagoan as Stu was a New Yorker. Son of an ad agency executive, Dick was especially an expert in grooming products. He was with Toni in Chicago, and I'm sure it was never as hard for him to figure out the answer to "Which twin has the Toni?" as it was what to do with all the members of the nutcracker suite, our writing department.

Stu had the new look approach to advertising, which always came first, of course, out of New York...especially the television. He wanted to completely revise the format of television commercials, an idea which nobody has yet done and which would revolutionize the sponsors messages...as much as photos did in newspapers over a century ago.

Chapter 7

(Reprinted by permission of Editor and Publisher Magazine, By Mary Ann Kelly)

If We Had Been Assigned to Create the World

Which brings me to something I've always questioned. Is there really such a thing as a creative director? Isn't that a contradictory term? To create is a subjective word. To direct is an objective. Nobody ever speaks of the creative director of the world. Just simply the creator. Which gave me an idea. The devil made me do it! Wonder what would have happened if an advertising agency had been assigned to create the world. Ummm. Let's see. The world certainly, certainly would have been wearing an eye patch. And we would have had until tomorrow noon to create it according to the account executive's requisition. Not seven days. Who needs all that time? Wonder if there are any competitive samples of the world floating around anyplace? Anybody else ever created a world? Any been test-marketed anywhere?

Guess this would have to be both a "space" and "time" campaign. The world will surely need both. But it really might need more time than space. Which brings up the point of billing. Wonder what the world will bill. Of course, this will have to include expense accounts in creating it. It's going to take a heap of material, especially staples. And art supplies, all that green for the grass and blue for the sea, except the Red Sea. Better make that yellow. Or we could just make the whole thing in black and white, like an old TV set. And put the leftover money in a convention center.

Now about shape. Should it look like an egg...or a Coke bottle...or a pretty leg? Better leave that to the art department. Better suggest they do a square overlay just in case the client doesn't buy the round. But on second thought, if we ever want to mail the world it will have to be flat. We don't want the world falling apart in some post office annex. Besides, it will never go through the meter machine if it isn't flat. Remember what happened to that bubble gum we tried to mail in letters. And let's not forget to mark the world "fragile." Maybe we'd better hand stamp and lick the million stamps.

If we do a lot of newspaper and magazine advertising of this thing, we'll have to find a printing press big enough to run off the world. Let's see...now for the headline of the world in the introductory campaign. Maybe something extremely creative like, "Love at first bite." Or maybe "Pretty as a picture." Heaven forbid! Which reminds me, wonder if anybody has ever created a heaven. Got to do a terrific job on this assignment. Understand that other outfit, Genesis, Exodus and Leviticus, has prepared some terrific material on the creation of the world. Don't want them to get the account.

Think the campaign should be an institutional one. Not a hard-sell. After all, how do you hard-sell the world? I mean, you either buy the world or you don't. That eliminates doing "Good news, ladies!" commercial. Or a parody to "Buffalo Gals." And better ask the art department if they are going to do the world in the house or send it out to some guys who do great worlds. Uh-oh...here comes the creative director. Always did think he creatively directs best who creatively directs least. Better jot something down on paper quick so he'll think I've been working on the world. "You'll wonder where the world went when you brush your teeth with rubber cement." No, that's no good. How about "I'd walk a mile for a world." Or "When better worlds are built, better world builders will build them." Or what rhymes with world? "You haven't lived 'til you've whirled through the world?" And we mustn't forget a diet world. "Only one calorie in every sphere."

Better get some facts and figures from the research department. Maybe the entire total of all the zip codes would help. 9876548765032183948573902984958765432198765432198765. Yes, that makes a big difference in the direction of the creation of the world. Yes, I can see it taking shape now. And what contests we might enter it in. Surely it will win at least an award of merit for its air pollution if not for anything else. And mustn't forget that most important line at the end: "The world is brought to you in living black and blue."

But wait! What is that noise? Is the world beginning to grind on its axis? No, that's only a short in our new electric pencil sharpener. Now what's this memo? "Stop all work on the world. The Client decided to create the world Himself."

I wonder why?

The Cleaners Was Never Like This

Is it any wonder that at the end of the day in the copywriting department the male members would migrate downstairs to the Arcade Bar to put finishing touches on the screwdriver and grasshopper

ROY MADISON — super duper "PR" man. All business and no baloney.

(Photo courtesy Bob Dailey WCLO, Janesville, Wisconsin)
GENE DAILEY - A broadcast news writer at heart, he blew in from the windy city of Chicago and CBS, manager of WBBM after being a reporter for United Press. He recalls his early mornings rounding the corner of the Wrigley Building with the wind and snow blowing up a storm. Among writers, the gentlest disposition. You could never pick a fight with Gene. He's written many beautiful public service TV programs, including his most recent, a nature study, *THE CREATION STORY*, in collaboration with his son Rob, manager of WCLO in Wisconsin.

141

campaigns, while I would be left alone to tend the pickle barrel and put the money in the sugar bowl? Before they were down in the coal hole very long, a voice would call on the wire from the depths. "Hellooooo, is this our little flower of the orient? Would you bring our topcoats downstairs? We're heading for home." I think they had to be headed for home by somebody else from the general tone of the vocal chords. So I obliged. Gathered up the topcoats in my "Paul Baby" shopping bag. Their hats I piled on top of each other and carried them in my other hand.

One day I was getting on the elevator with all this equipment from the copywriting department and who should follow me out and get on the same elevator but Mr. Bliss, our office traffic manager, who always made us toe the line to get our assignments in on time. In my frenzy to conceal what I was doing and hide my identity, I frantically put the pile of hats on my head. Naturally, they came down over my eyes. I stood frozen like this on the thirty-one floor ride with him down to the street level. He didn't say a word. But, getting off at the first floor, he turned and said, "We're being taken to the cleaners, I see." There was a dry cleaner i n the lower arcade where I was going next to the Arcade Bar. And I still wonder to this day if he thought... or do you suppose he realized...then again how could...or was it really his way of saying...on the other hand there wasn't...

Paul Dixon...the One and Only

Gene Dailey was a leveling influence in the department, a completely competent, experienced pro. A native of Milwaukee and a Marquette grad, Gene had formerly worked with WBBM, Chicago. He also had been a reporter for the United Press. And he, too, was a Crosley/AVCO Broadcasting alum, WLW radio program director. Gene was not a clown like some of the rest of the characters in the business, but had a great appreciation, nevertheless, of the clowns and discovered some.

Gene kept us all entertained with his interesting stories from his long career. Like the time he was with the Armed Forces Network in Frankfurt, Germany, during World War II. Mickey Rooney was also with the Network. Mickey and another actor, Gene related, did a skit about Mickey's return to Hollywood after the war. Mickey played Cecil B. DeMille. And the other fellow played Mickey. Rooney portrayed DeMille as not being able to recall who Mickey was after coming home from the war. Even when Gene told it, I started to cry. And seeing it first-hand, Gene said it was one of the most humorous, yet touching skits he ever saw in his many years in the business. But the climax came accidentally

142

(Photos courtesy WLW-T, Multimedia Broadcasting)

PAUL DIXON - How did a guy like you get in a place like this? Kneesville, of all places! Show me a guy that could do an hour show every day, 99% of the time without a guest star, and I'll show you a guy that could do an hour show every day, 99% of the time without a guest star! And for 20 years. From the sublime, like interviewing Robert Kennedy, to the ridiculous, like a wedding of some rubber chickens, Paul proved himself the one-and-only. The comics called him, the greatest comedian since Red Skelton. And the tragedians called him the greatest tragedian since the early days of the stage. Whatever you called him, this comic-tragic character of a man, when he walked into the wings, it was your loss. Dixon's talented helpers Bonnie Lou and Colleen Sharp.

A YOUNG MERV GRIFFIN with Paul.

PAUL DIXON, BOB HOPE, JOHN T. MURPHY, president of the Crosley-AVCO group of stations, got in a little game of golf for the benefit of "The Hope House" in Cincinnati. Paul claimed he won, which was par for the course!

144

WHERE'S SID CAESAR? Who but Imogene Coca could make such a comic face (except Sid !) and cause Dixon and Bonnie to break up.

BRUCE BROWNFIELD and "the Bellaires" make music for the Paul Dixon Show.

after the show. Mickey was tired and irritable, so he accidentally slammed his fist down on a table and a tube of shaving cream, which he didn't know was there. The shaving cream splattered all over him like a pie-throwing scene in an old silent movie. Everybody roared and Mickey most of all.

One of Gene's best friends, and friend to us all, was Al Bland, vice president in charge of programming for the entire Crosley/AVCO group of TV stations and radio. Al was one of the finest and most accomplished people in the broadcasting business, a southern gentleman by birth and by nature; a brilliant idea man, writer, executive producer and even performer. Before joining Crosley Broadcasting and the WLW Stations, he was program manager for WBBM-CBS Radio and Television, Chicago. Al was responsible for setting up program formats as they now are being used on television generally, including the local live programs with personalities, living up to the ever-Crosley credo that nothing comes alive like live personalities on the air. We worked with Al on many occasions, shows, and information background for our WLW stations national advertising campaigns in broadcasting magazines and the Crosley/Avco corporate group.

Nobody loved humorous and human interest incidents better than Al. The best one he played on himself, accidentally. We couldn't believe it was happening when we were monitoring the *Paul Dixon Show* show one morning. The odds for such an occurrence must be one million to one. Al had suggested that Paul have a mystery voice contest on the show. Paul thought it was a very good idea, so Al proceeded with plans to set up some well-known personality whose voice would be used on the phone from the show to some viewer at random. Such a contest usually runs for weeks, because rarely does anybody guess the voice early in the game.

Ralph Lazarus, chairman of the board of Federated Department Stores, agreed to be the mystery voice. After a mammoth promotion and build-up on the show, one bright morning Paul Dixon selected the first telephone number at random and made the first call to see if the person on the other end of the line could guess the voice. Immediately...without hesitating a second...the woman replied, "That's Ralph Lazarus!"

Dixon almost collapsed. As Al Bland put it, "They had to scrape Dixon off the boom." Crawling back to the mike, Dixon weakly asked, "Lady, how in heaven's name did you know this voice?"

The woman laughingly replied, "Why, I ought to know that voice! I used to be his private secretary!"

So there, out of a possible million or two million persons in the midwest televiewing area, Dixon had incredibly chosen Ralph Lazarus' secretary for the very first phone call. No mathematician could figure what the odds for doing this would be. It was something that couldn't be put down in figures, only fantasy. And only on the Dixon show, where the incredible always happened.

Dixon ran a unique program every day for an hour, but with no regular guests. Only Dixon with Bonnie Lou and Colleen Sharp by his side and the audience, studio and otherwise. He kept the audience in stitches. Who else regionally or nationally would try that and get by with it? He was so talented himself that he didn't need anybody else. The climax of his show came one day when he decided to marry off the two rubber chickens which had been props of the program for a long time, like the rubber chicken on Johnny Carson's show. He put on a full-scale wedding, sending out invitations to all the agencies, the press people, and advertisers. Even had a reception at the Lookout House, a classy restaurant and nightclub on Dixie Highway over in Kentucky. He outdid Red Skelton on this one as the classic clown, attired in wild tuxedo and zany top hat, the wacky minister.

Why did Dixon do it? Why did he act the way he did? Why was he so funny? The answer might be for the same reason Shakespeare wrote his comedies as well as his tragedies. This was a deep, compassionate, intelligent man who had to be helped to the stage the first day he returned to the show after his young son was killed in an auto accident. Thus was Dixon's cycle of life completed in the comic-tragic script of it all.

She Lived in the Land of Counterpane

What can be said about Ruth Lyons that has not already been said? The woman who had a talk show before anybody knew what talk shows were. The voice of the Midwest and then some. The subject of articles in national magazines: *American Home, The Saturday Evening Post, Cosmopolitan, Ladies Home Journal, Look* and others. She put on a superb show with a superb cast, superb guest stars, and superb assistants, like Elsa Sule, Mickey Fisher, Gloria Rush and Sue West.

But of all the things she did on and off the air, she was best with children, best with her Ruth Lyons Children's Christmas Fund to buy toys and equipment for hospitals. I had the privilege of writing the message for the fund over many years. One was a little boy who had traded his crutch for a clown. But my favorite of all was based on Robert Louis Stevenson's poem, "The Land of Counterpane."

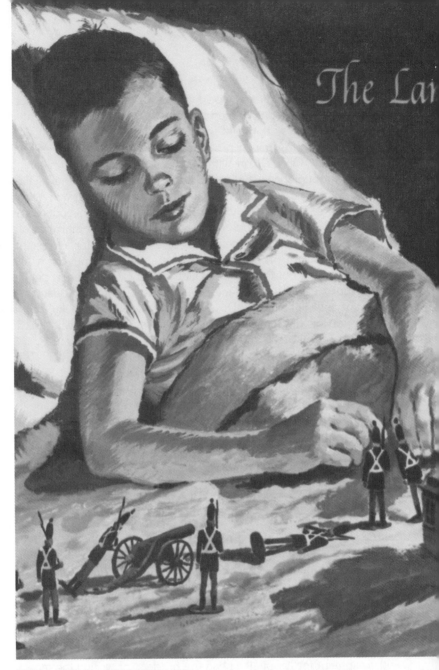

THE LAND OF COUNTERPANE–it was my pride and my privilege to write the Crosley Broadcasting account for twenty years. With the WLW Radio and TV stations and others in the group, we had so much to work with in the great Crosley tradition of broadcasting. This ad was very special to me and to Ruth Lyons for her Children's Christmas Fund, based on Robert Louis Stevenson's poem, "The Land of Counterpane," about a sick child playing with his toys in bed.

148

Counterpane...

When I was sick and lay a-bed,
I had two pillows at my head,
And all my toys beside me lay
To keep me happy all the day.

And sometimes for an hour or so
I watched my leaden soldiers go,
With different uniforms and drills
Among the bedclothes, through the hills;

And sometimes sent my ships in fleets
All up and down amid the sheets;
Or brought my trees and houses out,
And planted cities all about.

I was the giant great and still
That sits upon the pillow-hill,
And sees before him, dale and plain,
The pleasant land of counterpane.

— Robert Louis Stevenson

Maybe it's leaden soldiers . . . or ships in fleets . . . or little toy cities . . . sent by the WLW Stations to children in hospitals that help keep them "happy all the day."

We hope so. Over the past nineteen years, the Crosley Broadcasting Corporation Ruth Lyons Annual Fund has collected almost two million dollars for children in thirty-four hospitals, with last year's record contribution of over $315,000.00.

This is more than the policy . . . this is the spirit of the WLW Stations — to serve their communities in every way, especially to remember those who are forgotten . . . like the little "giant great and still that sits upon the pillow-hill."

Naturally, we are proud of our reputation in the communications industry. But we are most proud when our ratings and statistics, when our business and technology are pleasantly lost for priceless moments in such lands of counterpane.

Yes, this is our pride — but also our privilege.

Crosley Broadcasting Corporation,
a division of Avco

"When I was sick and lay a-bed,
I had two pillows at my head,
And all my toys beside me lay
To keep me happy all the day.

"And sometimes for an hour or so
I watched my leaden soldiers go
With different uniforms and drills
Among the bedclothes, through the hills.

"And sometimes sent my ships in fleets
All up and down amid the sheets;
Or brought my trees and houses out,
And planted cities all about.

"I was the giant great and still
That sits upon the pillow-hill
And sees before him, dale and plain,
The pleasant land of counterpane."

It was not only sick children but all children. Once when a member of her audience wrote to her that she herself had seen children swinging from a rope in the dirt because that was all they had to play on in a children's home, Ruth saw to it immediately that they got a well-equipped playground. And who can forget her when she marched around the studio with children carrying small flags. "Children are the fabric of freedom," she said.

Ruth went to California with Tyrone Power and Lee Wilson in an old touring car. Wouldn't you loved to have seen that! Lee and Ruth decided to come back and Ty stayed. You know the rest of the story.

Milton Berle described her as "The greatest showman I've ever met." And Mort Sahl made the routine of trying to get the cap off a bottle of the sponsor's bath oil a classic comedic ad-lib sketch with her.

One time on her show Ruth complained that her rocking chair wasn't just right. She needed a new one to use on her program. And in came an army of rocking chairs; so many that they didn't have enough room for them in the mail room or her office or anywhere in the building. So they left them on the sidewalk in front of Crosley Square until there were so many you could rock around the block!

A fine songwriter, too, Ruth will be best remembered for "Let's Light The Christmas Tree." Her own personal tragedy of her daughter's early death from cancer will always be remembered in her own lyrics to

150

Grouped around the piano are the performers heard five times each week over WKRC in the "Musical Memory Book." The program is heard Monday through Friday at 5:45 p.m. Pictured are Sam Rabinowitz, violinist; Ruth Lyons, pianist and director; Fred Edwards, WKRC announcer; Sylvia, the featured vocalist; Ely Chalfie, guitarist, and Gene Hoctor, pianist. (1936 Photo and cutline from Times Star)

(Photos courtesy WLW-T, Multimedia Broadcasting)

RUTH LYONS - Talk about a talk show! There wasn't a local, regional or national performer that could equal her. She invented the talk show. And the cry show. And the laugh show. And the music show. All rolled into one great daily adventure on the WLW TV and Radio Network. She had the Lyons share of talent to put it over for 30 years. No wonder Milton Berle called her the greatest performer who ever lived. Although she is no longer with us, her Children's Christmas Fund will go on living forever, her "Land of Counterpane."

RIGHT IN THE !MIDDLE! of Laurel & Hardy, Ruth could match wits with the best of them, even in the early days when this faded photo was taken. "Now look at the mess you've got us into!"

SHE ALWAYS MAKES THE DAY BEGIN, even on the Today show with Dave Garroway (r) and Jack Lescoulie.

THE GREAT DANE has a poodle pet! And note the expression on the dog's face as its master Victor Borge (r) and Willie Thall and Ruth go at it.

THE JOKE'S ON US ALL, when Bob Hope and Ruth go to it. She could really hold her own with any star.

ARTHUR GODFREY– looking for talent? Plenty of it here, but he's just paying a friendly call. Much to Ruth's and singer Ruby Wright's delight.

CLIFF LASH and the band– Gordon Brisker, Barney Yelton, Jack Crowder, Eddie Bennett, Jack Volz, Jerry Conrad, Bobby Keys.

154

On Ruth's show, produced by George Resing and Bill Gustin, she had a running gag about her favorite song, "I Love Paris," in which Eddie Bennett from the band tried to drown her out, even when there were guest-star-musicians like Doc Severinsen, Tony Pastor, Peter Nero, Al Hirt, etc., which caused hysterics among the audience. But it was the other extreme when her letter of good-bye was read for her on the program. From the second book of Timothy: "I have fought a good fight, I have run my course, I have kept the faith." Even a gimmick she once used on her show bowed his head, the old peppermint horse, and wept.

THERE THEY ARE! THE. WHOLE GANG! What wouldn't we give to see them all together again. Powerful local programming that has passed into history. Will it ever be the same again? Not without this group. Not without a heart. (back row—1 to r) assistant Bob Braun, newsman Peter Grant, orchestra leader Cliff Lash; (front row—1 to r) singer Bonnie Lou, Ruth Lyons' daughter Candy, Ruth Lyons, singer Marian Spelman, singer Ruby Wright.

"REMEMBER WITH ME" - the early 50-50 Club cast and their families. (l to r) Ruth's husband Herman Newman, Ruth Lyons, Rob Hund and wife holding baby, singer Dick and Eleanor Noel, little Noel girl holding rabbit, performer-emcee Willie and Hazel Thall, children Diane and Bobby Thall, Ruth's daughter Candy with her little dog, Marian Spelman, son Stephen Spelman, country music star Ernie and Jeanne Lee holding baby, Ernie Lee's two sons, Russ Brown and wife, daughter Marcie Brown, WLW staffer Eileen Martin and husband. Ruth began her career in 1929 on WKRC Radio. She later joined WLW in 1942 and began the 50-50 Club on radio in 1946, on TV in 1951, in COLOR in 1957. Early shows she emceed were *Women's Hour* and *Open House* on WKRC Radio; and on WLW Radio, *Pettycoat Partyline, Consumers' Foundation* and *Morning Matinee.* (Remember Frazier Thomas?!) (Photo courtesy Pat Lackner Mimicou, Cincinnati) (Identifications courtesy Elsa Sule.)

this song sung by Ruby Wright. "Somewhere across the snow...Hearts may still be lonely...Longing for those they love..:"

When Ruth Lyons retired from her show after more than thirty-five years on the air, she turned it over to Bob Braun, who carried on with the program and the Christmas Fund for seventeen years until he left for California a few years ago. A few bouquets here to Rob Reider and the rest of the cast who did such a superb job of helping the show continue its popularity.

That's the Most Insulting Waiter I've Ever Seen

Among Al Bland's many friends in show business is Gene Autry. Once when Gene and his troupe were playing in Cincinnati, Al invited him and his cast to lunch at the Crosley Broadcasting dining room. One of the members of Gene's cast was the celebrated character actor, Vincent Barnett. His father, Luke Barnett, originated the hilarious insulting waiter act. Vince was a master at this act, too. So Al cooked up the idea with Gene Autry for Vince to do the routine at this luncheon to which we were all invited. Naturally, nobody else knew that the waiter was not really a waiter. Gene and Al thought it would be a great joke on the invited guests, which included members of the WLW Television staff, advertising agency people, and the TV-Radio columnists of the local papers.

Al obtained a waiter's uniform for Vince and stationed him at the table of hors d'oeuvres. As the distinguished guests arrived, they started migrating naturally toward the hors d'oeuvres table. Unaware of who Vince really was, they began reaching for the tempting morsels. As they did so, Vince, in the waiter's uniform, slapped their hands and in a perfect stage whisper remarked, "No..you don't...not until the cocktails are served." Well, you can imagine the reaction! Everyone started mumbling and grumbling. One of the most outraged was Kiernan T. Murphy, then Crosley Broadcasting vice president and treasurer. K.T. shouted angrily, "Who the hell hired that guy?" And the surly anchovy, blintz blitz, spearing cheese spears, erring herring, tongue-in-cheek rolls, and open-face cocky cocktail routine continued.

A few minutes later, Vince Barnett started circulating around the room in his waiter's uniform. Among his roaming insults, he whispered to Mary Wood, TV editor of the *Cincinnati Post Times Star*, "Stop dumping your cigarette ashes in your empty martini glass!" Mary naturally was offended and complained to Al Bland about it. But undaunted, Vince continued his act. He told another guest he couldn't have a second drink. And to one he remarked, "Please don't lick your fingers. That's not nice."

MARY WOOD - Cincinnati's and the Midwest's best known TV-Radio editor. This must have been her reaction to a WLW-T party when an actor was hired to play an insulting waiter, unknown to Mary and the other guests. He said Clark Gable was the only one who took a swing at him. No, it's really at the Mike Award. Amidst all of her columns and books, the one for which she received the most mail was about the little stray dog she picked up on a bridge.

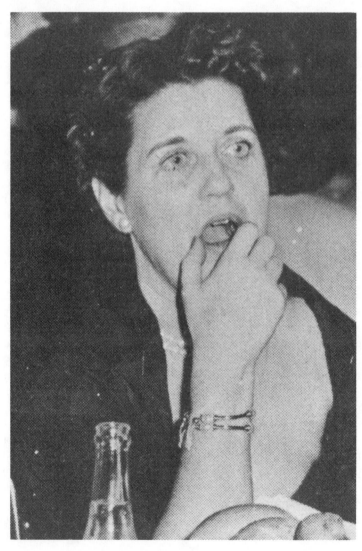

JEAN SHEPHERD - One of the most talented people who ever performed on Stations in Cincinnati. His Christmas Story, about when he wanted a gun as a child, has already become a Christmas classic. His stories on TV are taken from his books: *In God We Trust, All Others Pay Cash; The America of George Ade; and Wanda Hickey's Night of Golden Memories and Other Disasters.* His 14-part television series was carried on PBS. The head of the radio "underground" in New York, he also acted on Broadway.

(Photo by Art Baas, courtesy WLW-T, Cincinnati, and Al Bland, Chicago)
AL BLAND—vice president and program director of the entire Crosley/Avco group of stations. A real Southern gentleman, now in New York. Little did Al dream that things would get out of hand when he hired a performer to play an insulting waiter at a station-client-agency party. It's a good thing Clark Gable wasn't there! Al came to WLW-T after KMOX, St. Louis, and WBBM, Chicago.

So the affair was turning into a flip quip dip that was running out of chips!

But Vince kept at it. And to another, "It's impolite to drain your glass." Finally, Al decided it was time to give away the gag and introduce Vince to the crowd before there was a fist fight. Rage turned to applause. And Vince related that he had played this part many times, but only once did somebody actually try to take a swing at him during the hoax. "You might know who it was," he said. "The he-man of he-men who never took anything off anybody, Clark Gable."

The Governors Pardoned Us

This story of the great pretender is one among many in the world of make-believe in the broadcasting, advertising and performing arts business. Another was the day Dixie Lee, Dick Perry and I joined the great pretenders when the National Governors' Conference was being held in Cincinnati one summer some years ago.

I was on my way to lunch through the lobby of the Sheraton Gibson Hotel when I noticed one big, beautiful limousine after another driving up in front of the door. And who did I discover was alighting from them but one big, handsome governor after another. So I stopped to watch the limousine-governor procession. Everybody else in the lobby stopped to watch it, too, including Dixie Lee, well-known Kentucky political candidate, who will probably be the first lady CEO of the U.S. or one of the foreign countries she has not visited, which totals all of three. I spotted Dixie and she spotted me and we both got the same gubernatorial aspirations at the same time. Why wasn't there a welcoming committee for the fifty governors then in the lobby? So we appointed ourselves on the spot as the instant hospitality hostesses. We shook each governor's hand as he alighted from his limousine and welcomed him to Cincinnati, saying we were the appointed committee! But, of course, not saying who appointed us.

And who should walk in right in the middle of the governors? Dick Perry, another great pretender. He was wearing a defunct *Collier's* magazine press badge. Both the magazine and the badge. And looking very serious as if he really were on press-ing business to cover and report on the big conference.

"Dick!" I called out. "What in the world are you doing here, and with that old phony *Collier's* badge on?"

"Shhh," he whispered, "I'm going to send in a story to Horace Greeley that I really did go west and this is what I found!"

The whole jig was up, though, when I mistakenly shook the hand

160

of the hotel manager, thinking he was the governor of Alaska. Did I get a freeze! But that wasn't as bad as shaking the hand of the head waiter, thinking he was the governor of Rhode Island.

But we had to cut our fractured hospitality duties short because I had to get back to a meeting. It had already begun when I entered the office, so I hurriedly rushed to my desk to pick up my file for the meeting. It was a windy day and the breeze had blown some of it on the floor. As I reached up to shut the window, the whole file fell out! Thirty floors high! And the papers blew merrily over the skyline as "Dry leaves that from the wild hurricane fly...When they meet a big obstacle mount to the sky." And my heart flew with them...up..up...and away! How could I go in the meeting when the file of television scripts I was supposed to present was dancing gaily over the rooftops?! I was sunk...torpedoed.. shelled...Kamakazied!

Then suddenly I noticed that the wind had shifted. It was blowing around the corner of the building where our meeting was taking place. Could fate prove so kind! And the wind so westerly! So I rushed into the conference room to everybody's surprise, "Threw open the shutters, threw up the sash," and stood back as the scripts blew in the window! They landed in wild disarray all over the conference table before the astonished assemblage. I assumed the air that this was not an unusual occurrence and very pompously gathered up the television scripts and started to read them. I stood there, proud as the NBC peacock, and began: "This program is coming to you from the home of Adolphe Menjou and his wife in Beverly Hills, California..." At this point, somebody interrupted and mumbled, "For a minute there we all thought it was coming from the Mars afternoon flight."

MORT WATTERS – gets everybody to sign on the dotted line while Jack Kelly looks on. Mort was one of the powers- behind-the-throne that pioneered television in Cincinnati and helped make WCPO-TV a leader with a long line of credits and awards. And some outstanding shows, like Paul Jones news, Larry Smith puppets, Jack Moran sports, Juvenile Court, and Allen White news.

(Photo courtesy WCPO-TV)

"UNCLE AL" LEWIS - Best babysitter a mother ever had. He was certainly the answer to a mother's prayers. He'd keep the kids happy for hours every weekday morning on WCPO-TV, as he played his accordion and his wife, Wanda Lewis, "drew" their attention. More kids in this area grew up on Uncle Al than on Dr. Spock! Or Dr. Seuss and *The Cat in the Hat!* Well, maybe not *Sesame Street!*

JACK KELLY AND JACK KELLY! - The one on the left played James Garner's brother in the western TV series, *Maverick*. Bret and Bart! And the one on the right is the former WCPO-TV producer-director who drew a bead on the TV shows for WCPO-TV, including the *Maverick* series. Sportsman and man-about-town, the business could use a guy like him today.

WHO ARE THEY? - That's Jack Kelly and his wife Eleanor, in costume for the PBS Huckleberry Finn TV movie shot on location in Maysville, Kentucy,1984.

(Photos courtesy of Jack Kelly—former WCPO-TV producer-director-writer)

RECOGNIZE ANYBODY in this Dance Party! Popular teen-age record hop and jam session televised on WCPO-TV every Saturday afternoon, hosted by genial Myles Foland with famous guest stars as the Andrew Sisters, Edyie Gorme, Joni James, Frankie Avalon, Pat Boone, Ames Brothers, Pearl Bailey, Andy Williams. Personalities, performers, platters, prizes, and all the Coke you could drink!

WCPO-TV Sales Staff turns on the lights with their pretty secretaries for a special promotion of General Electric. What would Edison think of these bulb snatchers! (1 to r) Pat Crafton, what's-his-name, Pete Marino, Virgil Schmidt, Jack Hale, Jack Kelly, Paul Hodges, general manager Robert Gordon.

167

GIMME A BREAK during a movie matinee on WCPO-TV, (1 to r) station manager Glenn Miller, Judge Paul who dropped in while somebody else minded the store, "Mr." Starleton, Wanda Lewis behind that smile.

WCKY GANG - No history anywhere, especially in Cincinnati, would be complete without giving credit to the role WCKY played in it. Founded by L. B. Wilson, Covington, Ky., bank president, entrepreneur and showman, the station boasted such notables as Sid Ten-Eyck, the first announcer with his "Doodlesockers" shenanigans; the incomparable Leo Underhill; Paul Miller in Drive-time; Mark Neeley, forever the newsman; and many others.

Chapter 8

I Like Ivory Soap because...

A wonderful character in the communications business was Mary Elizabeth Jones. A fine writer and product expert because of her life-long hobby of entering contests in addition to her advertising and broadcasting background. We nicknamed her "Reasonable Facsimile." Her contest winnings read like an inventory of the Taj Mahal. She was the winner of twelve refrigerators...a half dozen automobiles...plenty of moola...and boola. In fact, just about everything ever offered in a contest, including a ton of flour, a mound of manure and lifetime supply of plastic worms.

If it had been left up to Mary Elizabeth, the Declaration of Independence, the Constitution, the Magna Carta, even the Yellow Pages, would have been written "in twenty-five words or less."

Mary Elizabeth gave me the contest bug, so I started entering with her. On our lunch hours we went all over town investigating writing competitions after writing all day in our jobs. We studied products, researched companies, analyzed anything and anybody from magazines to meat markets putting on a contest. No matter how lofty or how lowly the requirement or prize, we'd delve into the depths of the public library looking up things, including the history of the South America oola bird or Afghanistan dessert recipes. We entered every writing challenge and contest from "name Mrs. Schumtz's Pickle Juice" to "Was Hamlet-mad-or-not?" The result, of course, was that we both started winning in the same contests, which often caused an amusing episode if we had to go to the same place at the same time to accept our prizes. Then we'd pretend that we didn't know each other and we'd be introduced to one another over and over again.

"Haven't I seen you some place before?" I'd say. And Mary Elizabeth would reply, "Yes, you look familiar to me, too. Could it have been in the South American oola department of the public library?"

"No, I think it was in the Afghanistan recipe department. Yes, that's it. What a small world! Imagine meeting you here, winning a contest prize!"

In a sportsman's contest, we each won a portable radio by finishing the statement, "Why I like to shoot a rifle.." Yet neither of us could ever aim for the other side of the street on a WALK light and make it without incident or accident. One day I did make it, but turned around to find Mary Elizabeth had gotten only halfway across. She was standing in the middle of the street shouting down a manhole to a workman below, "Charlie, Joe said to cut it off!" The generous soul was relaying a message from a workman down the street who kept yelling, "Hey Charlie, this is Joe! Cut it off! Cut it off!" He was referring to a drill the men were using in the manhole. So Mary Elizabeth kindly obliged, and, in trying to help, was almost knocked into the manhole of Charlie, Inc., by passing traffic as a reward for her good deed.

Well, we finally arrived at the sporting goods store to pick up our radio prizes. We didn't realize, however, that the salesman would ask us to demonstrate our rifle-shooting ability before presenting us with our contest awards. He took one look at us and immediately became suspicious that we were not sharpshooters, or even square shooters, or any kind of shooters. "Well, well," he said. "Isn't this something! Ladies winning a rifle-shooting contest. Let's see a sample of your marksmanship." And shoved a rifle at me. I didn't know the barrel from the bullet. So I picked up the gun and aimed it right between his eyes. He ran behind the counter and nervously pleaded, "Now wait a minute, lady! Wait a minute!" I dropped the gun, we ran out of the store and headed for the hills; the same ones he headed for.

We decided that next time we'd better stick to something we were familiar with like the oola bird and foreign cookie recipes and African diamond mines and South Seas mermaids and judo and Juno. We were authorities on these subjects as long as the librarians held out and the two-by-four inch sheets of paper they give you to copy *Gone With the Wind*.

She Was on the Brink of the Great Caraway Robbery

In our hasty exit from the store, I lost Mary Elizabeth. When she returned to the office, I asked her what in the world happened to her. She proceeded to tell me that she was almost arrested with a bag of groceries.

"Why in the world would you be arrested with a bag of groceries?" I inquired. "You didn't steal them, did you?"

"No," she laughed. "But you would have thought so the way the Brinks men came after me."

I was afraid to hear the rest of the story, knowing the situations that the writers in our department were capable of walking into. And that's just what she did, walked into a real situation, a bank vault! She had

(Photo courtesy "MEJ")

"MEJ" - Good heavens! Could that be Mary Elizabeth Jones misidentified as Mrs. Duncan Hines attending a client dinner? It sure is MEJ! Among her many aliases and pseudonyms! A wonderful writer and very special friend. And, yes, that's Duncan Hines, (l) the host of the dinner. Still say he makes the best chocolate cake mix. Oh, about Mary Elizabeth, she was later vice president of the Cincinnati Women's Club under her own name.

171

stopped at the food shop to pick up a few things for dinner. And in darting across the street, she entered the wrong door of a building and walked right into the vault of the First National Bank...along with some Brinks Security Guards carrying guns and moneybags. Surprised at seeing her in there, one guard gruffly asked, "What the hell are you doing in here? And what have you got in that bag?"

Mary Elizabeth innocently replied, "One box of caraway seeds, a half dozen eggs, one bunch parsley, two..."

At which the Brinks guard huffed and puffed, "Oh, never mind! Just get the hell out of here!" And the Brinks men, with pistols drawn, proceeded to escort Mary Elizabeth with her shopping bag of delicatessen delicacies out of the vault and onto the street.

She certainly had a rare talent for being in the wrong place at the wrong time. I'll never forget picking up the newspaper one night and seeing her in a television group photo for the introduction of a new line of food products. The cutline under the picture mistakenly identified her as "Mrs. Duncan Hines!" And there she stood, looking every bit the part of the authority on room and board, with a kind of "recommended by" serene look on her face.

In another contest, Mary Elizabeth won two organs. She decided not to keep either one. So she advertised them for sale, giving our office phone number in the ad. That morning when the switchboard opened, the strangest calls started coming in. The first person said, "I would like to talk to the lady with all the organs." And another asked, "What condition are those lady's organs in?"

Well, the poor switchboard operator, like Lily Tomlin doing her famous Ernestine routine, was baffled for sure because she had not been informed that such an ad on the contest prizes of organs was running. The calls continued with persons very serious, non joking, "What make of organs does that lady have?"..."I had a couple of organs and got rid of them a few years ago. And now I'm sorry."..."I'm very interested because I would like to donate some organs to charity." Finally the switchboard operator, aged and gray by the time the morning was over, called the office manager to notify the telephone company that we were receiving obscene phone calls.

Now, I thought, it was surely my turn to win a big prize. So I entered a contest that required entrants to name a large, lustrous valuable, beautiful, magnificent, unique pearl. After hours of racking my brain, I finally came up with the great name, the one that would surely win the grand prize. Nobody on earth could have thought of this one. I'll go down in the writers' hall of fame for sure. This, above all, will make me a celebrity. Nothing else that I could ever undertake could equal this, even being the first woman on the moon. But somehow, my name for the pearl didn't win. I never could understand why. Surely nobody else submitted my suggestion, Big Pearl.

I was sure, however, I'd win a giant one yet. Then along came my great opportunity. A limerick contest. The first four lines were provided by the sponsor. All I had to do was fill in the winning last line.

There once was a fellow named Wright
Who was terribly, terribly tight
To save gasoline
He tried kerosene
"After you!" said the comet polite!

Well, maybe the next time I'd win. The next big contest would make me rich. It was for Dial Soap. Finish in a rhyming couplet the sentence, "I'm glad I use Dial...", that's a cinch! Money in the bank, sure.

I'm glad I use Dial for my bath main event,
It shines my bare back and fresh airs my tent!

I'm glad I use Dial for all-over freshness,
Now odor and dirt are sure bodylessness!

I'm glad I use Dial, it sure rings the gong
For striking up the whiffin' poof song!

But the next one would surely be the big haul. This would be it. The big daddy that would send me around the world. A rhyme for Fedders Air Conditioners.

Keep cool with this Conditioner
It helps the amour
No ricochet romance
When cool air is toujours!

Keep cool with this Conditioner
And sleep like a breeze
No hot bed of dozes
No toss and turn wheeze!

They're all probably still at the dead letter office...forwarded there by some discouraged contest judge. The least Uncle Sam could do is send me back my wrappers or reasonable facsimiles.

One of the most original contests ever put on was one sponsored

173

by *Harper's Bazaar* magazine. Contestants had to create some humorous women characters and state why they achieved their place in history. Mary Elizabeth created Madam Human Torch, the woman who invented the hotfoot. And I created Lean Towers Pisa, who perfected better foundation garments.

Oh, well, there was always another contest, just like another streetcar. And sure enough, one night Mary Elizabeth called me at home and excitedly proclaimed, "Guess what! I heard from Jackson China!" She was referring to a contest we had entered months ago. But I misunderstood her on the phone and thought she said, "I heard from Jack in China!" Jack was then her fiancé. An engineer and advertising manager of the Packit Division of the Stearns and Foster Company, one of our clients. A true-blue Sigma Sigma, one of whose ancestors probably invented the phrase "Liberty! Equality! Fraternity!" And a tireless University of Cincinnati booster. In fact, everybody says they should put Jack Grieshaber in the cornerstone of the next new University of Cincinnati building, holding a red Bearcat flag in one hand and a list of UC donors in the other. If there is such a thing as reincarnation, Jack will probably come back as one of the famous stone lions in front of UC's McMicken Hall.

But back to Jack in China. I knew he was away on business for his company at the time, but I didn't think he had gone that far! "What in heavens name is Jack doing in China?" I exclaimed. At that moment, something happened to our telephone connection and we were cut off. I was left with the horrible thought that Jack had defected to someplace behind the Bamboo or Pacific curtain. I knew he was a Russian scholar and teacher and wanted to see Russia someday. Maybe he'd gone by way of China. Poor Jack. He must have flipped. When we were reconnected, Mary Elizabeth was laughing hysterically.

"What's so funny about Jack being in China?" I asked. "I think it's dangerous and sad, especially since he doesn't like almond cookies and can't even play 'Chopsticks." But Mary Elizabeth continued laughing and tried to explain that she had said, "Jackson China." I continued to be concerned and baffled, not realizing she was talking about a brand name of china she had won in a contest. Then to compound and climax it all, she concluded, "Sure hope there's not a crack in it. If so, I'll just have to put china up for sale." By this time I thought surely she had slipped her sampan...or had sprung a leak in her rice paddy...or forgotten to fasten the seat belt in her rickshaw.

174

YES, THAT'S MARY ELIZABETH again! This time standing in front of the British Medical Association, which has just been sold by Parchman and Oyler! Her husband's idea, Jack Grieshaber, of a little joke in which he snapped a picture of his wife in various countries of the world standing in front of a famous building with the P & O sign! Yes, the Louvre in Paris had also just been sold by P & O... and the Taj Mahal in India...and the Kremlin in Red Square...and the palace of the Dali Lama in Tibet!

Hope Sprang Eternal

Our contest memory to top them all was the one sponsored by Columbia Broadcasting System for their television stations around the country. We entered the one at the CBS Station here in Cincinnati. I had written a lot of NBC promotion material in the last few years for the WLW group, so it was a breeze to do it! Only the names were changed...with a few additions here and there. Mary Elizabeth Jones and I were both lucky to win in the first week's contest...a trip to New York. Then we decided to enter the second week's contest for two friends, help them write their entries so they could go, too. And we won again! Then in the last week's contest, the rest of the writers in our department dared us to enter in a fictitious name, betting us we couldn't win again. Taking the dare, Mary Elizabeth and I pooled our efforts. Yet, we almost collapsed when the fictitious name proudly was announced a winner on a television show that weekend. Now what have we done? How do we get out of this one? Should we confess? Or should we try to rightfully claim the trip prize and give it to another friend? But our biggest problem was that the station was supposed to mail the trip tickets to the winners. How could they mail this last one to a fictitious name at a fictitious address?

We decided to claim the prize trip which was rightfully ours. We'd give it to Mary Elizabeth's fiancé, Jack Grieshaber, who was quite a contest winner himself. Several years before, he had won a six-weeks' tour of Europe. And we'd never forget his winning name for a mattress, "Hope Springs Eternal." But we still had the problem of how to claim the tickets at the CBS-TV Station here. So one day Mary Elizabeth and I decided to disguise ourselves and go up to the station for the extra prize trip ticket. We put on dark glasses and big hats and appeared at their door, hoping we wouldn't run into anybody in the business who would recognize us. Of course, that was like putting out a green flag on Orangemen's Day or Guy Fawkes Day. We received more than one strange look from strangers, and ever stranger from people we knew.

I calmly told the receptionist I was Hattie Carnegie. I just can't explain why I love that name. Maybe because it's so chapeauish. Every time I had to give my identification, and it didn't make any difference if I gave it right or not, I used to say I was Hattie Carnegie, as when calling the public library or in an introduction at a party. Nobody ever batted an eye. Batted me yes, but never an eye. Anyway, we had great success and got all our prize trip tickets.

In preparing to go, however, we realized one point we had overlooked and I do mean looked. The first name on the fictitious name we had used to win the last week was "Elizabeth" which caused Jack Grieshaber all kinds of hilarious complications on the trip. When Jack pinned on his name tag to start the trip, it said, "Hello, I'm Elizabeth Berg!" Well, we thought that would never do. At which moment one of the CBS station representatives came up to us and jokingly commented, "So, you're Elizabeth, huh?" But Jack, a quick thinker, snapped back, "Young man! This is a typographical error. I'll have you know my name is Eli Zabeth Berg. And I didn't appreciate your remark. If I thought there was going to be anti-semitism or any such kind of discrimination on this trip, I certainly wouldn't have come. I worked hard on this prize...nights and days I labored...wore my fingers to the bone on the typewriter. I'll report you to your superiors."

The poor fellow then fell over himself apologizing. "I'm so sorry, sir. No offense intended. I have many friends who are...Eli Zabeth's..." But Jack continued with a routine too good to let drop.

"Name one!" he demanded.

"Well..well..." stumbled the young man as Jack pursued him.

"Don't you know Eli Whitney?"

"No...no..no...don't believe I do. Maybe he's with NBC."

But Jack persisted. "He invented some kind of gin." And the rep thought and thought again.

"He did, huh?"

Jack wouldn't let it die. "Yes, made of cotton." Which really threw his prey.

"Made of cotton, huh? Excuse me, I think I better see a man about a..."

Episodes like this continued throughout the trip to New York with Jack wearing the "Elizabeth" badge. And when we arrived, Jack alias "Elizabeth" was booked in the room in the hotel with a very elderly lady named Tillie, (you'll never believe it) Hug! The scene with the busy hotel clerk as Jack tried to explain his way out of it was like a Groucho Marx skit. Television emcee, Bob Collier was host for the group and helped us out of many a predicament like this. Polly Bergen was hostess, the girl with the lovesong eyes.

Mary Elizabeth finally left our office and joined another agency down the street. We had worked on so many accounts together that when she joined the other company, we naturally continued to consult each other on ideas and campaigns. So I'd call her up and say, "Got any good ideas for a TV commercial on such-and-such a product?" She'd answer that she'd think up one and call me back. Then, the next day she'd turn around and ask me for some television situations for one of their clients. So we pooled the efforts of both agencies, unknown, of

177

THE MEDIA BUYER

(Photo courtesy Bill Frietsch III, Cincinnati)

BILL FRIETSCH - Unlike the station reps, the media reps of the magazine and print world were a more serious, less flashy crowd. Anyway, Bill kept them in tow - an all-around expert in the media business, plus marketing and research. One day he hurriedly entered a media contest of guessing numbers of circulation, jotting down something like 666,666,666 for an answer. Later he was notified he had won the grand prize of flying down to Rio de Janeiro! When asked how he arrived at the right figure, honest Abe Bill quietly said, "I just guessed."

course, to our employers, who were friendly rivals.

One day I called Mary Elizabeth and a very strange sound came over the phone when she picked up the receiver. "What on earth is that?" I inquired.

"Oh, that's Rand West singing one of his commercials over the office public address system," she replied. Which system or which phone, or maybe both, was not working properly at the time. It sounded like the Wichita lineman still on the line, or a distress signal from the Watergate Hotel, or the mating call of the white rhino.

In the confusion on the line, I started calling for everybody else I knew over there until Mary Elizabeth's connection could be straightened out. "Art department, Tom Austing, please. He's working with Snoopy on a rough layout of Woodstock, the singing sparrow? His phone's out of order, too? Then how about Charlotte Shockley? or Levinia? Ummm...that singing commercial must have blown out AT&T around the world..."

The Human Fly Was Green!

One St. Patrick's Day morning as I was walking up the street to the Carew Tower office building, something caught my eye high up on one of the floors. It looked like footprints walking up the side of the building and going over a sill in a window! Had I had too many green carnations so early in the day? Was I seeing things? And whose office did that look like it might be? Mine! Yes, that was our floor and my office! And to top it off, the large footprints were green! So I hurried up on the elevator and down the hall. And sure enough, there they were. Giant green footprints coming in over my windowsil! Some Paul Bunyan leprechaun, no doubt. Then I heard the snickering in the next office. It was dearest Maury Oshry and Bill Frietsch, our media buyers, our innerspace men, who handled the contracts for the advertising in the newspapers and magazines. This was their handiwork as being secretly divulged to the *Business Week* magazine rep, Dick McGurk, one of our all-time favorites. This eminent emissary of the McGraw Hill Publications should have won the Apollo award for space reps. Anyway, Gertrude Boegli, everybody's darling and house-mother in the office, smiled and said, "Nobody would have somebody green climbing in their thirtieth floor window but you." And I'm still wondering what she meant by that. Could it be that..? No, maybe it was just...Then, again...

That day I was going to lunch with Al Rebstein, grand knight of the New York LIfe Insurance Company, million-dollar roundtable and all

HAPPY 50TH ANNIVERSARY LUN-CHEON - Mary Jane Knolle, librarian, and Joyce Brach, secretary, help celebrate for the company. But where is the leprechaun to match the hats?

JIM LAWLER - one of the dearest, kindest persons in the business. Too dear and too kind to stay in it? Jim deserted the ship for the world of the classroom at Sacred Heart Academy, Louisville. Jim's father was president of Aeronca, subsidiary of Boeing, which made the nose cones for Apollo spacecraft. His father was in such demand by companies that they kept calling him for his services even after he retired. And even when the lawn mower was running. So he would reply "Sorry I can't hear you." And hung up!

QUITE AN APPETITE, you can work up in 50 years! Pass the Nu-Maid! And the Strietmann Saltines! And the Kroger everything!

180

that...plus lifelong family friend. So when he arrived in the lobby, I showed him the footprints, too. And what do you think he said? "Nobody but you would have somebody green climbing in their thirtieth floor window?" Then I was sure that...or could it be..no, maybe it was just...

I'll go over to the Maisonette for lunch at noon and drown myself in the chef's special from Stanley Demos, world-famous for his drown-your-trouble chef's specials. He was going to think up one for Durkee's Salad Dressing and give it to us. When I told him about the green footprints coming up the outside of the Carew Tower and in my office window, he replied, "I know I can't trust you to make this recipe. Now, I don't know if I can even trust you to take it back to the office."

Our Department Was Allen's Alley

Dealing with the stars adds up to many of the most memorable experiences in the broadcasting/advertising business.

When we were working on the Streitmann (now Keebler) account, we prepared a television campaign featuring a series of stars giving the cookie and cracker commercials. Lyle Allen, our account executive (ex-navy pilot and man about town), handled it with Harry Bailey from New York. Harry used to write for Fred Allen and appeared recently in a TV show about the big days of radio, as the characters who lived in Allen's Alley once again relived the days with the genius of Fred Allen...and the genius of radio. Harry is really a Connecticut Yankee, our big-city contact who really knew the sidewalks of New York and which ones led to the right agents and right people, including Mrs. Nusbaum, Titus Moody, Senator Claghorn and Ajax Cassady.

For our set of TV commercials, Harry lined up Burgess Meredith, Henry Morgan, Celeste Holm and many other personalities, including Hermione Gingold. We went wild in our department writing the scripts for Hermione. I put her in a castle setting wearing a suit of armor, trying to sit down in it. "Pip! Pip! Hello, there...and all that! Welcome to my castle. Borrowed it from somebody's attic for the occasion. Had it flown in from jolly old England. Simply love castles, even though they are drafty and damp, making it a problem to keep the crumpets dry for tea and crumpets."

But when Lyle and Harry went to film Hermione in the commercials, she was such a comedienne they couldn't get her to deliver a straight line. And, of course, ad-libbed rather than stick to the script. She had the camera crew in such an uproar they shook the cameras. Finally, they got her to settle down and do a few sensible commercials, but even these ended up with her calling the crackers "little beggar" and "fellow earthlings." They were afraid she'd bang around so in the suit of armor, they never did get around to that one, sparing the cameramen more convulsions.

She told us that one day when sitting by the sea in England, her wig blew off into the water. Two stalwart young men swam out after it. When they handed the half-drowned wig to her, they said, "Sorry, Mum, but your little dog died!"

Hermione's names of beggars and earthlings for the crackers was like the suggestion some anonymous character kept sending in. This slightly cracked-pot kept insisting that our client call the crackers brittle little vittles. Even the crackers cracked up at this. It could have been worse, though. Brittle whittle vittle. We should have given this one to Hermione to play with.

Following our star of the month campaign, we decided to do a campaign based on famous nursery rhymes. My assignment was to do Old King Cole for Zesta Crackers, one of the most famous saltines ever made. So my deathless poetry contribution came out:
"Old King Cole was a merry old soul
Who had his cupboard made of asbestos
In case of fire broke out in the palace some night
And nobody saved his Zestas!"
Then somebody else was assigned to Old King cole.

Perhaps, though, our greatest memory of this particular account was the wild-eyed woman commercial. Everything went just fine in the preparation of this minute spot. The script was easy to write, the perfect actress-model selected to announce it, the filming went off like clockwork. But when it was finished and we all sat down to screen it, we couldn't believe our eyes..or rather, the eyes of the woman doing the commercial. For some strange reason they looked wild! Stark raving wild! It must have been a light reflection. Anyway, no matter what it was, she looked as if she were going to commit murder. On whom or what? That was the question. Was she going to massacre the cookies and crackers before the televiewers' unsuspecting eyes and her suspecting eyes. Or was it the televiewers themselves she was going to let have it with a double barrel. Or maybe again, it was the innocent cameramen. Just as Hermione had bent them over with laughter, this gal was going to do like Lizzie Borden:
"Like a murderer she stared at you
And blew the tubes on Camera Two!
And when she saw what she had done
She blew the tubes on Camera One!"

(Photos courtesy Jack Kelly, sales manager of WCPO-TV, producer etc., and Jack of all trades!)

DOTTIE MACK - Queen of pantomime, the gorgeous gal in a scene from her popular WCPO-TV show which ran 1949-1957. Dottie married talented William B. Williams, rated the number one disc jockey in the U.S., on .WNEW, New York. "It's make believe ballroom time..." The little girl from Westwood, Cincinnati, once dated Joe DiMaggio. That's Colin Male and Bob Smith with her.

DOTTIE MACK

DOTTIE MACK

VICTORY HUDDLE - When the WCPO-TV softball team beat the WKRC-TV team. The score? 12 to 1. (Back 1 to r) Ed Hirsch, John Fiarini, Jules Leventhal, Jack Kelly, Jim Black, Jule Huffman, Ralph Cobb, Ed Weston. (Middle 1 to r) Dick Woods, Robert Gilmore, Skip Maddox, Joe Murphy. (Front 1 to r) Joan Gamble, Dottie Mack, Jack Sebastian, unidentified girl.

Chapter 9

The Under 121 Dance

Then came my big opportunity to work on an entire television package show, production, script, commercials, everything. It was my brilliant ideas.. Why don't we propose a program format to some TV stations on a special series of programs devoted to single people, their lives, their problems, their joys, their tables-for-one, their "his" or "her" towels, their no exemptions, their capped toothpaste tubes, their mini-laundry and maxi-landlady, their nieces and nephews, their single dogs, their blind dates and deaf dates, their little-or-no-garbage, when all their married friends are using giant plastic bags, their lives going through the under-12 items line at the checkout counter in the supermarket.

Everybody thought it sounded tremendous. So I sat down and listed every single idea I had in my head. The first show should be devoted to that noble American institution called, for lack of a better name or court battle, the "Over 21 Dance." This red-white-and-blue establishment among the foibles and fancies of boy-meets-girl in the United States is truly "Love, American Style." It is usually held in a hotel ballroom every Friday night. Any gal or guy over 21 may attend. Each pays his or her own way, because most came separately. And most leave that same way, too, having wished they had stayed home and cleaned out that basement storeroom. Nobody is sure what category this fling should be classed in, social..sport..blindman's bluff..or karate with music.

Anyway, I thought if I make this the subject of the first show, I'd better go to one of these things. So I talked another single girl, a TV producer who was also "over 21," into going with me to case the joint. Or joint the case, as it turned out. Some of our friends had forewarned us about this obstacle course, civilian American style. But many seemed to think it was worth it if you did happen to meet your Prince Charming there. But we were further warned to make sure it was not King Kong or even worse, Princess Charming.

Well, the big night came. We got dressed fit to kill to go to the "Over 21 Dance." I brought my tape recorder and note pad to record information as the evening progressed or retrogressed. This would be firsthand information-research for the big TV series on the single person.

When we arrived, it was so dark in there we couldn't see a thing. I couldn't even find the "on" switch of the tape recorder or see what my note pad looked like. We groped our way along the wall, bumping into people, falling over chairs, and finally passed through a swinging door into an even darker room. It looked faintly like a mop and bucket closet to me, but to my friend who had already lost one contact lens on the way to the dance, it looked like the stag line. "Gee, what a funny haircut on that guy," she remarked.

"Shhh...:" I whispered. "His handle might hear you."

"Oh, well," she consoled, "the night might get better as it goes along."

But then one mop turned out to be a wet one, which rubbed against her leg. "Eeeek!" she screamed. "Somebody's getting fresh already. Let's get out of here!" And she tripped over a vacuum cleaner, switching it on, which grabbed her skirt just like the wet mop did.

"Heavens!" she yelled. "This place should be raided!"

So we rushed through another door into a bright room where there was a wedding reception taking place. "My goodness!" commented my friend, "they certainly work fast at this dance."

In our hasty exit from the broom/mop closet, we intentionally brought two buckets with us, or was it somebody else who brought them? But there they were, rolling right out into the middle of the receiving line. I'll never know where they came from. Could they have followed us from the cleaning closet? Or was there a window washer's convention here the night before? Everybody kept staring at the buckets, the wayward buckets, the restless buckets, in bucket disbelief. But nobody seemed to want to be the one to usher them out of the receiving line.

"Come on," I said. "This isn't getting my research done for my TV series. Let's look for the dance again."

Finally, we found our way back to the ballroom where it was being held, after almost knocking over the waiter bringing in the wedding cake for the bridal reception, and after almost being caught up in the line of visiting football players checking in for the big game the next day.

"OOOOOOOOOOoooooo," my friend squealed, "this beats that other stagline with the funny straw haircuts and mop-like hairdos."

He Used to Mint Juleps

We groped our way in the darkness of the dance to a table in the corner and sat down. "Wonder why it's so dark in here?" my girlfriend asked me.

"So you can't see who you are dancing with or what you're dancing with," I supposed.

"Well, I'll fix that!" she exclaimed...and proceeded to take out of her purse none other than a coal miner's cap with a lamp on it!

"What in heaven's name are you going to do with that?" I shrieked.

"I'm going to wear it and turn the light on whoever asks us to dance!"

I agreed that was a fantastic idea. I had heard of bringing a flashlight to this coal hole of the "Over 21 Dance," but never a miner's light!!

"The United Mine Workers Union will never be the same after tonight," I commented, just for the record. And what a record. So far we were batting zero at the dance. Nobody even looked our way. And no wonder. They were blinded if they did. We hadn't turned a shovel of men or totalled a ton of masculinity for my research TV project. And my friend finally confided she didn't get the lightning bug headpiece from a miner at all, but a minter.

"You mean a counterfeiter who used to mint money in his basement at night?"

"Oh, no," she laughed. "He used to mint juleps!"

"A mintlegger! Or is that a bootjuleper? Great day in the evening! Not only the United Mine Workers, but the revenooooers will be after us!"

"I can't get my battery to work..."

Soon a very nice looking man approached our table. I told my friend not to give him the spotlight treatment because he looked okay even in the dark. So she got up to dance with him. When the music stopped, she came back to our table, politely escorted by the gentleman. And he was a gentleman. I could tell by the black satin stripe down the side of his trousers. My friend whispered to me that she must have made a quick hit with him because he already had asked her what she would like to have. A present already, and he hardly knew her!

"No wonder he asked you what you'd like to have!" I dryly commented. "He's the waiter!"

"Ohhh," she moaned. "You mean he was coming over to our table to take our order and I thought he was coming to ask me to dance. I thought it was funny that I kept feeling a towel hanging down by back as we were dancing."

189

Then we both embarrassingly mumbled our drink order to him, "Two single girls on the rocks," That was us, we both agreed. And I still couldn't find the "on" button of the tape recorder. And my friend still couldn't find her other contact lens. And to make matters worse, she lost the second one. So she actually put on the miner's-minter's cap and started looking under the table for it. Somebody passed by and remarked, "If you're looking for night crawlers, this is the wrong season."

I thought nobody would ever believe this if I recorded it in my research for my great TV series. I couldn't even believe experiencing it! Then suddenly I exclaimed to my friend, "Quick! Give me the light! Here comes a prospect. Let's spotlight him." While I was trying to get the thing to turn on, the fellow bent over and asked me to dance. Fumbling with the light, I replied that I can't get my battery to work."

"I'm sorry," he counter-replied. "I thought you were alive."

As he walked away, we agreed that the spotlight routine wasn't such a good idea. Instead, we decided if some fellows were heading in our direction with whom we did not want to dance, we'd just pull the tablecloth over our heads. So this we did. The result was as strange as the miner's cap. We attracted more attention than we did without our heads under the tablecloth, which must hold the core of a message in there somewhere. The guys just kept coming up to us and when we ducked under the tablecloth, they didn't ask us to dance, anyway. They just said, "Boo!" And we, hidden, mumbled, "Boo who!"

By that time, the poor waiter was ready for the waiters' rest home that specializes in "Over 21 Dance" patients. He pulled the tablecloth off our heads and slammed it back down on the table and exasperatedly remarked, "Laugh and the world laughs with you. Weep, and you weep alone."

"I love singing waiters," I remarked in return. "Don't you?"

"Do you suppose," my friend asked, "That he thought we were crying under the tablecloth. You know what I mean...boo-hoo...rather than boo-who?!"

Next on the agenda, a real swinger came up and asked my friend to dance. He swung her all over the floor. To get away from him, she slipped behind the drapery in the midst of one of his wild swings. He turned around on the dance floor and couldn't find her. As she peeped out from behind the drapery, the waiter went by. Our waiter. She lifted a drink off his tray unknown to him until he started to serve it at a nearby table. As he went by again to get another drink, replacing the one that mysteriously disappeared, her arm came out from behind the drape and put the empty glass back on the tray, unknown to him. He did another double take as he discovered the empty glass on the tray. He then put a filled glass on the tray and started back again to a table. My friend behind the drapery again lifted the glass off the tray as he went by and put it back again as he returned. By this time, I thought I'd better get her out from behind the drapery before it caught on fire like a crepe suzette.

We Were Russian to Conclusions

As I crossed the dance floor heading my friend back to our table, and by that time she did need heading because she was getting such a head on, an elderly man asked me to dance. This must be the "Over 121 Dance" I wrote down on my note pad, still not able to find the "on" button of the tape recorder. I thought they already had the last encampment of the Grand Army of the Republic.

That was not enough. Then we went to the other end of the rainbow. Two very young men came over to us. They had long hair and long beards. By that time we were getting very disinterested in the offering of male merchandise for the evening. "Where are Luke and John?" I asked. Such a remark was not a memorable lyric from a love song or conducive to romance. So they left as fast as they came.

It was time we rallied our forces or forced our rally. We were not doing too well at the dance and neither was my research for my big TV series. So we decided maybe we'd better go back to the miner's cap. But this time, rather than wait for the guys to come to us, we'd go to the guys. We'd try going around the room and spotlighting the Prince Charmings. As we did this, two very nice-looking fellows, who had been watching and laughing at us all evening, asked the bartender for a magazine lying behind the bar. They tore off the front cover and stuck the faces from the cover over theirs. As my friend, still woozy from the waiter-glass-tray-drapery, shined the light on their faces, she screamed, "The Russians are coming!" And we ran out of the ballroom...running into as we flew...no less than the waiter of waiters. And his tray went flying this time, not a glass at a time, but gracefully and generously, all at once!

The two faces from the magazine cover were really two Russians. So out in the lobby my friend shouts to the hotel guard, we were just attacked at the "Over 21 Dance!" The half-amused, half-confused guard asked, "By whom?" And we both moaned, "By the Russians!"

Chapter 10

"Rex" and the Single Girl

The investigation of the singles' dance turned out to be as much a fiasco as my investigation of a singles' apartment complex. Everybody kept telling me that I should move into one of those Swinging Singles apartment buildings. Lots of social life...everything's jumping...people all in the same boat...whatever that means. It's supposed to mean not married. But it probably means anchors away! Or maybe it's referring to the beer cans floating in the swimming pool to keep them chilled. Yes, everybody kept saying move out of that old house built by your great-grandfather during the Civil War and join the Swinging Singles. One look at the flotilla of buoyant brew in the swimming pool and I couldn't head for my old house and John Hunt Morgan fast enough.

"Well, you've got to do something," my friends at the office kept insisting. "You've got to do something to get married." Why is it that everybody else is always more concerned over a single person's state than that person is herself or himself? Their next campaign was for me to loiter around the drinking fountain. I wonder if girls did that in the Roman Forum two thousand years ago? Loiter around the water cooler coming out of the Tiber. Maybe that's why Rome wasn't built in a day. But, anyway, my water fountain campaign didn't do any good either. I just couldn't stand there and stare into space as men from other offices came up to drink. So I had to drink, too. The result was that I walked around all day with the swishing noise of a water-logged barrel adrift at ebb tide. I was afraid to use the electric typewriter for fear of getting electrocuted. And I didn't have to lick the stamps for the mail. I just breathed on them. Could have done the same thing for the window washer.

"But just think," everybody kept saying, "you're gathering such wonderful first-hand material for your television series idea on the life of single people."

Then I broke the news to them that I had changed my mind about proposing that kind of program format. I was going to narrow it down to that aspect of single living at which I had succeeded. At the dances, clubs, drinking fountain, apartment complexes, I was a singular failure, but in one single area of my life I was not.

193

"What is that?" they asked. "We can't think of any category in which you haven't failed so far...or succeeded."

Cheered by their confidence and unfailing faith, I set about to set up a series of TV program formats based on my one single success. With dogs! The title would be *"Rex" and the Single Girl*. With alternate title suggestions, *Behind Every Good Dog There's a Woman*, or *How Do I Love Thee? Let Me Count the Strays.*

At last? This was it! I had found my treasure where my heart was and vice versa. This would be my glorious contribution to over forty years of television. On my tombstone rather than a cross or a star or a crescent, there'd be a TV antenna with a dog bone hanging on it. And the inscription: "Here lies a good and faithful servant who was barked to death." What better way to go!

So I set to work to draw up the D-Day plan for the dog invasion of the vast wasteland. Programs, scripts, commercials, suggested stars, the whole bag of bones. On the first page I began my presentation with the most vital statistics on the bow-wow pow-wow...the barking minority in this country...the fact that there are about 26,000,000 dogs that are American citizens. That's enough to start another political party. This would give speechmakers of the present parties good reason at last to shout, "Don't let the country go to the dogs!" But if the dog's party did get elected, their administration could justifiably be in the doghouse. Then, too, politics could be called a dog-eat-dog profession. And, of course, the dogs liberation platform would be based on the appointment of a new government cabinet member, a dogcatcher catcher!

Indians Have Captured the Chuck Wagon

I was off and running. Where? I didn't know. But, anyway, it was with the dogs. Maybe a little foaming at the mouth in my excitement. This program, however, would surely win an Emmy. The lines in the scripts could be blockbusters. Just think of the campaign slogans that could get the dogs elected. "A mailman in every pot!"..."As Maine goes, so goes the Ken-L-Ration!"..."I like Spike!"..."54/40 or bite!"..."What this country needs is a good 5¢ bone!"..."Tippecanoe and Tippy, too!" And we could even drag in Shakespeare: "Let Hercules himself do what he may...The cat will mew and dog will have his day."

This is just great. The first program would be called *Man's Best Friend*, or should it be called *A Friend's Best Man*? After all, dogs probably do have weddings with vows they make up themselves. NO, better call it *A Man's Best Friend*. That goes best with the introduction:

"I never met a dog I didn't like, regardless of face, breed or color." This show would be about the Rover rovers. How do I love thee? Let me count the strays. Right! And I could count them right under my desk. These downtown strays used to be corralled by the candy-stand lady in the street-level arcade and sent upward thirty floors to my care via the building elevator guard. I ran the SPCA of the working world. An office is a white collar zoo enough without having stray dogs in it, too. My top file drawer always contained a stray can of stray dog food with a stray can opener for my stray canine clients.

One was a big black knight of the road. He must have been an inspiration for the original shaggy dog story. He was under my desk one zero morning, so I invited him to stay for a cup of coffee. I supposed even dogs took coffee breaks. And he stayed with me for weeks. The canine man who came to dinner. A real pooch-er. After I took him home, I did everything to get him to leave...to take another home in the neighborhood where he could be taken care of. I even made insinuating remarks. "Indians have captured the Chuck Wagon!"..."You're barking up the wrong tree!" But, alas, to no avail. He was not the sensitive type. Instead, he was very dog-matic.

He would be very good for the subject of my first television show about "Rex" and the Single Girl. In no time, he took over the house, and had me waiting on him hand and foot. Or paw and paw. I don't know who he thought he was. Maybe another World War I Flying Ace as in the Peanuts comic strip. Even the Red Baron himself. That's probably it. AWOL from the 1917 German army. I didn't mind him taking the best chair by the fire, but I did mind him resting his hind paws on my petit point footstool . . . even though his dogs were tired. That didn't get to me as much, though, as dropping cigar ashes on my new rug. I continued the left-handed compliments: "You really think you're the cat's meow." . . . "I have a bone to pick with you." But he knew he was on a Gravy Train and wouldn't budge. Finally, when spring came, he left me. Broke.

It began to be a habit entering my office in the morning and finding two woeful brown eyes peering out from under my desk. An early stray arrival. The problem was keeping the dog in the office all day until it was time to rush home in the rush hour I would get on at the back door of the crowded bus with a sweater over the dog's head so the driver wouldn't see the stowaway. But keeping the dog out of sight and out of sound under my desk was the neatest trick in a busy advertising agency.

Rose was especially a problem. She had a wheeze. Every time I started to concentrate on my work she would start to wheeze. The man next to me thought it was the plumbing stopped up and called the building superintendent. And somebody else across the hall offered me his tape

195

recorder, thinking mine was jamming. Here, all the time, it was just Rose, second-hand Rose, the stray cocker under my desk with her asthma.

But the stray dog I'll never forget was a wild Indian who shall remain anonymous, because he never remained at all. He came up on the elevator one day and almost chewed down the building by 5 o'clock. He chewed the shoes off my feet under my desk. That particular day one of our favorite printers, Howard Sunderman, was standing in my doorway talking to someone.

I Tossed Him a Bone in My Leg

As they stood there, the dog in hiding was ripping the soles off my shoes and off my feet. I tried to remain still by holding onto my chair, so nobody would know there was an animal under my desk eating me alive. But my bluff was not successful, because my wastebasket was not in the habit of making chewing-growling sounds. By this time, I was shaking from the workout I was getting in my lower extremities as the dog had gnawed his way down to the bare bone. My bare bone. Howard Sunderman began to notice my shaking state and desk-holding, as if a six-degree tremor on the Richter seismograph had just been registered. He stuck his head in my door and asked, "You cold or something?" I tremulously answered, "Yes, or something!"

This particular dog creature I had to take home in a cab for fear he'd chew the tires off the bus. He was the chewingest dog ever created. He should have been a cow or a goat, or been fed chewing tobacco instead of dog food. Even his ears were dog-eared from chewing on them. Like my other office strays, I had to leave him alone all day while I went to work until I found him a home. When I returned the first evening, he was sitting in my plastic yellow dishpan in the middle of the kitchen floor. He had chewed off the rim until it looked like a serrated crust on a fancy lemon pie. He was in the midst of devouring my aquarium fish book entitled, *Enjoy Your Gouramis and Other Anabantids*.

That night the dog disappeared. He was determined not to have a master. But he wasn't gone long when I heard the loudspeaker from the nearby baseball field blaring forth a frantic plea "Somebody get that dog off the field!" Oh, no! It's not him? I hurried down to the ballgame and there he was, chasing and chewing on the players. I had to run all over the field to catch him amidst the laughter and cheers of the crowd.

Finally, I found him a home on a farm. I suppose he's chewed up all the crops by now. And even chewed down the barn. I know he ate me out of house and home. He ate my house and home.

196

In discussing my scripts with Vern Schumann, a tip-top TV writer-producer in the next office, he said, "All I want to know is whatever happened to that last stray you had under your desk. I bet you that was going to be a large dog when it grew up. But you bet it was going to be a small one. Well, which of us was right?"

Then I had to confess what happened. I really did think the puppy was a toy breed. So I gave him to an elderly couple in a third-floor apartment. When I saw the people a few months later I inquired, "Well, how's the little toy dog?" The man growled, "Toy! Hell! He grew up to be a Great Dane! When he wags his tail in the living room, he knocks the dishes off the kitchen table!" I sighed, "Oh, dear!" What else could one do but sigh, "Oh, dear!" Maybe, "Oh, my!" at the thought of a Great Dane in a third-floor three-room apartment.

That was something like the one that grew up to be a Labrador Retriever. And he started retrieving everything within the vicinity of a thousand miles, including Labrador. This one I promised to a television engineer and his family. While I was waiting for them to come and get him, he retrieved the countryside. Anything he found in the neighborhood that was unchained...unclaimed...or unframed. This he'd dog-trot over to my doorstep. Now, I didn't mind the workman's lunch pail with the limburger-garlic sandwich...or the leaky hot water bottle...or the apache headpiece. But I did mind the cannon shell. That was carrying things a little too far. For some strange reason, don't like cannon shells lying around my yard. Although my property is no thing of beauty, I do try to keep it from looking like Bull Run.

How he knew when it was time for me to come home at night, I couldn't figure — unless he could tell by that calendar watch he wore. He was up at the corner waiting for the bus — that is, unless there was a cat around — then he was hiding someplace. Whenever a cat even looked at him, he'd scream at the top of his lungs to the great bewilderment of the entire cat population of the United States. He certainly would have made a great subject for one TV show in my series.

Just think of all this wealth of material for my dog TV series! The more I worked on it, the more I worked on it. First thing you know, it was endless. Tributes to dogs I found everywhere, even in the works of Goldsmith, Swift, Trowbridge, Ruskin, Kipling, Byron, Scott, Wordsworth, Browning, Terhune, Thurber and Snoopy.

"Listen to this," I announced to Joe Martens, our classy public relations man. "Even Pliny in his *Natural History* comments on the ancient Egyptian proverb: Treat a thing as the dogs do the Nile. Always act with caution as dogs do in drinking from the Nile, running along the bank rather than standing still, so the crocodiles won't get them. And

Seneca reminds us that dogs are not the only creatures that bark. It is the practice of the multitude to bark at eminent men as dogs do at strangers."

"That's all very well," Joe remarked. "Now all you need is a dog food account to sponsor your dog TV Series."

"Gee, I've been forgetting about the commercials," I agreed. "Let's look in the Standard Advertising Register and see whom we might get." As I paged through the book, I was still reciting dog quotations I had looked up. With one great sweeping gesture of dog drama or trauma, I expostulated Alexander Pope's famous quote: "I am his Highness, dog at Kew; Pray tell me sir, whose dog are you?"

As I said this, I looked up and there stood Harry Blaney of Central Engraving Company, one of the best-known and best-loved characters around. "You know," he laughed, "that's the nicest thing I've had anybody say to me all day!"

"And here all the time you were just getting me worked up about going to the SPCA to look for another Rin-Tin-Tin," Jack Lindsay exclaimed, one our favorite account men and producers. "I guess I'll just have to settle for some mutt with a bit part. Or Bite part!"

HULBERT TAFT - WKRC-TV - Chairman of the board of Taft Broadcasting Company and vast Taft enterprises. A member of the distinguished Taft family, his grandfather was a half-brother of William Howard Taft, 27th president of the United States. He was responsible for transferring the newspaper business, the old *Cincinnati Times Star*, into a broadcasting empire. He was tragically killed when something he had planned to save his life took his life, an explosion from a gas leak in his bomb shelter on his property. (Cincinnati Historical Society–Paul Briol collection)

199

(Photo courtesy WKRC-TV, Great American Broadcasting Co.)
SKIPPER RYLE - Sailed through his weekday WKRC-TV morning show for children
for seventeen years. It was a smooth, quiet kind of show with Glenn Ryle at the helm.
The children loved it! One little girl even ended her prayers with, "God bless Daddy,
God bless Mommy. God bless Skipper Ryle so he won't drown."

(Photo courtesy WKRC-TV, Great American Broadcasting Co.)

NICK AND NINA CLOONEY- A darling couple. Here's wishing him good luck whatever he does and wherever he goes. Always a gentleman and a scholar, right now a columnist for the *Cincinnati Post* and editorial news commentator for WKRC-TV. Former anchorman at KNBC in L. A. Brother of WLW's Rosemary and Betty Clooney, who died suddenly on the eve of her daughter's wedding in Las Vegas.

No Salute to WKRC-TV would be complete without mention of Charles Meecham, top man on the hill. A delight to deal with and even greater experience to work with as the WKRC-TV staffers well know.

(Photo courtesy Soupy Sales, NY)

SOUPY SALES - Imagine meeting you here! Behind that pie in the face. One of the early performers on WKRC-TV, he confessed they used shaving cream in the pie, because it held up better and didn't sour. Just another of the superb performers who were on TV in Cincinnati.

FROM THE "CUTTING ROOM" FLOOR - As children, we made our doll clothes with the scraps of the gorgeous gown materials of many movie stars, sent from Paramount Pictures in Hollywood to Ludlow, Kentucky, by a seamstress friend. Then we carried the dolls with dresses made from the materials and the patterns to see the stars come on the screen in the very same dresses! Dorothy Lamour, Barbara Stanwyck, Claudette Colbert, Carole Lombard, Gloria Swanson and many more. (Photos from Paramount Pictures, Hollywood)

(Photo courtesy Len Goorian)

LEN GOORIAN talks over show biz with Jimmy Durante. Wouldn't you love to hear this conversation between Lenny and the "Snoz!" Len was one of the powerhouses in Cincinnati television. He sang! He danced! He emceed! He acted! He joked! As Durante would say, "Inca...dinka...do...Goodnight, Mrs. Calabash, wherever you are!" And if you've wondered who was Mrs. Calabash? She was the nickname Durante gave his "clotheshorse" in his room, where he used to hang his shirt and trousers and coat every night. That "figure" of clothes, bidding it good-night, became his famous closing to his act, "Good-night, Mrs. Calabash, wherever you are!"

Chapter 11

Give My Regards to Broadway
and Robert Sherwood

Working with the artists is one of the great experiences in the communications business, advertising and broadcasting.

Bill Powers was head of our New York Office and art department. And how we did love the trips to see Bill...and the New York office and New York. I'll never forget the time he was taking the photographs for one of my Crosley Broadcasting national magazine campaigns. He apologized for the delay in getting the photos to us.

"We were held up at the photography studio," he said. "The photographer was taking shots for a promotion of a new biblical movie. Rather than a loin cloth, they improvised a towel wrapped around some extra in a crowd scene. Nobody paid any attention to the towel until the pictures were developed. And there, big as life, was the word "Waldorf" on the towel (supposed loincloth), on this guy in the Old Testament scene! Wouldn't that have been the towel howl of the century.

Bill said he had to leave the office early that afternoon because he was going with his wife and writer friend to the theatre. "Is he a TV commercial writer?:" I asked. And Bill just smiled and said, "No." So I proceeded to tell Bill that he should inform his friend to learn how to write TV commercials and programs. It was going to be the coming thing. Then only twenty-five years old, I knew it all and casually offered to give Bill's friend some tips on writing. Bill again just smiled and said, "I'll sure tell Robert Sherwood you said that."

Omar Sharif Said "Trick or Treat"

Clark Collard (he looked like Omar Sharif) was the artist with the most unusual and creative sense of color. Clark could make black stand out on black and white stand out on white. When he would suggest a color combination for an advertising campaign and television film storyboard, we'd gasp, "That'll turn out like a nightmare!" But it turned out like a dream. Striking and unusual.

But the most striking and unusual recollection I have of Clark was

(Photos courtesy Mrs. Clark Collord, Alexandria, Kentucky)
CLARK COLLORD - The artist with the unusual sense of color combinations and design. And with his great talent as a witty actor, he posed for many of his own TV storyboards and ads, like the crazy foreign general eating the hotdog shown here. Only Clark could pull this off! But he was visibly moved when on his silver wedding anniversary, the staff decorated his office entirely in silver foil.

one Halloween afternoon when I opened the office stairway door. There he stood on the darkened landing dressed as a lion, carrying a trick or treat bag. "Why, Clark! I'd know you anywhere!"

"Please!" he whispered, "no remarks from the writers."

"Are you auditioning for the MGM trademark or the next TV version of *The Wizard of Oz*? Remember, you gotta be a coward to get the part of the cowardly lion. You have to have lost your courage."

"Don't ever put me to the test and say, 'Women and children first!'"

"Well, anyway, would you mind crawling in out of that dark stairway and bringing your tail with you, or whatever?"

"I have a very simple explanation for my very peculiar attire in this very peculiar position at this very peculiar moment. It's merely a case of being out of afternoon snacks in the art department. I thought I'd just go around to a few floors dressed as the king of beasts, grrrrr, in this costume left over from a beastly television commercial, and by trick-or-treating, replenish our supplies. Whew! Am I hot. I think it would have been easier to have whipped up a batch of fudge on the hot plate."

"Gee! You've really made a haul! But wait a minute, how did that rock get in your bag!"

"Some crazy, mixed-up peanut must have thought I was Charlie Brown of the jungle!"

Clark was my father-confessor. I was always running in to his office unloading my troubles. "That dirty rat changed my headline,"... "The staplers in the copywriting department or lousy. Can I borrow yours?"..."Now when we go into this meeting, remember we gotta fight for our idea. Get in there and fight!"

Then Clark would console, "Now calm down. Remember the old saying, cheer up, things could be worse."

"Yes, and I remember the rest of that old saying, too. So I cheered up and sure enough, things got worse!"

"You sound like you're really wound up today."

"No, I'm really wound down because I thought of the television advertising campaign of the century. and nobody liked it. Listen to these fantastic headlines: What has bow legs, purple wings and flies the ocean. A bow-legged, purple-winged ocean-flyer!"

"Well..would you mind repeating that...for a minute I thought you said...?" Clark began to inquire with a slightly frightened expression.

"Now don't interrupt. You have to get these socked to you all at once for the full impact. Here's the next: What has polka-dots, fuzzy ears and likes grapes? A polka-dotted, fuzzy-eared grape-liker! There's more. Now, what has no hips, chews tobacco and grass hops? A no-hip,

(Photos courtesy Robert Cushman Hayes Photography)

BOB HAYES - Who was that car I saw you with last night? That was no car. That was my life. The lizzy I love! Bob sports one of his many sports cars and poses as the world-travelling old master painter with international exhibits plus his award-winning design for the Valvoline Motor Oil can and ads. But his masterpieces were his harrowing tales of raising his little boy, especially the day he took his son to kindergarten.

tobacco-chewing grasshopper! Aren't these sensational?"

"I'll have to sleep on them. But if I do, I doubt if I'll ever wake up," Clark nodded...already.

"Please don't drop off yet, Clark. I've got another campaign idea.

Look, we show a blank white piece of paper on the screen and ask the viewers if they can guess what it is. Then we say it's a ghost running through a cotton field waving a flag of truce! Next commercial is an orange piece of paper. It's a sun-tanned girl eating an orange at sundown. Then here's a plain brown piece of paper...it's a bear making fudge in the forest in the fall. And a black piece of paper — that's a chimney sweep putting in coal at night...Clark, you're snoring..and on your drawing board..."

He Painted the Globe

Bob Hayes, the master painter from the far-away hills, was the art department VP. And those hills have really been far away. As far as Saskatchewan or Afghanistan...Ludwigshafen or Chichicastenango...and somewhere west of Laramie. Bob was the paintin', packin', slide snappin', globetrotter who brought'em back alive. The sites of the world. They're going to make a movie about him and call it *If It's Tuesday, Bob Hayes Must Be in Belgium.* If you wanted to talk to Bob about a television storyboard layout, you had to catch him between Berchtesgaden and Mandalay. Then after you'd caught him, you were really glad you did and got to see some of his truly magnificent slides.

It's no secret that every year thousands of American tourists passport themselves off to all parts of the world for better or for worse. And they carry back as souvenirs everything from Italian museum stubs to Israeli Coke bottles to Irish telephone directories. But most of them, including myself, consider their best souvenirs to be their slides. That glorious collection of the face of the world which actually gives the photo developing companies the darkroom bends, gives the neighbors the yawns, and gives the tourists' families their jokes...like "They laughed when he took out his camera, they didn't know it was loaded."

Rarely does the courageous photoplaying tourist come up with a very good shot, including myself, among those slide masterpieces of nothingness, the mysterious double exposures, the cumulus clouds, the protruding poles, the unidentifiable bodies of water, the flecks in the distance or in the lens. So as all the acquaintances gather 'round to view them, the family and friends who have never cared to go any farther than the corner bottle opener, can conscientiously remark, "Deep in December,

it's nice to remember your slide showings were over by September."

But not Bob Hayes' slides, a first-class professional performance, which rate encore after encore, and Samuel Johnson's comment, "Let observation with extensive view...Survey mankind, from China to Peru." And his own paintings from his travels in thirty-six countries have won many awards.

Regardless, however, of all the souvenirs, slides, photos, paintings that American tourists return with...no time, no memory, no experience will outlast that supreme one:

"What though you hide it in your trunk
Ere sailing hour has set?
Jammed down beneath your old blue serge?
Don't think you can forget!
The face within that passport book
Will rise to haunt you yet.!*"
–*Your Passport Picture* by Laura Simmons

In appearance Bob reminds me of the unforgettable illustration by Caroline Williams' father, of Sekatary Hawkins in the wonderful youthful stories by Robert Schulkers, former *Cincinnati Enquirer* writer.

One day I was going out on a local picture-taking assignment with Bob and a photographer for some television promotion shots. Bob said he'd pick me up in his new car in front of our building. Well, not knowing anything about makes of cars...I can't tell a Duryea from a Furyea..I just didn't even bother to ask him what kind of car he'd be driving. After standing there for a few minutes on the corner, a Volkswagen pulled up with some strange character at the wheel wearing dark glasses and an Alpine hat with the brim pulled down all the way around. He looked like a Nazi escaping across the German border. He kept honking his horn and I finally realized it was Bob. "How do you like the get-up?" he laughed. "Bought the hat and car in Germany."

I replied, "It's great! But don't offer to pick me up on a street corner after a trip to the north pole, Mush!"

Bob Hayes had won many awards for his paintings in more than a hundred juried national and regional exhibitions in leading galleries. He was a member of the USA Exhibition and Washington, D.C., Water Color Club National Exhibition. He was also a member of Knickerbocker Art Society of New York and American Watercolor Society and represented the United States at the International Exhibition at Monaco.

While serving in a front-line unit of the U.S. Army during World War II, Bob Hayes carried his sketch pad and watercolors for two years in a 90 mm shell casing, even in the invasion of Normandy.

LARRY ZINK—what can I say but that the art awards were made of zink. He was the master of arts—fine art, commercial art, photography, sculpture. They good-naturedly called us the Betty Comden and Adolph Green of our world for our Crosley Broadcasting campaigns, often beating even the networks. I recently walked into a Madison Avenue advertising agency and there still hanging was the large bright red Christmas tree ornament we had sent out for the WLW stations years ago. And in another agency I saw the cartoon about the timebuyer-"the good and faithful servant who was talked to death." And I thought of the night we stayed until midnight decorating the office on Christmas Eve. When we turned off the lights to go home, one elevator door slowly opened. In the darkness it was the cleaning ladies from the entire building. They had come to see the sleigh we had decorated in the lobby by the light of the elevator. Like a scene from the cover of *The New Yorker*.

CONFERENCE CALL, to show our latest WLW-T and Radio campaigns, which Larry Zink and I had prepared, to Crosley Broadcasting president, Bob Dunville (center), and Jack Frazier, ad manager.

The Art Awards Were Made of Zink

Larry Zink was one of the most talented artists from here to Madison Avenue and back again by way of the world. The Art Director of *Cincinnati Magazine*, national first-place award winner for metropolitan publications, Larry had won so many awards he could shingle the outside of his house with them.

We were one of the pioneer copywriter-art-director teams. Our favorite account, of course, was Crosley Broadcasting...the WLW TV and radio Stations. We did the corporate ads for them in *Saturday Evening Post, Look* and other national magazines. The compliments from Jim Shouse, Bob Dunville, John T. Murphy...and even Victor Emanuel...made us know it was all worthwhile.

It was my pride and privilege, a line I used for Crosley, to have worked on the account. Among the memories of his or her writings, every writer has his or her favorites. Things he or she has prepared that will seem to be forever a part of him or her. My two were the General Electric Jet Engine Division and the Crosley AVCO Broadcasting accounts. In our General Electric *Miracle of America* broadcast series we touched on many wonders of the world and that sense of wonder that led to many great discoveries. Galileo wondering about a swinging lamp in a cathedral...Columbus wondering about the slant of the sun's rays on the supposed flat earth...Edison wondering about the magnified reflection of a kerosene lamp in a mirror...Einstein wondering about the fourth dimension of time...Voltaire wondering about all the armies of the earth being powerless before an idea that has come into its own...Hero of Alexandria wondering two thousand years ago about the spinning speed of a metal ball with escaping steam, discovering that long ago the principle of jet power. Such stuff as writer's dreams are made of...and artists'.

The piece of writing closest to my heart for the WLW Stations was my "Land of Counterpane," national ad for the Ruth Lyons Christmas Fund. It was based on Robert Louis Stevenson's poem about the little boy sick in bed playing with his toys. "The little giant great and still that sits upon the pillow hill..." and all the other hospitalized children who benefit from toys and equipment bought through the Ruth Lyons Christmas Fund.

We were in seventh heaven having a free hand with headlines and illustrations like these: "Never step on an ant in Atlanta...it might be building a mountain along with WLW-A"...and the giraffe in Indianapolis at WLW-I who ordered "some leaves of mimosa on toast for lunch"...and the bird building her nest on the windowsill of the television studio, unaware

(Photo by Terry Armor)

GOVERNOR RHODES accepts Larry Zink's famous award-winning painting of the Delta Queen as a gift to the state of Ohio.

The Delta Queen by Larry Zink

(Original in color) ©

> "Down the valley of a thousand yesterdays
> Flow the bright waters of Moon River
> Dream on, sleep on,
> Care will not seek for thee,
> Float on, drift on,
> Moon River, to the sea."

she was being televised, "A million people watched her build her nest on WLW-D"... and the anniversary of WLW Radio "When the flowerpot spoke..."

The mailing pieces were something else. Will we ever live down the piece of real fresh fruit! The day we went bananas. I got the brilliant idea to send out a real banana as a WLW-TV mailing piece to all the advertising agencies, advertising managers, etc., on the big five-thousand-name mailing list. So I told my brainstorm to Gus Lemperle, our print production manager. "Where in the hell are we going to get five thousand artificial bananas?" he calmly yelled. He didn't realize the worst of it...they were going to be real!

"Now don't get excited," I cautioned. "They're not going to be artificial."

"Thank heavens!" he exclaimed. "They're going to be just illustrations of bananas. For a moment there I almost had a heart attack!"

"Uh, Gus..." I quivered. "They're not going to be illustrations."

"Well, then what the devil are they going to be? Not artificial?? And not illustrated pictures?? What other kind of bananas are there???"

"There are real bananas," I weakly whispered.

"Real bananas! Real Bananas! Are you out of your mind? Mail out five thousand real bananas?"

It almost caused Gus and a little old Italian banana merchant down on the river front to head back to the old country, any old country. But the mailing was a great success as we sent out, one at a time, five thousand Chiquitas! A success, that is, except for those on the mailing list who did not open their bananas right away! One ad manager from the West Coast sent us a polaroid picture of himself reenacting the crime of opening his banana mailing, which had sat on his desk for two weeks unopened. What was that black, mushy blob in the picture? His note simply said, "Now please don't send me a mailing saying that your television stations are the apple of my eye or a peach of a buy!"

To sooth Gus' ruffled feelings about the big job of sending out the five thousand bananas, I told him I was going to write a book someday and put him and the bananas in it. "No, no," he pleaded. "I can't be in your book! I've got a printer waiting!"

Better than a Paste in the Mouth

As is inevitable with all art directors and writers, Larry Zink and I would occasionally disagree over the concept of an advertising campaign for television or print media. One such disagreement took place on the phone and I slammed down the receiver. For some strange reason, it flew in a million pieces! Meanwhile, Larry was trying to ring me back. With the collection of phone pieces hanging around my head, I tried to answer him. "Hello, hello...stop ringing my phone..it's broken...hello...hello..." Finally, in desperation, I charged back to his office, which he had just left to charge back to mine. Somehow we missed each other on the way.

When I arrived at his north light creative corner, I spied a jar of rubber cement by his drawing board. This is one of the most diabolical weapons of war in an advertising agency, or the whole world, for that matter. If aimed properly, a wet rubber cement brush would wipe out an army and even jinx the "hot line." So with this in mind, and in hand, I proceeded to politely paint the seat of his chair, using the weapon with the purpose of dry mounting him in his place. But what happened?! He returned with Art Volk from Frank Hulefeld's Art Studio. This worthy gentleman just missed sitting in Larry's chair by the skin of his...

Finally, Larry himself sat down and as he realized his posterior position, the look on his face changed from a rough layout to a finished award-winning piece in an art directors' show. But Art Volk's coincidental remark really made it the best of show. He told Larry "to stick to it to the end" and the television commercial storyboard he was working on would turn out just fine. Larry, realizing what was on his chair, was frozen in his position. He could do nothing but woefully reply, "I think that's what I'm doing." So I had finally gotten even with Larry for the time he poured the rubber cement in my paper clips.

I was always telling Larry that I had a great idea for a best-selling book. This one particular brainstorm came to me one evening as I was passing a newsstand and looking at the magazine covers. Often the title of a story inside was splashed across the cover in big type which, if identified with the cover photo, was quite a gasser. One book showed Lassie looking over a fence, or maybe it was some other collie.

Anyway, the title of the story inside, which had nothing to do with the dog on the cover, was in bold type on the front: "Why I am proud to be an American." Another cover showed a girl in a bikini with a military story title underneath: "Look what's happening to our U.S. Army." And another cover had a fellow dressed as a hobo with the title of a story inside over the picture, which had no bearing on the photo: "Why so many wives leave home." Another writer and I were going to combine our research efforts on this but it got lost with an agent someplace. We were going to call it *Gags on the Mags* or *Taking All the Covers*.

Another idea I had for a book was to take candid shots of people throughout the country. And anybody whose picture was in the book received $1000. The books couldn't be opened until they were bought. I

Sure glad we finally hired somebody who could figure out those Station Rate Cards

the famous Crosley group

the famous Crosley group

(Photo and Artwork courtesy "Whitey" Fisher—Steinau–Fisher Art Studio)

"Whitey" Fisher - The master artist-cartoonist. He illustrated the Crosley campaign for which Time Buyers around the country are still asking years later, especially the one with the tombstone which reads, "Here lies a good and faithful Time Buyer who was talked to death." And the giant colorful Christmas ornament that read, "Shining Best Wishes from the WLW Stations."

219

CHARLIE HARPER - Charlie, with a boyish happy grin that was a prediction of things to come. Did anybody have such a unique talent? What a thrill it was for me to have him do one of my Crosley Broadcasting campaigns. It sure beat my "copywriter's roughs," the "joke" of the advertising business. The artists would say, "Here she comes again. The Picasso of the writers. Who thinks cubism is a form of Latin American government."

221

(Photo and various material courtesy Alex Schmitt)
SCHMITT, MOFFET & GEHRING - That's multi-talented Alex Schmitt at his drawing board creating an early Crosley Motors ad or a Cincinnati Milling Machine folder or a General Electric Jet Engine TV storyboard. He often "flew" right out the window, as the art department had the habit of flying homemade airplanes with little men in them out the 31st floor window, the first jet engines made of papier-maché!

GENE BOTTS - So shy and so humble that he first submitted for this book a picture of himself and his back turned. Such a mild-mannered creature in this business is a rarity. A beautiful disposition and equally beautiful work. No back-talk, no back-biting, a truly wonderful person. Peace! He did the beautiful artwork for the final cover.
(Photo courtesy Gene Botts, Artist, Cincinnati)

MORE ART DIRECTORS - (1 to r) Fred Potschmidt, Ed Steinau, Sam Lipson, Charles Jacobs, Phil Goyert, Elmer Koenig, John Zeigler. Oh, what these distinguished artists could do with a copywriter's rough. With trees with no leaves! Little men with no eyes! Skies with no clouds!

WHO'S WHO IN ART about town, some of them that are or were. (1to r) Bill Barker, Ray Brown, Larry Zink, Henry Wilder, Ed Steinau, Charles Gerhart, Bob Helmick, Sam Lipson, Ed Betz, Vern Rader, Noyes Strout. Those were the days! And who poured the rubber cement in the paperclips!

(Photo courtesy Hank Mott Art Studio)
THE ART DIRECTORS CLUB - The yuppies of their time! That young men-about-town group with talent to spare. Here are some of the club's art award winners: (1 to r) Hank Mott, Dick Lewis, Ed Betz, Don Baker and Bill Sontag. Also billed as the closing act on *The Ed Sullivan Show.*

SHAKE THEIR DRAWING HAND, what a lineup! The best of the best. (back row 1 to r) Vern Rader, Alex Schmitt, Dusty Rhodes, Don Baker, Clint Orlemann, Clark Collard; (front row 1 to r) Stan Thal, Charlie Harper, Henry Saensy, Larry Zink. Other wise known as the Brooks Brothers.

224

told this to Larry one fine day. His only comment was, "And it'll be just your luck to pick public enemy number one and some unregistered alien and some escapee from Old Bailey to snap in crowd scenes."

Larry was the first art editor of the St. Anthony Messenger, national awards winner. His work is seen in numerous national and private collections. He was elected to the prestigious MacDowell Society.

Best of Show

What would we have done without the outside Art Studios! Those savers of the day. That magnificent bunch of talent who belong with their finished beautiful layouts in a special niche in the Louvre. Just like the Poets' Corner of Westminster, there should be a special hallowed spot in every one of the world's great museums for masterpieces of commercial artwork produced by the impressionists of the earth's businesses.

And they, too, are great characters. Who could ever forget the episode with Whitey Fisher. He's the top cartoonist in town and that sort of thing. Whitey was in a terrible hurry to get back to his studio, but somebody in our meeting kept dragging it out, talking about his aches and pains. Whitey couldn't take it any longer, listening to the state of health. So he started squimmering, a better word than squirming, to get going. But when the hypochondriac began on the ingrown toenail he had cut out, Whitey blurted out, "We don't want to hear about your sex life! Good-bye."

Others who have rated best of show are Alex Schmitt, Jim Moffett, Hank Mott, Frank Hulefeld, Dave Diehl, Johnny Johnston (our man in London), and Sam Lipson, all supreme examples of masterful creativity with, as Van Gogh once said of true art, shades of gold always showing through. That's especially true of Charlie Harper's work.

And an honorable mention always to the suppliers — the printers, engravers, lithographers....including J. W. Ford, Bud Janszen of Amity, Hennegan, Westerman, Cincinnati Typesetting, Central Engraving and Cincinnati Graphic Art. And our favorite photographer, Austen Bewsey. Austen and his wife are British and as charming as a cotswold cottage. When you'd call up to make an appointment, their reply was like a breath of fresh English country air in the middle of the hectic business world. One time I called for a photographic session about a television commercial. Austen answered as if inviting us to a cup of tea. "Oh, do come!" he said.

"Deelighted to have you, you know. Jolly well."

Many thanks, too, to Ed Colina, the all-around entrepreneur, for

BILL HETHERINGTON– What are you doing in that bathtub!? Another case of the artists posing as models in a client ad or TV spot. This one was appropriate for The Ohio River Company, but hope it didn't cause the account to go down the drain!

"YESTERDAY WHEN I WAS YOUNG" - Country star Roy Clark reminisces with "Pappy" Taylor, old-time star of traditional and country music on the fiddle and banjo, who once played on WLW and WCKY in Cincinnati, WLAP in Lexington, and other stations around the country. He also opened for Roy Clark and toured with *Hee Haw* celebrity Grandpa Jones. He made records on Capitol and Broadcast labels as a member of the Kentucky Mountaineers. He said his mother sold ten pounds of geese down to buy him his first fiddle.

226

his encouragement along the way and especially his powerful autobiographical book, *Hour of Dreadnoughts*, the story of the *U.S.S. Maryland* in the Pacific during World War II.

The Keystone Kops Had Nothing on Us

When someone was temporarily located in the writing department, they were dislocated in more ways than one. Bill Hetherington, a senior citizen artist, then eighty years old and still going strong, was one of the such unfortunate DP's who got lost among the copywriters. Bill had worked as artist on everything all the way from the Keystone Kops to modern TV. Being the only artist in our part of the office at the time, he was constantly besieged to lend us his supplies so that we might do our usual masterful copywriter rough layouts, which always looked like phony treasure maps. Or we'd prevail upon him to do a better rendition for us before we turned in the assignment to the account executive.

Bill proved just what we needed in every way, an artist in our midst, a storehouse of supplies, and best of all, a sounding board for all our ideas. The routine went something like this:

"Bill, I've got an assignment today to do a television commercial for Arbor Day. You know, when the little tree seedlings are given out to the school children to bring home and plant."

"Okay, I'm listening. What's your idea?"

"The little green thumb will be coming home from school tomorrow..." I began.

"What is this, a little kid from Mars...a little green kid..."

Never mind, Bill, I can see you're going to be an editing artist. I'll just..."

"No, go ahead!" he laughed. "Tell me more about the little green thumb coming home from school."

"Never, never mind. But I will try you on another one. Now, how about this one? This is for the zoo no-littering campaign.

A camel would walk a mile to get himself a drink...
So you can walk a thousandth of a mile
To the trash can, don't you think?"

"I'm trying to be brave. Continue."

"The lion is the king of beasts
And he commands that after feasts..

Folks leave tables clean as before
Or else he'll roar and roar and roar!"

"Oh, these are rhymes! I get you now. What's the next one?"
"I'll read it as a rhyme:
When the ostrich hides his head,
It's of trash he has a dread;
So give the zoo a helping hand
And put all rubbish in the can!"

"Did you do one about the zebras? They're my favorite. I
always..."
"No, I didn't do one about the zebras. Now listen:
No dinosaurs are in our zoo,
So let's not act like cave men new;
Don't scatter rubbish for and to,
It's not the modern thing to do!"

"Are you sure you didn't do one about the zebras?"

"I'm sure. But here's one about some guy we know:
Monkey see and monkey do
If you were them and they were you,
You'd be screeching all day, too,
Please don't litter up our zoo!"

"I think I've had enough. Good-bye"
"But you haven't heard about the tiger, tiger burning bright in the
forest of the night...or, if you could have the autograph of Mr. Long-and-
Lean Giraffe..or, see you later, alligator...Bill, where are you going?"
"If I find out I have to do television layouts for these, I'm going to
the zoo and drown myself in the octopus tank. After while, crocodile!
Just one more artist killed by a well-meaning copywriter. Oh,
well, next target is an account executive. And here comes an
unsuspecting victim down the hall right now. It was Dick Jones, who
handled the Streitmann-Keebler account...the kings of the cookies and
crackers. Maybe I should try some of my more serious poetry on him.
"Say, Dick, have you got a minute? Like you to listen to
something."
"Sure thing. How long is it?"
"Only as long as it takes you to get away."
"Shoot! But I'm warning you, I'm keeping my motor running."

"Now this against soft organ music in a beautiful garden on late night television:

If you could but travel in the Milky-Way light
'Til you reached the man in t he moon,
Or you made a wish with the fireflies some night
In their magic sleepy lagoon..."

"Very nice, very nice," Dick smiled. "Go on."

"That's all there is," I smiled, "There's no more to go on."

"What's this for? Any special program or assignment?"

"No."

"Ummm...." Dick began to squirm. "Well, I've got an appointment with..."

"But I have others entirely different."

"How different?"

"Listen to this: When a piece of paper changed the course of history. The Declaration of Independence. The Constitution. The Star Spangled Banner. The Gettysburg Address. And did you know that paper was invented almost two thousand years ago in China, but it took more than a thousand years for it to get from China to Europe by way of Baghdad."

"What is this for?" Dick suspiciously asked.

"Maybe for Champion Paper Company."

"Does Champion know it's coming?"

"No, I think I'll surprise them."

"I think somebody better warn them. Or rather tell them. I mean I think.."

"Now, don't leave," I pleaded, "until you hear this one. Among ancient oriental legends, there's a mythical figure known as the story-teller, also known as the figure of long life and happiness. And legend has it that he lived seven centuries, collecting many stories as he lived and many objects in his pack as he traveled. Children would swarm around him to hear his stories and see what he had in his pack. And the legend says that even now when the moon is full and the only sound is the stars twinkling, elves tiptoe in from nowhere and gather round the storyteller. And they say if you listen, you can hear him telling his stories of long life and happiness."

"I'll listen all right," exclaimed Dick. "And if I ever hear some creep with elves telling stories on a moonlight night, I'll call the paddy wagon! I've got to go and look up that number. Good-bye!" I told this to Jean Jones, his darling wife. And she, too, didn't know whether to laugh or cry.

229

(Photo courtesy WCPO-TV, Scripps-Howard Broadcasting)

JACK FOGARTY - The Irish wit and wisdom of TV NEWS interviews President Lyndon Johnson for WCPO-TV, Cincinnati. When asked what he would like to contribute to this book, he answered, "My six children. To the highest bidder!" To which his wife, Agnes Devaney Fogarty, as Irish and humorous as he is, replied, "Oh, Jack, not all of them." But that's John Wiethe, Hamilton County Democratic Chairman (back to camera) and William Doherty, president of the Letter Carriers' Union.

THE NEWS PEOPLE

(Photo courtesy WCPO-TV, Scripps-Howard Broadcasting)

AL SCHOTTELKOTTE - He was the who, what, when, where and how of NEWS in
Cincinnati and the Midwest for many years on WCPO-TV. He's now president of the
entire parent company, Scripps-Howard, with corporate headquarters here in Cincinnati. Here Al talks over old army days at Ft. Knox with former vice-president and 1984
presidential candidate, Walter Mondale. Al has been the last word in news ever since
he helped solve the famous taxi cab murders by the clue of an earring, which was later
reenacted on Pall Mall's famous TV program, *The Big Story.*

Bouquets to the new breed of news people -- Jerry Springer, Norma Rashid, on
WLW-T; Randy Little, Carol Williams, Paul Shaeffer on WCPO-TV; Rob Braun,
Deborah Silberstein, Kit Andrews, Terry Jessup on WKRC-TV.

PETER GRANT—and the NEWS and the personality. Unforgettable Pete. What a voice and command of language. And he's read every book ever written. The man who came to work every day in his Volkswagen carrying his lunch in a brown bag. Humble and happy. NEWS will never be the same without him.

(Photo courtesy Mount St. Joseph College, Cincinnati Office of Public Information)
(photo by Peter Edles)
MARIANNE O'REGAN - The superb *Cincinnati Post* editor, fellow alumnae from Mt. St. Joseph. She wrote and covered and told many a wonderful story. But the most memorable of all was the one about the little village of Illeg...

H. L. MENCKEN, the great writer and newspaper man once said of F. Scott Fitzgerald, that his biggest mistake was to wait for his royalties. He believed that writers suffer from "black dog," black moods, periods of despair. That's why paper airplanes were shot out the windows of the 31st floor of the Carew Tower in downtown Cincinnati. Anything to relieve the pressure as "black dog" is after them again. Beware the dog— pit bull with AIDS!

"THE OLD REDHEAD" - yes, that's Red Barber in the middle, broadcasting the early Reds' games. One of the legacy of sports announcers from Cincinnati that helped make the city a legend in baseball. With his soft, sweet Mississippi drawl, he began his career with the Reds. Later, he spent fifteen years doing the Brooklyn Dodgers play-by-play, and twelve years as the Yankees' announcer. He's one of the few non-players or managers inducted into the Baseball Hall of Fame.

Who will ever forget that night at Cincinnati Riverfront Stadium, Sept. 11, 1985, when Pete Rose beat Ty Cobb's record of 4191 hits.

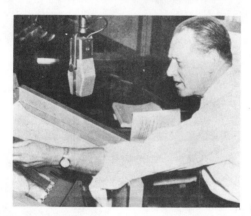

"BURGER BRINGS YOU BASEBALL", with who else but Waite Hoyt, spinner of tales, some tall, some short, but never equalled. Hoyt was a leading pitcher on the Yankees' dynasty teams of the '20s, considered the greatest ever assembled in 1927. Also a Hall of Famer, an accomplished painter, the best friend of Babe Ruth and Pete Rose. At Ruth's funeral, in the sweltering August heat, Joe Dugan, the third baseman of "Murderer's Row" whispered to Hoyt, "I'd sure like to have a big glass of beer." And Waite replied, "So would the Babe."

DICK BRAY - who could forget his "Fans in the Stands" pre-game radio shows? He also did play-by-play with Red Barber and Waite Hoyt. He covered the bases on WSAI, WCPO, WCKY and WLW-T in Cincinnati, and WHIO in Dayton. His reporting was not flambuoyant but simple, like talking face-to-face with his listeners, and without an ego. A devout, sincere sportsman, as well as an announcer.

235

THE SPORTSMEN
(Photo courtesy George Brace Baseball Photos, Chicago)

NO-HIT VANDERMEER, Reds' pitcher who hurled two no-hit games in a row, a record unique in baseball, against Boston on June 11 and against Brooklyn on June 15 in 1938. But as children, we never got the pitch that we were throwing him a curve ball with the girl next door by waiting on her front porch every time he came to take her out! He did autograph a ball for us on his no-hit historic occasion, which we still have.

THE LITTLE MAN BEHIND THE MASK? Who is it? It's Johnny Bench as a boy, who grew up to be the Reds' great catcher and hitter and Hall of Famer and TV announcer for the games. Maybe there's a little guy behind a mask in your family just like this!

GRAHAM MCNAMEE with the Babe! Wonder what they're saying. Who's on first? What's on second? No, that's those two other guys. Here's a pair of champs. One of the smoothest swingers and smoothest talkers in baseball. (Photo originally from the NBC files)

A tip of the Reds' cap to the sports announcers: Greg Hoard, George Vogel, WLW-T; Denny Jansen, John Popovich, WCPO-TV; Ken Broo, Walt Maher, WKRC-TV. Not to forget the old-timers like Red Thornburgh, the first Reds' TV announcer . . . to WLW Radio's Marty Brenneman and Joe Nuxall, "This one belongs to the Reds!"

BO ROHAN - More ballplayers came from the old hometown, per capita, than any other part of the country. With its many scenic ballparks along the river, Ludlow attracted the crowds and the teams, even the Reds. After all, wasn't the idea for the National League born in Ludlow? Sure it was!

(Photo courtesy Mrs. Jane Law Rohan, Ludlow, Ky.)
(Photo courtesy Mrs. Bert Rich, Boone County, Kentucky)

HOMETOWN BOY makes good! Pitcher Neal Brady who lived next door in Ludlow Kentucky. King of 1915-1917 New York Yankee fame and 1926 Cincinnati Reds king on the mound. When playing for Xavier University he struck out 28 batters in an 11 inning game against the University of Cincinnati. And later pitched a record 45 consecutive scoreless innings. No wonder that the National League declared a Neal Brady Day!

FIRST BALLGAME ON TV was a game between Princeton and Columbia at Baker Field, New York, May 17, 1939.

The Grand Opening

The grand opening of the ships and the safes got to be too much for human consumption to bear. For instance, Geraldo Rivera and Al Capone's safe. I could have told him there was nothing there in Geraldo's Hideaway. Anybody who ever lived in Chicago knows that. What did he expect to find, anyway? Some old St. Valentine's Day cards? Or maybe some white felt hat cleaner? Or some bootleg Metamucil? Maybe the first-AIDS kit.

Then there was Telly Savalas and the safe from the *Titanic*. On TV, it looked like it contained some octopus squid, or soggy cornflakes, or mud mush, silt scraps, seaweed souffle, or floundering flounder. If that's all that's kept in the bursar's safe, then somebody must have made off with the crown jewels, or else it was a poor man's cruise to the poorhouse.

Not to be topped, there was George Plimpton's rapturous discovery of the sunken *Andrea Doria*, which promoted me to promptly dispatch a letter to the local TV editors.:

Don't Be Half-safe!

Dear Editor:

Well, now we've seen everything on TV. After all the hip hipe, the big night arrived! The safe of the Andrea Doria was finally opened! And what to our wondering eyes did appear? Oh, for a sleigh full of toys and eight tiny reindeer! Instead, the comedy of the year! It should have been a Marx Brothers movie called *The Safe Crackers*. Andy Rooney, Steve Allen, Art Buchwald, Sid Caesar...couldn't have written a funnier script.

To add to the hilarity, the sound went awry...so some of the crew sounded like Donald Duck. We expected to see his three nephews, Louis, Dewey, and Phooie, or whatever, waddle in. I missed the apology for the sound failure, so I thought the cast had been obtained by a casting agent who specialized in tracheotomies.

Any why was the safe kept submerged in water. It looked like the new underwater birthing tanks for mothers and babies. Or at least for mother and baby whales. (We pause here for George Plimpton to be struck by lightning.)

And why was not the safe simply turned upright like all upstanding safes, especially full-blooded Italian ones? Then open it, let the water run out and soaked bills? Why did it have to give birth lying down the old-fashioned way? And at Coney Island? Was this supposed to be more thrilling than a roller-coaster?

Whatever made them think they'd find jewels in the safe? This was no ancient Spanish galleon. The wealthy New York department store owner, Peter Gimbel, surely knew that modern luxury liners use individual safety deposit boxes for passengers.

The most hysterical part was the diagram of where the safe was on the ship. It appeared to be in the bathroom! Behind the tub! It looked like a portable commode! Then we were shown how it might have moved in the crash. If there's anything I like to beware of, it's a commode on the move! A toilet on the prowl! An outhouse on the rampage! Worse than the Jesse James gang! A whirling dervish bedpan!? A rock-and-roll john on rocks and rollers.

Then how about the big yellow octopus diving tank, very unruly. And they had to keep knocking on the window to see how some inside were getting along with the bends. At this point, it was the TV audience who was suffering from this vertical/horizontal malady. If the Jacques Cousteau group were watching, they must have thought they were seeing the underworld of the undersea world underworld.

Now we come to the great discovery which the diver made of the hole in the side of the sunken ship. Of course, there was a big hole! That's why it sank. You'd have a big hole in your side, too, if a large Swedish vessel crashed into your side between your gizzard and your gut. That's why the big boat was lying down there and not floating up on top. The diver also made an announcement of the discovery of the ocean floor. Well, we didn't expect to find the tan bark dance floor of the Paragon Ballroom there. And a fish almost bit him. He tried to pet it.

Meanwhile, back at the ranch at Coney Island, everybody still had hands soaking in the opened safe's murky water like a Palmolive Dishwashing Liquid commercial with Madge, the manicurist. There was great hugging and joy in Mudville throughout for discovering nothing.

Hey, Culligan Man!

Sincerely,

Daffy-Nitions

Some enterprising anonymous soul took the time to write this for the staff:

ALLEN, Lyle - Brother of Sportscaster

BEST, Dick - The kind of work he tries to get out of his writers...good, better...

BOTTS, Gene - Things artists see before their eyes when they've been working too long on a layout

BURPEE, John - A brand of seeds and seedlings

BOAM, Al - Something that is dropped (as in atom boam)

BRACH, Joyce - Something good to eat, like chocolate-covered cherries

CARDER, Ed - Worker in woolen textile mill

CASE, Virginia - Something in which to store books about the South

CHASE, Bud - What Cincinnatians call a French-type lounge

COLLARD, Clark - The greens so popular with southerners

CROSS, Newton - A state of mind

DAILEY, Gene - part of the name of his former Chicago newspaper

DOERR, Shirley - Right next to the one marked "Ladies"

DOUGHMAN, Dorothy - Someone who works with batter at Streitmann

ELFERS, Ed - Little people who bustle about at Christmas time.

Fahnestock, Bill - Shares in Disney, Inc.

FALLON, Carol - Someone who commits a crime in Russia

GANNON, Stu - Thing is shot off on all occasions in the writing department

GEIS, Richard - What a Cincinnati waitress asks, as in "Have youse geis been served?"

GICK, Art - What the creative department gets in the pants for their efforts

GILBERT, Larry - Part of a fish; and Ernie's partner on Sesame Street

GRIESS, Bill - What is always greener if it's on the other side of the fence

HALEN, Laura - Descriptive phrase of a young lady calling a taxi

HARMON, Connie - What she thinks most men are doing when they speak to her

HAYES, Bob - Semi-obscurity behind which we work

HENSE, Marcia - A group of agency girls

HERINGHAUSE, Charlotte - A place for salt fish to go

HETHERINGTON, Bill - Two thousand pounds of anything purchased in Hetering, England

JONES, Richard - Obviously a nom-de-plume. Or the name you put down on your income tax

JONES, Mary Elizabeth - Another non-de-plume! Or what you tell the police your name is.

KEATING, Jack - What account execs say when shown copy, as in "You must be Keating!"

KEATING, Norma - As in Mrs. Jack, or things have returned to "norma."

KELLY, Mary Ann - An imported whisky

KENNEDY, Rita - Rio Rita, things are sweeta when you are here

KNOCKLEMAN, Elaine - Former Newport hood who only used fists

KNOLLE< Mary Jane - The top of a small hill

KRAUSE, Walter - Name of shooting match with birds

LEMPERLE, Gus - Song from *My Fair Lady* as in, "Wouldn't it be lemperle?"

LAUGHLIN, Mary Jane - Something left over from Laugh-In

LESHNER, Don - if it were spelled with a "u," it would be exactly what this guy is not

LINDEMAN, Lee - Someone who can only do one kind of dance

LONG, Jo - A chinese waitress

MAHER, Pat - What La Guardia was in New York

MARRIOTT, Jack - What people better get after they've been engaged awhile

McENTYRE, Kelly - The pneumatic wheels used on Mack Trucks

McVEY, Mary Ellen - The Scottish Rites password used in place of "Oy Vey."

MORRISON, Virginia - What someone tells a kid who is pouring beer for his dad

MUELLER, Gertrude - Cowboys who don't ride horses

MYERS, Paul - Something we tramp through along with the mucks

NAUDEAU, Lois - Everybody's usual condition

NELSON, James - A TV rating service

OSHRY, Maurice - What falls over a crowd when the conductor lifts his baton

PALMITER, Jay - A former lotus Bater who lives in Florida

PERRY, Dick - His brother discovered the South Pole, or was it the North!?

RANSDELL, Charles - A wooded area near Robin Hood Dell

REGGIN, Eula - Asking directions while driving to client home office, as in "How far do you reggin it is to Ashland?"

REUTER, Mae - Someone who produces short stories and novels

ROBERTSON, C. M. - A kid whose dad held up candy stores

SCHUERMAN, Marlene - Reply of a beatnik chick when asked if she wants to dance

SCHUMANN, Vern - The first name of Madam Heink, the opera star

SCOTT, Viva - What Mexicans cry out about imported toilet paper

SCHMITT, Alex - As in Schmitt, Moffit & Gehring Art Studio

SEIBERT, Mary Elizabeth - Direction for Sesame Street, or see Ernie

SCULLY, Judy - How a Japanese mouse runs for its hole

SHERMAN, Helen - Had a tank named after her

SULLIVAN, Sheila - The order that is given to dirty-up only one of something

SMITH, Ann - Under the spreading chestnut tree the village smithy stands with big hats, big shirts, and big deals.

TELGATER, Jean - She did and he replied, "After while, crocodile!"

TOTIS, Kathy - What lovers do when they run out of lips

VEHR, Elmer - to the right and to the left, that's where you go for the money

VINES, Ralph - The things animals grow on, like gray apes

VORDENBURG, Rosemary - Last message from *Titanic*, as in "We're avorden burg.."

WILLER, Stanley - Best kind of wood for making charcoal

ZINK, Larry - The "mettle" art awards are made of

YAUCH, Ronald - A helluva good laugh

YORK, Linda - Where everyone wishes they were at one time or another

Proposed Agenda For Groundbreaking Ceremonies For Mausoleum

1. Band starts program with musical selection, "Massa's in de Cold, Cold Ground."

2. Mayor extols beauty features, comfort, luxury of new Mausoleum, reveals for the first time what Mausoleum will be called "Mausoleum Hilton."

3. Reservation blanks are distributed to assemblage, making sure that those over 70, those who are pale and hollow-eyed, those who are smiling heavily, and those older men accompanied by young ladies, get first attention.

4. President of bank, speaking in grave tones, tells of cemetery credit plan, assures assemblage that no one need fear passing away because of finances. Explains "Go now, pay later," or "Family Lay Away Plan."

5. Band selection: "Bye-bye Blues."

6. Soprano (unobtrusively dressed in black) sings, "I dreamt I Dwelt in Marble Halls," then leads assemblage in singing new Mausoleum Jingle, to the tune of "Oh, Them Golden Slippers."

Oh, that Mausoleum...oh, that Mausoleum

That's where this body is dying to sleep

Oh, what high class comp'ny I will keep!

Oh, that Mausoleum..Oh, that Mausoleum

I'll go "Top Shelf" in every way, so I'll sign up today!

7. Brief skit by Mort Sahl, with Mort making humorous allusions to his first name.

8. Groundskeeper points out superiority of Mausoleum burial as compared to regular type interment, as band plays softly, in accompaniment "How Dry I Am."

9. Governor speaks briefly, explaining why he intends to fire all grave diggers.

10. Visiting celebrity, radio and TV's Sam Spade, breaks first shovelful of earth.

11. Bank closes program with rousing rendition of "I'll Be Glad When You're Dead, You Rascal You!"

From the Mailbag

We received some lovely letters from those we did business with, like this one of appreciation:

From: Henry Morgan
        336 West End Ave.
        New York, N.Y.

Dear Mr. Allen,

I am not a plumber, steam fitter, nor corporation. I am an actor. I have been employed solely by advertising agencies for thirty years and have never made out a bill in my life. Please just send me the check owing and have done. You may recall that the last time we had dealings I had to go to the union to collect. Let's not have any more foolishness. I am too old and too tired for this kind of shenanigan. In short, and at the risk of being boring,...just send the check, please.

Yours truly,

(signature)
Henry Morgan

Royal Order of Liars

We awarded any employee, deserving that is, with the following certificate of merit or demerit, as the case may be!

This is to certify that (name) has been duly nominated and accepted in to the Royal Order of Liars, the Official Organization for those who would spake the truth with imagination, who would practice artful exaggeration, and who would honor veracity when convenient.

Thou shalt pledge thyself to follow the Father of our Country as thy guiding example of honesty, and admit any chopping down of cherry trees thou shalt do during thy entire lifetime.

Membership is hereby granted (name) for thy following meritorious services to our cause:

1. For the stories you've trumped up. (Sketch of playing card)
2. For the yarns you've spun. (Sketch of spinning wheel)
3. For the tall tales you've handed out. (Sketch of giraffes tail)
4. For the fish stories you've lined up. (Sketch of fish)
5. For the things you've cooked up (Sketch of something cooking)
6. For the bull you've slung. (Sketch of bull)
7. For the truth you've stretched. (Sketch of corset)
8. For the stories you've counterfeited. (Sketch of money)
9. For the humbug you've related. (Sketch of Scrooge)
10. For the facts you've juggled. (Sketch of juggler)

Signed, sealed and delivered this eleventh day of the twelfth month of the sixty-second year of the twentieth century.

(In form of big seal)

OFFICIAL LIAR's CLUB
CERTIFICATE
Be it known that from this day forward no living person will ever take your word for it.

(Photos courtesy "Bud" Janszen, Amity Unlimited)

GIMMEE A BUD like Janszen! Here's an expert printer, an expert Lieutenant-Governor of the Fifth District AFA-Advertising Federation of America, an expert in charity drives, an expert in the arts, an expert "supplier" of anything you need from a printing company to a ticket for the Reds' ballgame. What would the glorious communication business have done without Bud Janszen and Amity. A super-duper generous guy who turns any ceiling into one made of balloons to dance on.

Chapter 12

The Grey Flannel Underwear Had to Go!

I can't stand it any longer. I've got to get away from it all. The busy business world...the pressure of the huckster trade, these characters in the grey flannel underwear...and above all, that demon from the deep known as television, which devours programs, commercials and mammals called "people," especially the species named "televiewers"....and "telewriters."

I'll go to the closest place to heaven on this earth. Ireland! It really is, geographically speaking. Surely there I'll get away from it all. And I'll look up my ancestors while I'm there — because, after all, I'm 100% Irish. Never a taint in the pure Gaelic strain. Never a Hindenberg or an Amerigo Vespucci in the family. I'm sure some relative was the original Rose of Tralee....and a great-great aunt must have been Macushla...Macushla...and some cousin Mavourneen...Mavourneen...and a great-great-great-great-great-great-great-great-great-great-great-great-great-great-grandfather no doubt was a glorious Irish king...or at least lord mayor of Dublin. Yes, this is what I'll do.

Going to Ireland is like falling in love. There's a time and a place and a person.

"Oh, Ireland, isn't it grand you look,
Like a bride in her rich adornin',
And with all the pent-up love of my heart
I bid you the top o' the mornin'."*

*Locke, John. "Dawn on the Irish Coast" — Recitations and Readings, Vol. III.

I'm coming! I'm coming!

But first I'll have to go down to the Irish Building and Loan on the corner here and get some money. Everybody knows the Irish Building and Loan, founded among all the Germans in Cincinnati by Irishmen for Irishmen years and years ago...in back of a saloon! And with the original guarantee sticker still thumbtacked over the door. A holy picture of St. Patrick! It wouldn't hold up in any court, but it's held up over the doorway, and so has the Building and Loan, glory be to St...!

I took off on the flight for Erin on the shamrock-decorated Irish

248

Airlines, Aer Lingus, with all the Irish from New York and Boston returning from America after spending part of the summer with relatives here. The Irish planes are named after saints, which I didn't know — neither the fact nor the saints. So when the airline representative at the New York ticket counter said, "You'll be going with Lawrence O'Toole," I replied, "There must be some mistake. I'm going by myself. I'm traveling alone."

"Oh, you Americans," he laughed in his Irish brogue, "always joking."

"It would be a bigger joke if I go with Lawrence O'Toole!" I added.

"Never fear, ma'am," he continued, still laughing. "Mr. O'Toole is a saint. Not a man."

"Well, that's a good start for the trip, anyway," I agreed.

"He's not only a saint. He's an airplane," the airline rep continued.

"Good heavens!" I mused. "This gets more confusing all the time. I was beginning to think he was your version of Lawrence of Arabia. And instead of a sheet, he wore an Irish worsted coverlet."

After the long flight, the plane left the dark night of the ocean behind and approached Ireland as dawn was breaking over the Emerald Isle.

"...but there it is,
The dawn on the hills of Ireland!
God's angels lifting the night's black veil
From the fair, sweet face of my sire-land!"

Many thoughts and feelings rushed over me. As...

"Ho-ho upon Cliona's shelving strand,
The surges are grandly beating,
And Kerry is pushing her headlands out
To give us the kindly greeting..."

How Lindbergh must have felt in another dawn years before when he first sighted the Irish fishermen watching for him and wildly waving as they spotted the *Spirit of St. Louis* speck in the sky.

"Into the shore the sea-birds fly
On pinions that know no drooping;
And out from the cliffs, with welcome charged,
A million of waves come trooping..."

I knew I had made it, too — in another way. I knew I had come home, and thought how strange it is that all things come home...inevitably.

"O, kindly, generous Irish land,

So lean and fair and loving,
No wonder the wandering Celt should think
And dream of you in his roving!..."

Looking out over the soft green velvet dawn-hushed land, I know
this surely was from "whence I had come." I had truly come home.

"The alien home may have gems of gold,
Shadows may never have gleamed it,
But the heart will sigh for the absent land,
Where the love-light first illumined it.."

I looked around in the plane, hushed in anticipation and
reflection, even for those returning who had done so many times. Still
that feeling was there.

"Now fuller and truer the shore-line shows —
Was ever a scene so splendid;
I feel the breath of the Munster breeze;
Thank God that my exile's ended..."

"O Ireland, up from my heart of hearts
I bid you the top o'the morning'!"

Then I was doubly sure that I had made it when I heard two
Irishmen arguing over a seat in the bus at the air terminal. As my great-
grandfather from Kilkenny used to say, "Even though St. Patrick and the
lord mayor of Dublin are both Irish Catholics, you should never put them
in the same pew." And so, too, to put a bunch of Irish in one crowded
bus is asking for it. A John L. Sullivan fifteen-rounder on wheels. With
no referee but the poor busy driver, who is of the same national origin
himself. Which doesn't help matters. When it comes to telling somebody
to go to a neutral corner, or counting the fares by the count of ten.

"O Ireland, don't you hear me shout?
I bid you the top o' the mornin!'"

I Met with Napper Tandy...Watching Gunsmoke

And I had not gotten "away from it all." The first signs of
advertising began to pop up. An ad inside the green bus read, "Don't
keep you money at home. Keep it in the Galway bank." But, anyway, off
we went over the Irish countryside. It seemed like every five minutes
everybody on the bus but me blessed himself as we passed churches,
country graveyards and heaven knows what. The little old Irish lady sitting
next to me finally turned and asked, "Era ya a Protestant?" I answered,
"Well, up to now I didn't think so."

250

What a beautiful ride it was from Shannon to Galway. Emerald green velvet hills sweeping down to the sea...white thatched-roof cottages, each looking like a little music box...rich fertile farmland filled to the tip...an Irish tinker gypsy cart passing..and endless rows of rocks left strewn over the land from the ice age, now nice, neat walls that had been standing for centuries and centuries. So what did we do? We knocked one down! The bus ran too close to one and over the rocks went.

Well, I thought, now we have to wait for the highway patrol, the insurance adjustor, etc. etc. But no, not in Ireland. The bus driver stood up and announced, "Now we'll all get out and put back the wall!" So we all got out and put back the wall — and drove off! What a wonderful way to solve things. Maybe I had really gotten away from it all...after all.

During the ride the old Irishman in the seat behind me leaned over and whispered, "Have you ever seen himself?" Thinking he'd been living too long in the Irish Mist, I didn't answer. But he leaned over again and whispered, "I'm askin', have you ever seen himself?"

So this time I turned around and thought I'd better close this conversation fast by asking in turn, "Who's himself?"

The old Irishmen beamed, "President Kennedy, of course!"

"Oh," I smiled. "Yes, I did see him once. And was even mistaken for one of his sisters by two men from Boston who had bet each other $5 that I was a relative."

This pleased the man tremendously and everybody listening on the green bus. They all kept nodding and smiling at me the rest of the way. When I alighted from the bus in Galway, an Irish cabbie approached and said, "Here comes another American lookin' for her ancestors." I wonder how he could tell. It surely couldn't have been because I was wearing slacks, a Cincinnati Reds sweatshirt, white Indian moccasins, sunglasses, carrying a transistor radio and being strangled from my camera straps. Anyway, I hired him to help me look up my "ancestors:"...my father's relatives in Tuam, Galway. As guidance I had only the verbal instructions from my grandmother before she died. She had left Galway as a young girl and settled in Kentucky "because it looked so much like Ireland."

Her description said "there is a lovely winding road that leads to another garden-like road with a wall that comes to some cottages near the great white house." I read all this from the back seat to the Irish cabbie and almost drove him wild. "Saints be praised! Is that all the directions you have, girl?" As I could then plainly see, there were many winding roads and garden-like roads and stone walls. So we drove all over the countryside, drenched in a blowing Erin downpour. Finally, when we were just about to give up, I spotted a sign that read, "Ballygaddy Road." It struck a familiar chord. From it, we found one that said "Gardenfield" and followed it 'til we came to a stone wall.

From here, I could see three men in the distant field. In the wild Galway wind with the racing rain blowing a banshee's howl, I called to them...above the gale..."Helooooo, there. Hellooooooooo..." They stopped and looked in my direction with great curiosity. Then one started slowly walking over the field toward me...cautiously..apprehensively. As he approached, one of the most tremendous feelings of my life came over me. Then I knew for sure...for sure..I had come home. Because his form and face looked just like my brother's.

"Who are you, girrrlll?" he inquisitively asked. "Out here in a rainstorm?"

"Who do you think I am?" I asked in turn, overwhelmed with joy at knowing I had found my "ancestors" after a century or more of separation across the seas from our family.

"Well, now!" he brightened up, "you look like one of us, but you talk like an American."

"Right you are!" I proudly answered. "I'm your cousin from Kentucky."

"Holy Mary!! Mother of God!" he started ejaculating. And the Irish cabbie started to conclude, "Pray for us sinners..."

"Quiet, please," I reprimanded. "Don't interrupt this great homecoming scene in history."

Then Peter McHugh called to his uncles in the field, "Tom! Lawrence! Come quick! It's a cousin from America!"

They came running in their black suits and caps, which Irish farmers wear. Each shook my hand with the hardest grasp and thickest brogue as they all kept repeating, "Our cousin from America! Welcome home, girl! Welcome home!"

We all walked up the Gardenfield Road as they described the land to me.

"Far over there beyond that hill is where Queen Mab lives. And did you know that Columbus landed in Galway on his way to discovering America. That he did. That he did."

I was simply carried away with it all. We would sit by the Irish firelight that evening, I was sure, and listen to old stories of the land. As we arrived at the little cottage, eight pink-cheeked, blue-eyed children came running out to meet me. But what greeted me inside that quaint Irish cottage? There stood the monster. A TV set! I had not gotten "away from it all." I tried to ignore it.

"Now we want you to stay the night with us," they warmly said, "We think you'll love sitting here with us by firelight and.."

252

"Oh, yes! I will! I will! Telling stories, old Irish lore, and reading from *Casey!* How glorious! And what are your favorite stories?" I asked the children.

"*Gunsmoke* and *Bonanza!*" they shouted.

"Ugh...uhg!" I groaned. This is what I have "come home" to. After all my poetic thoughts...my great anticipation..my escape to the last outpost of the world. As the traditional turf fire from the legendary white thatched roof Irish cottage curls into the air over the Emerald Isle on a story-telling Erin night, what drifts over the moon-drenched, green velvet country side? The sounds from *Bonanza* and *Gunsmoke* coming out of the chimney!

There was no escape, no escape at all from that big black Cyclops eye of the iconoscope. No escape from the American way of life. As the cab raced back down the road, passing a little store, the window was filled with all the brands back home on TV commercials. Not one Leprechaun Soup among them.

As I climbed back on the green bus for the jitney jaunt to the airport, I did notice one thing different. A sign reading, "Bar & Undertaker" on a building. Who could resist wondering if that was where the check for a short beer, bier originated. Oh, I was getting despondent! Then a knight of the Irish road came up to me with a goat standing on a donkey and asked if I didn't want to take the goat's picture?

"No!" I snapped. "We got a kid like that in every neighborhood!"

Of all the stories of Americans looking up their ancestors in Ireland, my favorite is the one told by Marianne O'Regan, an editor of the *Cincinnati Post* with whom I worked on many a story. She said they went all over Ireland looking for the little village of Illeg, only to be told by a priest, "There's no such place. That means illegitimate!" Oh, to think of it! After relatives' names, that was what it meant. There was no little village of Illeg!

The Scotch Had a Flavor of TV About It

Well, I won't stop here. I'll continue on. I'll search the world for an escape. Surely in the Scottish highlands, the Sir Walter Scott country, the Robert Louis Stevenson land, there'll be a refuge from the tube...and the tuba of modern living. I'll even look for those verses of Sir Walter Scott he scratched on an inn windowpane. But first I'll wander up and down Princes Street, Edinburgh's heartline. Whatever happened to the Stone of Scone, I wondered, on which the Scottish kings were crowned. Was that what they used i n the last commercial we did for a false teeth adhesive? What am I thinking of? My mind is still cluttered with my "old life" and I'm still seeing sixty-second spots before my eyes.

Surely there's a performance of *Macbeth* here in Edinburgh someplace. And sure enough there was. But as I entered a man said, "Sorry, it's not open to the public. Being prepared only for television." So then I'd have to go back home to see *Macbeth* with Bill Nimmo and Willie Thall dressed as the witches in a Bavarian Beer commercial, one of my own. "When the hurlyburly's done...there'll be brew for everyone."

I wandered on into the district where the famous statue of Greyfriar's "Bobby" sits on its pedestal. The little stray dog that was made an honorary citizen of Edinburgh and for whom a state funeral was held. Some children were playing near the statue. I told them I knew all about their little dog. And all about Peter Pan, too, created by their own James Matthew Barrie. I had seen them both on American television. They all began to giggle. "What's so funny about American television?" I asked. "We saw them, too, on television from America. That's where we first heard about them." That reminded me of the Indian moccasins I was wearing, which read "Made in Japan" on the back.

But I forged ahead past the bonnie banks, the heather, the bluebells. After I met myself coming through the rye for the second time, I arrived in merry old Englandia.

I Wandered Lonely as a Cloud Among the TV Antennas

I came into the immortal English "lake country." Ah, the sweet, sweet lake country. That is it. This the escape from the modern world. I walked the road which Wordsworth walked and could hear the countryside echoing, "I wandered lonely as a cloud...And then my heart with rapture fills and dances with the daffodils." As I entered the cotswolds, however, all the charming cottages had TV antennas on them...picking up the lake poets, I supposed, on the BBC.

And finally to London. Didn't it say in Boswell's life of Dr. Johnson, "When man is tired in London, he is tired of life"?

"O gleaming lamps of London, that gem the city's crown,
What fortunes lie within you, O lights of London Town."*
*Sims, George Robert. "The Lights of London Town" — *A Book of Fireside Poems*. edited by William R. Bowlin, Albert Whitman & Company, Chicago, 1937.

Ah! This at last is really it. In this glorious city I'll find a hallowed corner for meditation away from the madding TV crowd. I took refuge in

Westminster Abbey. Here, if any place, will be my island of freedom. In this cool sanctuary away from the world. I sat in its hallowed atmosphere drinking in its peace and history and culture...amid the lofty tombs of Chaucer, Tennyson, Johnson, kings and queens. But then suddenly a voice awakened me from my reverie.

"Sorry to disturb you, lady, but would you kindly move so we can get this television cable through here. We're setting up a remote telecast from the Abbey for a special Churchill memorial program. Righto!"

And in they rolled the TV cameras, the dollies, the lights, the wires, the crewmen. "Sure, I'll move, Oliver, old chap. By jove, you just can't escape it!"

Later as I walked down the famous London mall, I looked to see if Buckingham Palace had a TV antenna on top of it. If it did, there was only one recourse...Westminster Bridge. No, I wasn't going to jump. I was just going to drown myself in Big Ben, the bobby and the bowler hat while the passing parade of London flowed by. As I was watching the reflection of London life in the Thames, a group of British teenagers rushed up to me for my autograph! They had mistaken me for some star they had seen on BBC television! But as soon as I opened my mouth, they knew I wasn't English. "That ain't her! She's a phony!" one shouted and they all ran away. There was only one thing left to do. Lock myself in the famous Tower of London. I begged the guard to do so, but he only laughed, "Oh, you Yanks are something else!" Then take me to Piccadilly, I ordered a cab driver. As I was alighting from the "handsome," another mob of teenagers came running up. When I saw them, I started to run the other way, yelling, "No, I'm not that BBC television star. I'm not! I'm not!" But they ran on past me and went screaming after the Rolling Stones.

Well, I've had it for the day, I thought. So I went back to the hotel, got on the elevator already occupied by several young men, and rode with them up to another floor. On the way, I just casually turned around only to find I was on the elevator alone with the Rolling Stones...in their heyday, too. From seeing the crown jewels in the Tower of London to seeing the Rolling Stones in the elevator — that was my gem collection for my first day in London.

Later, when I came down to dinner in the hotel, there was quite a crowd gathered in the lobby watching a TV set. It was a news report on some of our first American astronauts who orbited the earth. As I joined the crowd, they all started congratulating me on the tremendous space achievement. "It was the least we could do," I commented. I accepted with great humility the acclaim in behalf of the entire United States space program. Wasn't it Churchill who commented on that unique effervescence for life which Americans have? Was it really just Coca-Cola as documented in its constitution of Coke television commercials? But, anyway, jolly old England did have its Friday Street and town named Christmas Pie. Which to many is more important than a sign reading "Moon Rover Boulevard."

Was TV the "Hans Across the Sea?"

Maybe in the fairy tale kingdom of Denmark, I'll find asylum from the modern world of the machine age, especially the channel machine. On to "wonderful, wonderful Copenhagen...salty old queen of the sea..." Oh, yes, neath your harbor lights and your starry nights — it's Copenhagen for me. Surely in Tivoli Gardens I'll find a quiet nook...or I'll go down to the water's edge and commune with the Little Mermaid sitting on her rock, who became immortal because she wanted to become a mortal. As the Hans Christian Andersen story goes: "More and more she began to love human beings, and more and more she wanted to rise up among them. Their world seemed far larger than her own. For they could fly over the sea in ships, and mount up the high hills far above the clouds. And the lands they owned stretched out in woods and fields farther than her eyes could reach." And what would she have thought if she could see television, the new window to the world?

Filled with the spirit of the great storyteller, I actually found him — Hans Christian Andersen himself — a lifelike statue in a shady quiet spot sitting all alone as if he were thinking up more tales. So I took out a book of his stories, which I had just bought at a little bookstore, and started to read them aloud. Soon a crowd of little children began to gather around me. They couldn't understand what I was saying in English, but listened nevertheless in childlike attention. "Well," I said to them, "I suppose you've met this great gentleman here who wrote these stories. So, Hans, I'd like you to meet your admiring public, the little children of the country and the world." At which, they started to climb all over the statue and sit in its lap. After they had nestled around him, they indicated for me to go on reading to them as they affectionately held on to Hans. When I had finished, they all began to screech and clap their hands, "TV...TV...TV!" What in the world this meant I didn't know. So I thought I'd better call it a day. But they ran after me continuing to yell, "TV...TV...TV!"

*MacMillan Company, New York, 1963.

256

THE FACE OF THE WORLD ("painted" by the author)

NBC!They're everywhere! As Kipling said, "Such gardens are not made . . . by sitting in the shade."

AT THE MONTMARTE -- ah, to paint, perchance to dream, with all of Paris at your feet!

AN ERIN LAD in his beautiful hand-knit Irish wool sweater, going home with baskets of peat cut from the fields for fuel. Note the donkey has the latest headwear! And another donkey in Lourdes! And another donkey in Jerusalem!

THE COLOR GUARD passes in review in Seoul, Korea, not far from the DMZ.

THE LITTLE MERMAID -- Hans Christian Andersen made her immortal because she wanted to be mortal, in the Copenhagen harbor.

HANS CHRISTIAN ANDERSEN, seated in a shady nook in Copenhagen, Denmark, looks as if he is listening to a story himself. *The Red Shoes, or The Fir Tree, or The Little Match Girl, or The Snow Queen.*

"ETC., ETC., ETC.", a colorful gathering of Thailand monks before the temple of the Emerald Buddah near the Bangkok royal palace, setting of *The King and I.*

I BRING YOU PRETTY FLOWERS -- a colorful sight on a Cairo street amid the drab surroundings to brighten someone's life.

SINGAPORE JEWEL SELLERS -- The highwaymen of the East. "I would not trade my daily swoon . . . For all the Rubies in Rangoon." "Cat Naps Are Too Good For Cats", Ogden Nash.

NOT A CHINAMAN'S CHANCE to forget this memorable character up in the New Territories. What are the 1000 words worth this picture?

AND A CHECK FOR A SHORT BIER, Cork, only in Ireland!

BALLOONS -- balloons, and more balloons in Manila Gardens with a Philippine flare about them. Up, up and away!

NOW SMILE, CHEOPS, look this way. Who knows the mystery of the pyramids? The camel knows.

MY SHOULDERS ACHE BENEATH MY PACK, in the shadows of the Via Dolorosa in Jerusalem, as a man bent with his burden of the world carries his cross and people too busy with their lives pass him by.

And Was TV the Thumb in the Dyke?

Strangely enough, a similar "TV" episode happened in Holland. Many of the Dutch people were walking along near the dykes wearing wooden shoes. And I was wearing those throw away cellophane rain boots, a mile of dyke too big for me. As I sloshed along and they clacked along, they all kept pointing to my feet and laughing hysterically. Their wooden shoes were just as funny to me as my American emergency rainboots were to them. But I didn't get hysterical about it. Then they started to shout in Dutch...or whatever.." TV..TV...TV!" What in the world they meant I had no idea and couldn't find anybody who could tell me. Just as in Denmark with the little children. Why was everybody shouting "TV" looking at me? Did I have a face like a bygone 9-inch screen? Or a shape like an antenna? Or knobby knees? Or was I losing a grip on my vertical/horizontal control?

Fifty Million Rollers Can't Be Wrong

On to France and Lyon...where they throw the bodies off the trains in the late-night murder movies on TV. That will never do, so Paris here I come! City of light...of love! Ah, Paris... "no matter how they change her, I'll remember her that way." I checked in at my hotel and headed straight for a sidewalk cafe to "drink in" the French atmosphere. This is it at last. This is really it! Sitting here along the Champs Elysees... surrounded by the Louvre one way and the Montmartre the other...and Napoleon's tomb within shooting distance..and Versailles and the sun king within beck and call...and Fontainebleau. I'll take that drive down there today after I go back to the hotel and roll up my hair.

And what to my wandering, wondering eyes did appear as I entered the lobby? Was I having hallucinations? Are those my hair rollers piled on the registration desk in the grand lobby of this grand hotel? Not even one's BVD's are of a more personal nature than one's hair rollers. It is m'lady's most intimate possession. And how mysterious, how maternal it is that a woman can recognize her own hair rollers anywhere in the world, like a mother seal her baby among the hundreds and hundreds on Seal Island. Maybe hair rollers are made of seal blubber.

"What are my hair rollers doing here?" I demanded of the desk clerk.

With his most polished French accent, he apologized and explained that I had been given the wrong room mistakenly and had been moved to another room. But the maid didn't know who the hair rollers belonged to.

"So she piled my hair rollers up on the reception desk?!" I

screamed at the desk clerk. "Is this where you usually keep lost and found hair rollers?!"

"Please, madam...we are so sorreee...so sorreeee..."

"Never mind. Never mind. Just tell me as calmly as you can why my room has been changed while I remain as calm as I can."

"Because there was a big television set in your room and you did not reserve a room with TV in it. No?"

"Yes. No. I do not want TV. I don't care if tonight on TV your local French Station is going to show Napoleon live marching under the Arc de Triumphe, I don't want to watch it!"

"Merci, madam. Merci."

"You're welcome. And mercy to us all. Now would you kindly give me a knapsack for my hair rollers? I'm going to join the French Foreign Legion."

Maybe Switzerland...peaceful Switzerland. The Alps. No TV cameraman could dolly up that high. In a little Swiss chalet outside Lucerne I met a wonderful dog. And what a coat! For those Alpine winters. I thought he might be thirsty so I gave him some ice out of my Coke. The carbonation got up his nose and he started to act like a cat with catnip. His owner laughed and in broken English — really broken — said, "He saw TV." What in the Alps he meant by that, nobody'll ever know. Did he see Coca-Cola on TV or did the dog see ice on TV or did they both see...?

Batman? On the Balcony of St. Peter's?

Maybe in Italy...yes, Venice.
"The gods returned to earth when Venice broke
Like Venus from the dawn-encircled sea.
Wide laughed the skies with light when Venice woke..."*
"Gaspara Stampa." – by William Rose Benet

And Milan and La Scala...do...ra...mi...fa..so...la...ti... Then Florence, beloved Florence, birthplace of the Renaissance. And Roma. The fountains and villas and churches and ice cream cones of Rome. And here is one of the greatest, simplest pieces of "copy" ever written. On the tomb of St. Peter, only recently discovered beneath the great church of St. Peter, beautifully and simply, "Peter is in here."

The most unforgettable experience in another way was the Italian train ride. Otherwise known as Excedrin Headache #92. Packed in a small train compartment with Italians eating salami, strong cheese, garlic,

258

etc., etc., etc. One could speak English, so I gave him a Kennedy half-dollar. You can buy your way around the world with Kennedy half-dollars. The Italian sitting next to me kept trying to tell me something. Or ask me something. I thought he was trying to ask me if I had ever met the pope. So I tried to explain that I had not, because he is a very important and you have to make an appointment. He is very closely sheltered and guarded. Tourists just can't walk in and meet him anymore than Italians can. He is so busy, and meditates and prays much of the day. But I did see him appear on the balcony of St. Peter's. By this time the translator was doubled up with laughter.

"What's so funny?" I asked.

"The man is not asking you if you have met the pope; he is asking you if you have ever met Batman!"

One Moment Please. One Maalox Moment.

Surely in Greece there is a sanctuary of the soul away from the word or thought of television. The answer to the riddle of the ancient Grecian sphinx: "What walks on four legs, then two legs, then three legs?" is man himself. Crawling as a baby, then walking upright by himself, and finally walking with a cane as a third leg in old age. But some walkie-talkie Greek tour conductor joked that it was an American watching TV. I still haven't gotten the joke. But the rest of the goggling, gaping tourists giggled gaffawingly...at our leader's "funny." Maybe if I went back to Delphi, the oracle there would let me in on the little secret.

But, anyway, on to Spain and Portugal. Maybe this Hibernian would find solace in the Iberians. In Bercelona one morning, I walked into an impressive-looking church and wandered through it. And there over the baptismal font was a plaque which read, "Here the first Indians were baptized whom Columbus brought from the New World." One could just imagine what a sight it was when he arrived marching through the streets of Spain with such creatures as the Indians, the like of which was never before seen or even imagined on the face of the earth that Europe then knew.

Spain and Portugal, of course, are very religious countries. So stories frequently appear in the newspapers of such a nature. Since Bernadette at Lourdes in the Basque country on the Spanish border and the three little children at Fatima, many youngsters think and hope to see apparitions. So I couldn't help but be amused when one old Portuguese fisherman at the colorful fishing village of Nazare told me that the next apparition was going to be televised...even be on Telstar live to the United

States! Having been so closely associated with the broadcasting business for many years, I could just imagine the things that might happen trying to cover such an occurrence. It would pre-empt highly paid prime time commercially sponsored programs. But if the heavenly apparition didn't appear, then an earthly announcer would have to come on and say, "Due to circumstances beyond our control, we cannot bring you the apparition this evening. We will resume our regular programming with the movie *Hell's Angels*, sponsored by Chef's Devil's Food Cakes. However, if the apparition does appear, we will return immediately to our man in the bushes. And the sponsors will relinquish their commercial message so that we may bring you uninterrupted the apparition. But before this happens, telling when the world is going to end, we'd like to remind you that our alternate sponsor is Leako Ballpoint Pens that are guaranteed not for life but forever."

They Were Well-Oriented to TV

Even though I agree with Ogden Nash that "Cat Naps Are Too Good for Cats"* and I, too, "would not sell my daily swoon for all the rubies in Rangoon"...I thought I'd have a look at the rubies anyway! On to the Orient — Japan, Hong, Kong, Korea, Taiwan, Thailand, the Philippines, Singapore.

"The one great God looked down and smiled,
And counted each his loving child;
For Turk and Brahmin, monk and Jew,
Had reached Him through the gods they knew."
"Ad Coelum" – by Harry Romaine

And in addition, one new little tin god the world over was the TV set. One word the world over remained the same, even in the oriental writing scripts it nevertheless remained the same...spelled "TV." The same in every country, every language...the new universal language of television.

One day I went to a Japanese home in a remote village to take pictures. There, seated on the floor in typical oriental fashion, was an old man wearing Japanese robes and smoking a long Japanese pipe in a very oriental-looking living room. Quickly, I focused my camera and was about to snap the picture when lo! and behold! I noticed what he was doing. There into camera range came a TV set with an American western going full blast. East meets west and...

"Let me take you to my garden..."

Well, I hadn't tried Egypt. Surely the pyramids didn't have a TV antenna and the great sphinx a microwave relay unit on its head. Our Egyptian guide said we would stop someplace as a surprise. So down the Cairo alleys and back streets we went through the bazaars and finally to what looked like a crude hut. But inside we were transported to a setting like something out of the Arabian knights. A fairy tale perfume shop straight from the world of Scheherazade. And there sat the master perfumer. His name...yes, his name was...no less and no more..than Omar Khayyam! He greeted me with all the formalities of the sheik of Araby. I was sure he was going to tell me I had Rubaiyat lips.

"Ah, my lovely lady, enter my humble dwelling. You are a vision to behold!"

Well, I was finally making some progress, anyway, because I hadn't been told I looked like a vision since I left Ireland.

"Let me kiss your hand."

The trip was getting better all the time.

"Let me show you my rare collections of rare perfumes. Rare, just like you, my dear."

And a day in June and a good beefsteak.

"Many of these exquisite perfumes are made from the delicate lotus blossom, which I grow in my garden. Let me take you to my garden."

How far away is the garden, I wondered? And how far away from the garden is the lotus blossom? And how far away from the lotus blossom is the nearest police station for help?

"I'm going to the United States next month...to New York to try to get business for my perfumes. I am going to Macy's and Gimbel's."

"Well, that's interesting," I commented. "I write radio and television commercials for Sears. Why don't you see them, too, while you're there?"

"Ah, my lovely divine one, I will do that. I will say you sent me. And whom shall I ask for in your glorious name?"

"Why don't you contact Jack Schmitz, sales promotion manager of the Greater Cincinnati area? He'll tell you whom to see in New York."

"A hundred thousand thank you's. I will take him to my garden, too. The lotus blossom will smile on him."

When I returned home, I told Jack Schmitz at Sears that Omar Khayyam wanted to take him to his garden so the lotus blossom could smile on him. Jack's only comments was, "Oh, my god!" (Sears, one of our clients, owned WLS, Chicago, whose initials mean World's Largest Store!)

THE TIME BUYER

(Photos and identifications of station reps and others courtesy of Eula Regan Casello)

EULA REGAN CASELLO - My time is your time! The gals who buy the time and the shows on the TV and radio stations and the networks around the country for the sponsors. Sharp, smart and sophisticated. Eula Regan Casello was one of the best in the business. The wheeler-dealers who had to out-wheel and out-deal the stations. Unlike the national magazine reps, the station reps came from a world of show biz. Always ready to take a time buyer to lunch and close a deal. The Ralph H. Jones Company did its share for the NAB - National Association of Broadcasters, including a toast at many of the national conventions, and officers and board members of the organization. Here Jack Schmitz, ad manager of Sears, presents a gift to Eula.

Chapter 13

Eggs on the Rocks

Eula Casello was our crackerjack broadcast media director, our time buyer par excellence. And every remark you got a "prize." A master with a quip with a whip. Eula should have been in the writing department. She once described somebody as looking like a drunken owl. And she was right. This guy came into our office to deliver a dozen artificial eggs to be used in a television commercial. He appeared in my doorway. Slightly once-over-lightly from a one-too-many yolk in his eggnog at lunch. He was holding the carton of eggs gingerly under his arm as if they were the real thing.

"I tried not to break them," he slurred with a silly soft-boiled smile.

"Thank you," I silly hard-boiled smiled back. "We appreciate your effort," all the time wondering how anybody could break artificial solid rock eggs.

"I really handled them with care," he continued and gently placed them on my desk. "See, none broken, I mean broken." Then he proceeded to take each one out, fumbling open the carton and fumbling open his mouth with a strange "bamb-bang" noise as he hammered them on my desk to prove his unbroken vow of unbrokenness. They really did sound as if a "Rock" Cornish hen had laid them..."See, none broken," he repleated...or repeated.

"Wonderful," I congratulated. "Don't know how you did it!" If he had dropped one, it wouldn't have broken, but his foot would have.

"It was nothing, nothing at all," he BEAM-ED.

"Now would you like me to head you in the direction...I mean show you to the elevator?"

"Thank you," he said in gratitude. "I guess I will be leaving now."

"Thank you," I said in gratitude. "I guess you will, too."

After he left with the "down" button, I commented to Eula Casello that I thought sure I'd never get rid of him. "Neither did I," she answered. "I've heard of 'bottled in bond,' but never saw it walking! Or talking!"

As I was back in deep concentration with my work, who should shatter the stillness? Who should appear again in my doorway? None other than the leaning tower of pizza. And that's just what he was carrying this time. A frozen pizza, not eggs. "Yoo-hoo!" he gurgled. "Would you do me a favor? I can't remember where the taxi stand is. Will you call me a cab?"

(Photo by Ben Rosen, Cincinnati)
CINCINNATI ROYALS basketball luncheon attended by (1 to r) Charles Barnham and Pete Petersen, The Ralph H. Jones Company account executives; timebuyer Eula Regan Casello; Cincinnati Royals' Bob Cousy; Bob Zinn, WLW sales rep.

REDS OPENING DAY, afforded to the Cincinnati Reds each year because they're the oldest team in the National League. Joining in the celebration are (1 to r) Charlie Murdock, general manager of WLW Radio; Eula Regan Casello, timebuyer of The Ralph H. Jones Company; Bill Scott, V.P. of Central Trust Company; Brady Louis, sales manager of WLW Radio.

(Photo by Ron Schuller, Cincinnati)
WSAI DELTA QUEEN—Timebuyer Eula Regan Casello and her husband Johnny Casello join the WSAI gang for a station break from business as usual.

OUR GLORIOUS LEADERS in their fields of broadcasting and advertising: (l to r) Bill Scott, V.P of Central Trust Company; Elmer Weber, V.P. and marketing-advertising manager of Miami Margarine Company; Ann Brown; Eula Regan Casello, timebuyer for The Ralph H. Jones Company; Robert McDowell, V.P. and senior account executive of Stockton, West, Burkhart Advertising Agency; Paul Myers V.P. and senior account executive of the Ralph H. Jones Advertising Agency; Jerry Hurter, V.P. and public relations director of the Cincinnati Gas and Electric Company. (Correction: Bert Schloemer states that he is not the third man from right as indicated in first edition of this book; and that correct identification is Robert McDowell as noted here.)

"The taxi stand," I moaned, "is right in front of the building. You must have passed it coming in. Just back out and you'll run right into it. Or it will run right into you."

"Gee, thanks," he said. "You're so nice. I'd bring you something, anything. You deviled egg, you."

As he leaned on the "down" button...and I do mean leaned...that closed the episode of the eggs on the rocks.

Just a Big Sponger

The great stories that could be told about the development of products are endless or containerless or something. There was one we labeled "The Mysterious Case of the Disappearing Sponge"..or.."Who Is Sponging on Our Sponges?" One of our clients had just put a new abrasive cleaner on the market with a "sponge included." But when the women opened the product, there was no sponge! So they complained to the dealers, who complained to the wholesale houses, who complained to the distributors, who complained to the salesmen, who complained to their company. Well, the company management just could not believe it. They went down into the plant and watched with their own eyes the sponges being inserted in the packages. And we also went out and watched the sponge insertion act. So how could they disappear by the time the packages were opened? Were they stolen enroute? No, because the packages were checked at the end of the line and the sponges were in them. Could they have been taken out in the stores? No, because the seals weren't broken. Then how could they just disappear?! That was it! They just disappeared! Somebody finally realized that the abrasive cleaner was so strong it ate the sponges in the air-tight containers!

There Was Always a Bullet
Aimed at the Bulletin Board

I used to wear an old pair of red wooly socks under my desk in the winter because of the draft from the hall. When spring came Idecided to wash them. Or rather they decided to wash themselves. They walked stiff-legged to the sink and dove in. To dry them, I laid them out on my office windowsill of the thirtieth floor. When I returned from lunch there was a note on the bulletin board put there by Jim Lawler, one of our young darling account executives. It simply read, "She has jumped. Notify next of kin." My wooly red socks dangled merrily like the old wind socks at the old airports.

266

Such were the indignities suffered by the office bulletin board.

It bore such other memorable memorandums unofficially (and unlawfully) put there by the hired help. Masterpieces of prose and historical records of the then flourishing uncivilized civilization known as the Ding Dong Dynasty or TV Stark Ages, which were really the Peerless Period compared to what's on the television screen today. How could any of us forget those missives of the genius generation that were thumbtacked up on the bulletin board for all the world to see and cherish or perish: "Who took the key to the sandbox?"..."Dear Garcia, sorry I won't be able to make it in person with a message for you. But will send a Xerox copy air mail special delivery."..."What idiot put the unabridged dictionary in my pill box?"..."Where is the book of cliches?"..."Who put the cement in the deodorant?"...

Jim Lawler, who put my socks on the bulletin board, got everybody's vote for being one of the grandest young men in the old business. He had been with the United States Armed Forces Broadcasting Network in the Pacific area and was certainly a chip off the old block of his well-known father, John Lawler. Mr. Lawler, Sr., was the retired president of the Argus Comany and because of his business ability was constantly besieged by other companies to become the president of theirs! One afternoon he was cutting his grass and the phone rang. He picked up the outside extension and it was another company wanting him to become president. Not being able to hear with the noisy powermower, he just shouted into the receiver, "Can't hear you! Lawnmower's making too much noise. Call me back sometime when I'm not cutting grass."

Executions Were Scheduled Daily

The greatest masterpieces of writing in the entire business of advertising, broadcasting, the entire communications business are in account executive requisitions. Here are some I saved for posterity to be put in a time capsule to be opened a thousand years from now so nobody will still be alive to be responsible for the acts. So be it:

"I hope I have made clear to you what is not clear to me."

"When we finish this campaign we will not have anything to do but start on another one."

"I have no information at this time. If you have any questions about the missing information, ask me."

"By the time you get this, you already will have done the work. So ignore it."

"If you don't have time to do the assignment, will you ask someone else to do it to see if he does not have time."

"There are three things we must remember in these television commercials: always use the company names...never mention price...and the third I can't remember right now."

"Please submit all your ideas to the contact department. We do not want the writers running around to the clients. You can count on the contact men to *execute* your work as they usually do."

I was saving these to send over to WCPO-TV for Jack Fogarty and Al Schottelkotte to use on the news as a feature on St. Patrick's Day. But then the next thing they'd probably do is forward them to Roger Read, Sam Johnson, Don Chapin and the rest at WKRC-TV, or to elephants' graveyard, which is another name for File 13.

Then the follow-up TV feature story would be on mistakes that the copywriters have made, which would blow out all television transmitters from here to Mount Olympus. The real one.

The Big $999,999.99 Idea

Everybody in this business and out of this business thinks he has the brainstorm, the big million dollar idea that's going to make him famous and rich. Me, too. So here's a bouquet of them for Madison Avenue to take its pick and pay as they go:

For Braniff Airlines — "What Has Four Wheels and No Flies?"

For Anacin — "Grow Up to the Adult Pain Reliever for Big Relief."

For a Kraft Barbecue Sauce — name it "Sauce of the Border."

For Lucky Strike — "Give Yourself a Lucky Break."

For Wrigley — a diet gum or mint called "The Executive Sweet."

For *Time* Magazine — "How will the news of today be the history of tomorrow? Only *Time* will tell."

— "Take *Time* to keep up with the news."

— "More people read the news in this magazine — *Time* after *Time* after *Time*."

— Read this magazine for the news. It's *Time* well-spent."

For the national Heart Fund campaign — "Donate any amount...a heart won't stop on even a dime."

For Ford Automobiles — "Who was that car I saw you with last night? That was no car, that was my life! The lizzie I love."

But my really big, big idea I reserved for Cincinnati Milling Machine Company. Send out a mailing of 25,000 fortune cookies with some masterpiece message in them. So I contacted our supplier of such unearthling things as that quantity of fortune cookies. To find one fortune cookie around is quite a feat, much less to find 25,000. I'd contact Virginia Carlson, one of novelty and speciality experts. She could locate any gimmick for any television show, salesman's presentation, or advertising mailing piece. And she could sell Grant his tomb. She was not a walking Abbey Rents, but Abbey Sells. She must have sold the Greeks the Trojan horse. When I asked her if she could get 25,000 fortune cookies, she didn't even blink. "Sure can," she snapped. "And what do you want to say in them? There's a tall dark antenna coming into your life!"

On a Serious Note

One cannot write about the field of communications in our lifetime without some mention of the assassination of JFK. Dorothy Kilgallen, who wrote her "Voice of Broadway" column for the *New York Journal American*, claimed that she would break the case. She would disclose the whole story. But Dorothy died suddenly and mysteriously after she or someone else mixed her medicine with alcohol. So did eighteen others connected with the case, die under strange circumstances. Eighteen within three years of the shot that day at Dallas, thirteen of whom committed suicide or were murdered or died by accident. *The London Sunday Times* figured that odds on this happening were 100,000 trillion to one!

Jim Kilgallen, chief of INS and Dorothy's father, was a great reporter in the old Hearst tradition. He had obtained an exclusive interview with Al Capone and with Thomas Edison. Dorothy had been a panelist of *What's My Line*, a popular early TV show. What did she know? Did she have a story? If so, it died with her.

THE CLIENTS AND THE CAMPAIGNS

(Photo courtesy Mrs. Mary Elizabeth Jones Grieshaber Wright)

STEARNS & FOSTER - The mattresses, the Mountain Mist Quilt Filling, the Packet division. When they wanted a slogan for their Riviera mattress, we came up with, "How would you like to spend every night on the Riviera!" Or better still, "Hope springs eternal!" That would get a smile, especially here from Jack Grieshaber (second from right) who was always giving everybody else a chuckle with his antics. The biggest booster the University of Cincinnati ever had. And Sigma Sigma Nu.Owner of the company, Foster Stearns (r) is all smiles, too, as is President Jim Carruthers (1) and Superintendent Bob Buck.

Three times the impact!

Just a little momentum—the famous Crosley Television Stations offer the triple advantages of top shows . . . top audience . . . top promotion through the exclusive Crosley client service department. So rock and roll!

Crosley Broadcasting Corporation, a division of AVCO

WLW-T *Cincinnati*   **WLW-D** *Dayton*   **WLW-C** *Columbus*

10
CANDLES
IN
THE
DARKNESS

271

LOOK OUT BELOW! HOW TO SELL A ZULU AN IGLU! How to sell King Kong ping-pong! How to sell a fishwife a steak knife! How to sell a sailor a trailer! Of course, we prepared these for the Crosley Broadcasting and the WLW Radio and Television stations.

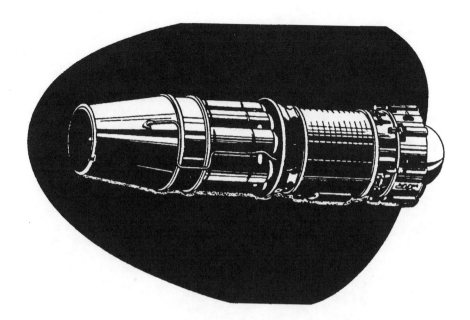

GENERAL ELECTRIC JET ENGINE division, Evendale, Cincinnati. On October 2, 1942, two of GE's new jet engines were mounted in a Bell P-59, marking the first
time in this country that a plane was flown by means of jet powerplants. Why was
General Electric selected as the first prime contractor of jet engines? Actually GE's
turbine history dates back to 1902, when the first successful steam turbine was
completed. In 1918 General Electric altitude-tested the first turbine-powered super-
charger in the U.S., after GE engineers the year before literally hauled on foot the first
jet engine 14,000 feet up Pike's Peak to test it at high altitude.

THE CROSLEY CAR - 40 years ahead of its time, as was its creator. Price tag: $337. Looks much like the compact cars of today. But I got a buckboard-bounce ride in the back seat, one of the early writers on the Crosley Motors account. Powel Crosley "folded up" his tall frame to sit in front and drive, with the account executive chewing his nails, as we went whizzing along in and out of traffic to show the car's ease of handling in passing and parking. Reminded me of newsman Peter Grant squeezed into his Volkswagen. And to think that I named Crosley's hydrodisc brake and quicksilver engine. And have never even driven a car! There's a very exclusive collector's club of Crosley cars now.

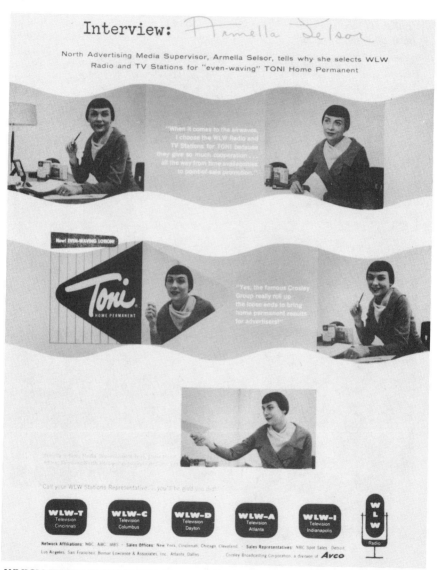

Interview: *Armella Selsor*

North Advertising Media Supervisor, Armella Selsor, tells why she selects WLW Radio and TV Stations for "even-waving" TONI Home Permanent

WHICH TWIN HAS THE TONI? - Neither one! Wouldn't you know they'd send a timebuyer with a bowl haircut for a home permanent ad!

275

THE JOLLY GREEN GIANT - Imagine finding him in a place like this! Ho! Ho! Ho! A bean stalk and a sprout!

276

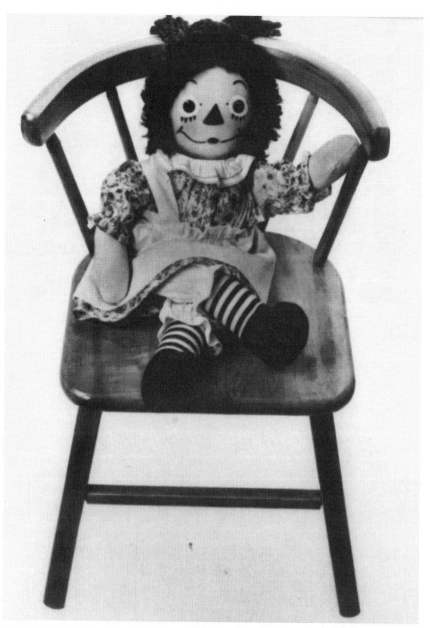

SHE'S A DOLL! - She is for sure. But she almost got us in trouble for using a copyrighted trademark figure without giving credit and getting permission. But the lawyer who called us was appeased when he realized so many of these dolls were given to sick little girls every year through the Ruth Lyons Children's Christmas Fund.

277

THE FIRST WATER COOLER - Another campaign featured "firsts" around the office. Need I say more?

STRANGE COINCIDENCE - We ran this ad in one of the leading national magazines, not knowing that another insurance company was running almost the exact same ad with the same headline just a few pages away. This should've been caught by the magazine advertising director. But we were glad it wasn't because of the attention and publicity it caused.

cracking the cat ...

with Powell Valves holding the "whip hand" over flow control in the petroleum industry . . . a position Powell has enjoyed since the first United States gusher came in a century ago. You'll find Powell's leadership in flow control extends itself to virtually every industry and industrial application. Leadership, through never-ending research, through constant pioneering in design and metallurgy . . . resulting in valve designs that have exceeded industries' demands for reduced maintenance and operational life. Whatever your industry needs, remember that Powell provides outstanding valves in the widest choice of metals both ferrous and non-ferrous for dependable flow control of virtually any corrosive or non-corrosive element . . . fluid, oil, gas, air, steam, missile and rocket fuels. If you have a flow control problem, call your Powell Distributor. Or, contact us. Powell Engineers will help you solve it.

This 600 lb. steel gate valve, sizes ½" to 24", is found in refinery catalytic towers, steam plants and nuclear systems—typifying Powell's wide range of valves for almost any flow control job.

POWELL VALVES

THE WM. POWELL COMPANY · CINCINNATI 14, OHIO

World Leaders in the Valve Industry Since 1846

Chapter 14

"The best is yet to be...Robert Browning"

Everybody who has ever been in the advertising and broadcasting business, the whole communication arts business, should publish a list of "THINGS I'LL NEVER FORGET." Certainly I'll never forget:

— the little typist from our general office who commented, when looking at the retirement gift presented at a farewell luncheon to an employee, "but this inscription on the gift says 'The best is yet to be...Robert Browning.' And his name is Robert Bliss."

— the day Joe Martens, our public relations man, returned to the office in a rage and exclaimed, "Did you all see a guy fly out the latrine window of that office across the street? He had the nerve to complain about some publicity I had written which was none of his business. I almost wrapped him up like a mummy in the roller towel!"

— the newsboy who was always trying to convert everybody, including me. "Bet you don't even know enough about religion to explain what B. C. and A. C. means," he said. "Why, that's easy!" I laughed. "I do know that much! It means the electric currents they used in the old biblical days." Then he gloated, "Ah-ha! SEE! You don't know!"

— the cleaning ladies from all of the forty-eight floors of the building standing in the lighted elevator at night, stopping to look at the crib and holiday decorations on our darkened floor one Christmas Eve, like a cover right off the *New Yorker*.

— trying to get the waiters at Wong's Restaurant to write a message in Chinese for inside 25,000 fortune cookies to be sent out for Cincinnati Milling Machine Company.

— the escape from it all under the hair dryer at Elsie & Irene's Beauty Shop, down on Fourth Street, on my lunch hour. What is it about a hair dryer that makes one drift off into the realm of peace, far from the madding crowd, and ad agency and television and everything. Like Huckleberry Finn and Jim on their raft way out on the river, far from the land and its woes.

— the character who used to come into our office among the television reps, always smoking a crossed-eyed cigar.

— the train that rode south carrying boxcars filled with a new batch of baking powder biscuits in cardboard containers. And when the engineer rounded a bend he looked back, and the boxcars were bulged out

.

swollen with the cartons swollen with the containers swollen with the biscuits from the Dixie heat! When they stopped and opened the boxcar doors, the dough poured out like a Buster Keaton movie. We didn't get that account either, because it was our suggestion that this potential client test-market this then-new-idea in biscuits in the biscuit belt of the warm South.

— the time I wrote the home decorating newspaper and television campaign for a wallpaper company and spelled "borders" wrong. The ads and the TV posters read, "Big sale on boarders! Get'em while they're cheap! You've never seen any like these! In all colors and sizes! Wallflowers and plain! Hurry! Hurry! Hurry! Last chance to take advantage of this big shipment of boarders!" It turned out like the old joke of the explosion in the boarding house — rumors are flying!

— the client picnic at Coney Island when we couldn't get Jim Coombe, multi-millionaire industrial valve expert, off the "Teddy Bear" ride. We had planned great publicity shots of this big industrialist whose company was supplying valves in the lifelines of the free world. But what appeared in the newspapers? A picture of him on the "Teddy Bear" with the caption. "Youngster enjoying himself." When somebody asked him, "Why in heaven's name wouldn't you get off that kid's ride?" he replied, "I was just trying to figure out how that doggone thing worked." This was the fabulous man who wore pure cashmere at a Coney Island summer picnic.

— playing cards in Ruth Lyons office at the coffee breaks with publicity gal, Betty Tevis Balke...when Ruth's little girl then a tiny tot, Candy, stuck her head in the door and said, "I love you."

— the day Walter Bartlett became the big chief at the WLW-TV Stations, now Multimedia, and he said to us, "I feel like Truman when FDR died, the sun and the moon and stars just fell on me."

— Jean and Lee Hornback, two of the finest people in business, upholding the Ralph H. Jones Agency and Crosley traditions of knowing it all but not letting anybody else know they know!

Yes, the ones I'll never forget:

— Jean Shepherd, former emcee on WLW, author of many books, including *In God We Trust, All Others Pay Cash; Jean Shepherd's America* series on PBS, in which he plays everybody from a southern plantation owner to an American at a baseball game; the Christmas classic, *A Christmas Story*, about his childhood when he wants a bee-bee gun for Christmas.

— Al Schottelkotte. WCPO-TV former newscaster, and the time as a young reporter he helped solve the famous taxicab murders around northern Kentucky by an earring found as a clue, realizing that it must be

THE ROOTS

(Photo by J. W. Rutter, Marietta, Ohio, courtesy of Dorothy Frye, Cincinnati)

THE OLD QUEEN floats on the Ohio River and into memory as the graceful white swan with the paddlewheel wings. The mansion on waves. The floating wedding cake. The big canoe, as the Indians called the steamboat. The great ship that passed in the night of American history. The Island Queen, with home port in Cincinnati, glides through the memory of childhood and brings back the day we travelled on her up the Ohio River to Coney Island. When the news came that she had caught fire in Pittsburgh, we all grieved and mourned her passing, for she was so much a part of this river, this life, this love. Photo was taken by Woody Rutter, son-in-law of Fred Way, Sewickley, Pennsylvania, editor of the S & D Reflector, a quarterly magazine of Sons and Daughters of Pioneer Rivermen. His wife is secretary, Betsy Rutter, named for the steamboat Betsy Ann, which her father owned. Lawrence Walker of Cincinnati is the treasurer of the S & D group.

JUMBO! - The pet of three continents! World's largest elephant, almost eleven feet tall, weighed eight tons. Captured before full-grown in Abysinnia, now Ethiopia, in 1861. Taken to Paris and London and kept growing and growing! Finally to America, causing an international situation when bought by P.T.Barnum for $10,000. Even discussed in Parliament. Our great-grandfather wanted Barnum to bring Jumbo to our little town of Ludlow, Kentucky; and parade him through the streets with all the children, like the Pied Piper. But our great-grandmother said, "NO!" And threatened that he, with Jumbo, would have to pack their trunk! Jumbo lay down in the street and wouldn't go into the transport cage in London. Even Queen Victoria's grandchildren had ridden on Jumbo. But the story had a happy ending. He loved his new home in America and lived to a ripe old age.
(Photo courtesy Circus World Museum, Baraboo, Wisconsin)

a man disguised as a woman because of the large opening of the screw-on.

— Marian Spelman singing "The Star Spangled Banner" to a height of beauty seldom before reached in the song.

— Nick Clooney, intelligent, talented, honorable, a real gentleman. One of the few people on camera who gave credit "to those you see, and those you don't."

— Ed Kennedy, the voice of the Bearcats in their basketball.

— Pete Mathews and his *Music 'til Dawn* broadcasts, which carried you to "the other side of midnight."

— "Lafe" Bill Harkness, humorist, ace radio salesman, entertainer, harmonica player on WLW, WCKY, WSAI, WKRC. He did it all with a smile.

— Bob and Janet Roger, the PR people at the Public Library, who saw us through many crises on television, advertising, publicity, news, with their research and support, especially the time we wanted to call Bob Taft "Buckeye Bob" to take him all the way to the White House.

— The Emmy, named for the image orthicon camera tube; the Oscar, named for an uncle named "Oscar" of one of the stars; the Tony, named for English actress, Antoinette Perry.

— Michael Feinstein's cat named "Bing Clawsby," who proved his master isn't the only one in the family that plays the piano at his home in Hollywood. He tiptoes up and down the keys playing his version of the scales!

— Rosemary Kelly and Jack Lescoulie doing parades and other remotes for WLW-T, recalling that in 1925 WLW did the first remote from their studios, twenty-two miles away in Harrison, Ohio.

— The newscasts and commentary of Gil Kingsbury. There's nobody like him today even on the networks.

— Stan Matlock, the story-teller, master of the trade on radio, WKRC, for 27 years, whom we'll never forget or his stories.

— Jerry Thomas, likewise and likewise, on WKRC in the morning, who must be doing "something right" as he says because he's been on for almost 20 years.

— Richard King, rounding out the big WKRC radio big three. King of the mike and madness and meaning. We should be so funny!

— Teddy Rakel and his WLW-T music; Dick Mergatroyd and his productions of the Ruth Lyons and Bob Braun Shows; Mike McConnell, my favorite of the talented WLW gang, with Gary Burbank and Bill Cunningham, the Big One on Radio; Pat Barry, seems like the weather's never been the same without him; Tony Sands, and his weather reports, to whom Ruth Lyons used to say, "Forget all those machines and radar and barometers and just look out the window!"

THE PERILS OF PAULINE? No, it was just Fireman Blake's idea of early women's lib when he took this picture of Southern Railroad "guys and dolls!' (1 to r) Ed Fleming, Mrs. Blake, Tom Rohan, "Pauline" Keith, L.H. Presnell, Engineer Holly Graves in cab at Ludlow, Kentucky.
(Photo courtesy Ludlow City Building)

WHO ARE THEY? - Where did they come from? Where did they go? The children in this priceless old photograph, found on a glass negative in the Ludlow, Kentucky City Building. Like a scene from the Our Gang movies who knows their story!

Bing Crosby — more people have heard his voice than any person whoever lived. One of seven children. His first movie was *Reaching for the Rainbow*. The first song on his first radio show was "Just One More Chance." He revolutionized the world of popular music with his mellow-baritone-crooner style, recording 1500 songs, selling a half-billion records in twenty-seven countries, making seventy films. He sang with Tommy and Jimmy Dorsey in the days of the big bands and wound up singing the best-selling record of all time, "White Christmas." He got the name of "Bing" from a comic strip character he loved as a child. He even had the ears that stuck out, which were taped back to his head in his first movie. But they popped out! So he left them that way. He did for America what the diplomats could never do. In his *Kraft Music Hall* program he sang and said it all, "When the blue of the skies meets the gold of the day, someone waits for you..."

Bob Hope — the man who never won an Oscar yet gave plenty of them away. He said, "I guess I'll just have to have Mickey Rooney bronzed." But he loved emceeing the big show of shows. "I never felt so much electricity in the air since I backed into Glen Campbell's guitar." He claims he wrote his original acceptance speech in Latin; he'd been waiting that long to win an Oscar. Bob gave us some of the funniest scenes in the movies, like the time he and Bing got in bed with a live bear in *The Road to Utopia*, and in *Son of Paleface* with Trigger, Roy Rogers' horse. He called himself a way-station between Paramount and Pepsodent. And along the way met Dorothy Lamour (and her sarong), who he said did more for a piece of cloth than any woman since Betsy Ross. From the Ziegfeld Follies to his 85th birthday party beamed around the world by TV satellite, Bob Hope has seen it all. But I'll never forget the contest my brother Jack entered years ago. You had to fill in the line to make a rhyme, "My favorite blonde is.." Jack wrote "My favorite blonde is a brunette named Toots, I can tell 'cause she's dark at the roots!"

Sid Caesar — he came, he saw, he conquered. John Crosby of the *New York Herald Tribune* wrote, "Sid Caesar is one of the wonders of the modern electronic age. He has more funny comedy sequences than he knows what to do with. His routines are even funnier the second time around and he has restored the art of pantomime to the high state it enjoyed before the talkies and radio." Larry Wolters of the *Chicago Tribune* wrote "Sid Caesar doesn't steal jokes; he doesn't borrow ideas or material." And master of them all, Alfred Hitchcock, said, "The young Mr. Caesar best approaches the great Chaplin of the early 1920s."

Jackie Gleason — admitted to the "noblesse oblige" of being talented. He said if God gives you a talent, you are obliged to do something with it. And it never lets you rest until you have done it to the

287

greatest degree. The story goes that some people went to heaven and were told upon entering that they were about to see the Beatific Vision, the sight of God, the "Great One." And one man commented, "Oh, I do hope he does his 'How sweet it is' routine."

Milton Berle — "Oh, we're the men from Texaco...we work from Maine to Mexico...I wipe the pipe, I pump the gas..I rub the hub, I scrub the glass..." About the most famous introduction any star ever had on his TV program. Even Archbishop Fulton Sheen, who was Berle's competitor on his time slot, said "do it again!" in his 1973 tribute at Friars Club of California banquet for Berle's 60th anniversary in show business. Berle's affection for his mother was well known. She went with her son to a Miami Beach hotel to hear the great Billy Daniels sing and he included a special song to her. When he had finished and everybody was applauding her, she leaned over to Milton and whispered, "I wonder who in the hell he was singing about!" Of course, the most famous line by Berle himself was the one he used to exclaim at rehearsals when he would get mad, "Jesus! Mary! And Irving!" This comic genius sums up best his life and his love and his longing in his dedication to his book, *Milton Berle, an Autobiography*: "To the funnymen who wore, who are, who will be...heroes who face the world naked but for the weapon of laughter." *

As It Happens an Autobiography by Milton Berle, Delacourte Press, New York, 1974.

Jeannette MacDonald — what lovely remembrances: Noel Coward's *Bittersweet* — "I'll See You Again"... *Rose Marie* — "Indian Love Call"...*Naughty Marietta* — "Oh, Sweet Mystery of Life"... *The Firefly* — "The Donkey Serenade"...Hammerstein's and Romberg's *New Moon* — "Wanting You"...Victor Herbert's *Sweethearts...Maytime* — "Will You Remember"... *The Merry Widow*...When Jeannette married Gene Raymond, Nelson Eddy sang at t he ceremony "I Love You Truly." And at her funeral the minister said of her, "One of the loveliest forms of expression that God's life has ever taken." In her eulogy Lloyd Nolan said, "She will be with us...as long as there are soft winds that caress the tops of tall trees...as long as there is sunlight on fields of swaying wheat...as long as there are moonbeams shimmering on blue green seas.."

Jimmy Stewart — He was George Bailey, the character he portrayed in the film that became a classic, *It's a Wonderful Life*. He often tells the story that the studio called him after World War II and offered him the part in a movie about a man who is saved from committing suicide by his guardian angel named Oscar. Stewart wasn't too keen on the idea but thought it would get him started back to work after the war and so he said, "Okay, I'll do it." Little did he dream that the dream would come true, "Every time a bell rings, an angel gets his wings."

One critic wrote of him, "Where other leading men simply stared, Stewart had something to say." He is known to have had the broadest range of an actor in Hollywood, always underneath a fundamental righteousness. His unrelenting professionalism never lets you down in the movies. He has taken more creative risks and conveyed more human emotions than anybody else, somebody wrote of him. I suppose that's why he loved his pictures by Frank Capra best. They were about you and me, about the average man, about the faith that was restored to him. And nobody could restore it any better than Jimmy Stewart.

Jack Webb — It is said of him that he set the stage for all the cops-and-robbers shows to come after him. But he really did more than that. He set the stage for the one-and-only *Dragnet.* There was nothing like it before and since. "Just the facts, ma'am." No wonder the flags at all the Los angeles police stations flew at half-mast when he died. He portrayed an old-fashioned heroic idealization of the cop on the beat. And because of it, his badge, LAPD No. 714, is enshrined forever for Joe Friday. "We need heroes," he said. "You and I are both endangered species." He didn't like policemen portrayed as drunks or stooges or renegades, as they were in later TV shows under the guise of "they're only human." Joe Friday was only human, too. And that's why he could "get the facts" so straight...so appealingly..so entertainingly...so enduringly.

Frank Sinatra — what more is there to say about "Ol' Blue Eyes?" The man who faked an arrangement of "South of the Border" for an encore on his first job with Harry James' orchestra, because he had only two arrangements, which he had already sung. Later, when he was with Benny Goodman, he was billed as "added attraction." He got the title of "Chairman of the Board" from the New York disc jockey who married Dottie Mack, William B. Williams. The thing I like best about Sinatra is that he always gives the writers credit by name in introducing each song. You never hear him called a "singer-songwriter." He leaves the song writing to the writers and song singing to himself.

Humphrey Bogart — The tough guy who appeared as a baby on a baby food package, painted by his mother, a well-known illustrator for many products, including Ivory Soap. During his funeral, a minute of silence was observed on all movie lots in Hollywood. John Huston said in his eulogy, "He has lasted so long and will last forever." Lauren Bacall placed a gold whistle in his urn as a symbol of their eternal connection. Bacall had married Bogart at Louis Bromfield's farm near Mansfield, Ohio. One of his most famous lines was, "May you never die 'til I kill you." Bogart got his start in movies when Leslie Howard insisted he be brought to Hollywood from Broadway to play the part in *The Petrified Forest* he had played on the stage, instead of James Cagney or Edward G.

Robinson. And when George Raft rejected *The Maltese Falcon* and *High Sierra*, Bogart became a star, a superstar. "All he had to do to dominate a scene, was to enter it," one director said. An injury in World War I from a ship shelling left him with an upper lip and mouth defect which added to rather than subtract from his presence. In the conclusion of *The Barefoot Contessa*, he said, "Life every now and then behaves as if it had seen too many bad movies...you fade out where you fade in." And his greatest, most unforgettable line of all at the airport to Ingrid Bergman, "You can't go where I have to go or do what I have to do..." As he turned and walked away, one critic said it best, "He never wore a trench coat, it wore him."

David Niven — one of the best books ever written by a performer is *The Moon Is a Balloon* by David Niven, with introduction by E. E. Cummings:

who knows if the moon's
a balloon, coming out of a keen city
in the sky — filled with pretty people?
(and if you and I should

get into it, if they
should take me and take you into their balloon
why then
we'd go up higher with all the pretty people

than houses and steeples and clouds:
go sailing
away and away sailing into a keen
city which nobody's ever visited, where
always
it's
Spring) and everyone's
in love and flowers pick themselves.
E.E. CUMMINGS

In his long, distinguished career ranging from *David Copperfield, Wuthering Heights, Charge of the Light Brigade, The Lives of a Bengal Lancer*, Niven recalls what Humphrey Bogart once said to him, "Keep going somehow, mortgage the house, sell the kids, dig a ditch, do anything but for Christ's sake never let them think they got you running scared, because somewhere in somebody's desk is a script that's right for you and when they dig it out, it's you they'll want and nobody else and everything'll be forgotten."

M*A*S*H — my personal experience with M*A*S*H could be

290

called "Why Did Hawkeye's Tent Collapse??" or "Who Stole the Pole from the 4077th?" I plead guilty to both counts. I was taking a professional tour of the M*A*S*H set when I noticed a pole on a tent was unattached. So I thought I would take it home for a souvenir; but when I lifted it up that part of the tent collapsed! The guard came rushing over to see what was the matter with Hawkeye's tent that it had partly collapsed. I was standing there with the pole in my hand, leaning on it with a frozen expression on my face. The guard immediately called someone to fix the tent, not noticing that I was leaning on the pole! I remained frozen in that position until they ushered us on to the next site, carrying the pole just as I had originally taken it. The guard looked at me kind of strangely, to say the least. So I leaned on the tent pole until the tour was over. Then I set it down to pick up some souvenirs of M*A*S*H at the gift shop. When I turned around, it was gone. So that's what I get for causing such a casualty among the 4077th!

Among the episodes of M*A*S*H the most memorable were: "Iron Guts Kelly," about a general who dies, not on a battlefield, but an aide insists he be propped up on one for appearance sake; "The Late Capt. Pierce," in which Hawkeye is pronounced dead by the Army, but he tries to convince them that he is not dead; "Period of Adjustment," when Mike Farrell goes to pieces as a father separated from his daughter; "Old Soldiers," when Harry Morgan toasts his dead comrades from World War I and leaves the cast in tears; "Dear Dad" letters from home; "Point of View," about the wounded through wounded soldiers' eyes; and the brilliant "Dreams" episode. M*A*S*H was surely a collection of varied characters and their astonishing decency and dedication to their profession and to each other under great pressure. Judith Christ wrote, "The laughter is blood-soaked and the comedy cloaks a-bitter and terrible truth."

John Ford — who gave us the classics *How the West Was Won,*

James Cagney — He told the story of his mother, half-Norwegian and half-Irish, "She had the guts of an army." He gently broke the news to her one day that he wanted to be a fighter. "I can lick any guy down at the ring," he boasted. "Can you lick me," she calmly replied. In recalling his stunning career in the movies, he remembered that the bullets were real in those days and the actors were real. No substitutes in either case. No pellets and no stand-ins. One bullet went right through his hat! It was Al Jolson who brought Cagney to Hollywood. *The Public Enemy* was his first big hit. Jimmy Cagney was the first actor to win the American Film Institute's Life Achievement Award. Pat O'Brien said of him, "He could tell a phony in a fog." And Cagney himself said of life, "Like performing, when you're on, you're on...you've got just so much time to make it in."

Donovan's Reef, The Man Who Shot Liberty Valance, The Horse Soldiers, The Rising of the Moon, The Long Gray Line, Mr. Roberts, The Quiet Man, What Price Glory, How Green Was My Valley, Tobacco Road, Young Mr. Lincoln, Grapes of Wrath, Stagecoach, Steamboat' Round the Bend. Orson Welles said of him, "John Ford knows what the earth is made of." And Ford himself liked to quote Jean Renoir, "If it doesn't show the glory of man, don't do it." Frank Capra described him best, "Half-genius, half-Irish, half-saint, half-satan!"

Barbra Streisand — In 1961 Mike Douglas erased the tapes with himself and Barbra Streisand to use them for something else. He paid her only $1000 for five shows! Paul Williams said that working with Streisand was like having a picnic at the end of an airport runway. So much was going on! The once ugly misfit, who slept on the floor in Brooklyn, sang songs to the neighbors out the window, and play-acted on the roof of the building. She went to the library and read the great plays. "*Anna Karenina* changed my life," she said. She also studied the tapes of the great singers — Morgan, Waters, Etting, etc. First big Broadway hit was *I Can Get It for You Wholesale*, followed by *Funny Girl, Hello Dolly*, and the rest. "The dream, you never achieve it. The excitement of life lies in the hope, in the striving for something rather than the attainment." Her performance in *Yentl*, an Isaac Singer story she dedicated to her father, exemplified her belief, "All we have is what is in our hearts, what is in our souls, what is in our heads...You can accomplish your dreams if you have to."

Fulton Sheen — the main competition to Milton Berle on Tuesday night! He received 10,000 to 30,000 letters a day on his program, *Life Is Worth Living*. It was said of him that he was the G. K. Chersterton of his day. In fact, Chesterton praised him. I will never forget my own personal experience with this mystic man. I had the assignment of obtaining an interview with him when he was speaking in Cincinnati at the Taft Auditorium. As part of my journalism course in college, it was up to me to find out how to contact him and how to get the interview. Well, it was quite a job. He wasn't going to arrive in town until the last minute, so I stood in line to get a ticket at Taft, still wondering and worrying how I was going to achieve this feat. When what do you think happened? None other than Fulton Sheen himself suddenly appeared out of nowhere and tapped me on the shoulder saying, "Would you like a ticket? I have an extra guest ticket." This was the man who worked miracles. He told the story once of an Englishman who got in a cab in New York and said, "Take me to Christ Church." The old cabbie absent-mindedly took him to St. Patrick's. When he pulled up in front, the Englishman said, "My good man, this isn't Christ's Church!" Then slowly the taxi driver turned around and said, "Buddy, if He ain't in there, He ain't in town."

Edgar Bergen — He discovered his ability to throw his voice when he was thirteen years old. And studied it in his Wizard's Manual. He named Charlie McCarthy after an Irish newsboy he knew and also after the woodcarver who made the original model, Charlie Mack. Bergen gave birth to a new, dramatic, literate art form — the art of ventriloquism. He went to a Fifth Avenue tailor, a Park Avenue silk hatter, and a British supplier for the monocle...all to outfit Charlie McCarthy. Rudy Vallee discovered Bergen and his wooden creation who became the most preposterous, impertinent, deceitful, egotistical, hypocritical, and lovable character show business has ever known. Bergen left $10,000 in his will to be administered by the Actors' Fund to keep Charlie in good repair. And Charlie would surely have something to say about that! But then, with Bergen gone, he would always be silent.

Ethel Merman — George Gershwin once said to her, "Never go near a singing teacher!" Toscanini said of her, "Her voice is like an extra instrument in the orchestra." "There's No Business Like Show Business" and nobody was ever in it who could equal Ethel. Her simple code to live by was, "The presence of God watches over me. The light of God surrounds me. The love of God enfolds me. The power of God protects me. Wherever I am, God is."

The Beatles — John Lennon said it. He was the dream weaver, but the dream is over. The Beatles' mystique enchanted a generation and enhanced the world. All you need is love. Love is all you need. Even Radio Moscow devoted ninety minutes to his music the night Lennon was killed. When I was in Liverpool, I went down to the Cavern Club near the Mersey River where the Beatles got their start. From this cavern came the music and the voices that would be heard around the world. They lived and performed when music and voice of the young people had shifted to them. The cultural heroes of their time. The creative center of their time. The consciousness and conscience of their time. John Lennon himself was the Beatles' spirit and the driving force behind their culture and their music. He was the poet-comedian. The teaser-healer. The passion and the compassion. The controversial yet mercurial. They wrote and performed an astonishing number of varied songs. Two of the finest songs by John Lennon and Paul McCartney were, respectively, "Strawberry Fields Forever" and "Penny Lane." In these they showed their remarkable talent of blending utopian dream with tough reality. "The burden of fame," John said, "it's like a drug." And he wrote and sang. His music will live on. "Strawberry Fields Forever." He was the beginning and the end of music. The alpha and the omega. The Genesis and the Apocalypse. Imagine all the people living life in peace...

Gene Autry — made ninety films, 500 records, and owns part of the California Angels. He said of Will Rogers that Will had a face and a voice of a man chewing on a cactus. When he was only twelve years old, he ordered his first guitar out of a Sears catalog. With his first movie, *In Old Santa Fe*, a new art form was born — the horse opera! John Wayne, under his real name of Marion Morrison, was Singing Sandy in *Riders of Destiny*. Tom Mix, who fought in a South American war, the Chinese Boxer Rebellion, the Boer War, and was a cowpuncher in Mexico, left south of the border a few hours ahead of a firing squad. Stone-faced William S. Hart had lived with the Sioux Indians as a boy. Meanwhile, back at the Melody Ranch with Gene Autry...and Champion, his horse. John Wayne on his photo to Autry wrote, "A lot of water has run under the bridge. Whiskey, too!" Gene had hired Whitey Ford, the Duke of Paducah, and Steve Allen in a radio show on KOY in Phoenix. And he picked up Merle Travis out of a coal mining camp in Graceburg, Kentucky. "Smoke, smoke, smoke that cigarette.." which made Phil Harris famous; and "Sixteen Tons" helped launch Tennessee Ernie Ford. In 1946 Gene was looking for a new Christmas song as Grand Marshall of the Hollywood Christmas parade. He heard kids along the route of the parade shouting, "Here comes Santa Claus." So he sat down and wrote that song. Later Johnny Marks sent him "Rudolph the Red Nosed Reindeer." Gene's wife liked it and urged him to include it at the last minute as a fill-in on the flip-side of the recording. It took ten minutes to record and no retakes! As they say the rest is reindeer history. It has sold over 100,000,000 records by all artists. Rudolph was first conceived by Composer Johnny Marks' brother-in-law, Robert May, who was a copywriter for Montgomery Ward in Chicago. He was the originator of the first Rudolph, the Red Nosed Reindeer, in a Christmas ad. This part about Gene begins and ends with Will Rogers. When leaving with Wiley Post on their ill-fated plane trip, Will said, "I'll see you when I get back."

Hank Williams, Sr. — found dead in the back seat of his car one cold winter day on his way to a performance. Only twenty-nine years old and one of the stars of *The Grand Ole Opry*, he left a legacy of song and sorrow reflected in his music. This son of an Alabama dirt farmer brought so much joy out of it all to so many people with his "Wabash Cannonball"..."Your Cheatin' Heart"..."These men with broken hearts..." And break it did that New Year's Day in 1953 in Oak Hill, West Virginia, when he was heading for Canton, Ohio. While shining shoes and selling papers on a street corner in Greenville, Alabama, he had picked up guitar licks from a black man. And when he went to the Acuff-Rose Music Publishing Company in Nashville, the man who interviewed him for a job couldn't believe he had written his songs and ordered him into a room to write one. Hank came out of that room with "Mansion on the Hill." Among the other lines of music he made famous, "your cold, cold heart" were all prophetic of his end.

Roy Acuff — like Hank Williams, Roy will probably be remembered best for "The Wabash Cannonball." "Hear that lonesome whistle blow...I'm so lonesome I could cry." Another of the Nashville greats who made music out of the loneliness of the mountains and hills, the echoes like the sound of a train at night, telling their story in the haunting refrain of its lonesome whistle. He started out to be a ballplayer and later played a fiddle with a medicine show. Gene Autry gave him the title of the "King of Hillbillies." That's when country music was country music, before it became the country's music.

And the list goes on — Woody Guthrie, named after Woodrow Wilson, said he wanted to sing songs of hope for human beings, "This land is my land"...Boots Randolf with his club in Nashville, forever playing "Danny Boy"...Tom T. Hall, who arrived in Nashville with $46 in his pocket, now "the storyteller" of country music with "Old Dogs, Children and Watermelon Wine"...Charlie Daniels and his million bestseller, "The Devil Went down to Georgia" from his album "Million Mile Reflections"...

Johnny Cash — "the man in black" who "because you're mine, I walk the line." It was Johnny's mother-in-law, Mother Maybelle Carter, who made the first real country music recording at Bristol, Tennessee, "Will the circle be unbroken?!"...

Bradley Kincaid — among my fondest recollections was our father with his bluegrass banjo from Kentucky playing the songs of Bradley Kincaid he heard over the WLS *Barn Dance* in Chicago. My three brothers and I would join in the chorus as children, much to our parents' delight. It brought back to them memories of Kentucky as no other singer had done. "In the hills of old Kentucky where the birds sing merrily and the mountain breeze comes blowing through the trees that's where I long to be..." Bradley had been a roommate of Scott Wiseman, brother of Lulu Belle & Scotty fame, at Berea College in Kentucky. His son Jim is a director of the American Music Association. In 1971 he was elected to the Nashville Songwriters Hall of Fame. Born down in Garrard County, Kentucky, he was raised about twenty miles from Renfro Valley. Famous for his hound-dog guitar, his father had traded their dog for a guitar for his son. His famous song "Barbara Allen" was named after his twin daughters.

O.O. McIntyre — said his column to which he received the most response was the one on the death of his deaf Boston bull; the same can be said for Arthur Godfrey on his radio show describing the day he took his dog to the vet to be put to sleep...Harold Ross, the great editor of *The*

295

New Yorker, claimed that "writers have sinking spells. They can't ride on trains, drive after dark, live above the first floor, eat clams, stay alone at nights."..the widow of the great Irish tenor John McCormack found among his papers after his death, "Now, like the old Irish minstrels, I have hung up my harp because all my songs are sung."...Sammy Davis, Jr., "Who can take a sunrise, sprinkle it with dew, cover it with love and make the world taste good?" — the Candy Man can...Dave Garroway in the daily closing of his show, quoted Edna St. Vincent Millay's poem "Renascence" —

"The world stands out on either side
No wider than the heart is wide;
Above the world is stretched the sky,
No higher than the soul is high."

Bill Cosby, in describing how you're supposed to use psychology in dealing with a child today, said his father's technique to get his attention was throwing a shoe at him; and if that didn't work, his father would shake him by the collar until his eyeballs rattled...The father of the Marx Brothers, whom they called "Frenchy," used to hire "boosters" to applaud the early acts of his sons in vaudville...When NBC was remodeling, they tore out a wall and found early versions of the Muppet faces on the pipes put there by Jim Henson...When Marc Connelly was asked if conversation today is as scintillating as it was back in the days of the famous Algonquin roundtable in New York, he replied, "Mine is."...The famous makeup artists, the Westmore Brothers, declared Ava Gardner to be the most beautiful woman of all...Ben Turpin of the early days, "The Keystone Kops," had his cross-eyes insured for $1,000,000 by Lloyds of London...Bob Newhart, in his act at Mr. Kelly's in Chicago, did the funniest monologue ever with his Lincoln and the Gettysburg skit...Alfred Lunt and Lynn Fontanne, in reply to a reporter's question about their long marriage and their career, said, "Divorce, never. But murder, yes!"...

Picasso — His father, also a painter and art instructor, put away his own art supplies for good when his son brought home his first assignment from school. Picasso had completed the work in a fraction of the time the teacher had allotted for it. When he took it back to school, the teacher wanted to know what he was doing back so soon. Had he forgotten something? Did he have any questions about the subject matter? When he showed the teacher that he had already completed it, the man was speechless. From then on, Picasso concentrated on a variety of styles. "Does God have only one style?" he asked. "He made the dog, the cat, the dove, the harlequin." In his early period he painted like the old masters — Lautrec, Gauguin, van Gogh and others. He, too, had a rose period and a blue period. When he began, he kept a fire burning in

296

his room with discarded rough sketches. Later he said wealth disgusted him. He thanked God for giving him poverty as part of his life. After all, he concluded, "Life with its torments is the basis of art."

D. W. Griffith — said, "All I try to do is make you see."...Joan Bennett sent a live skunk to Hedda Hopper...One of Elvis' first songs recorded at Sun Records in Memphis was "Blue Moon of Kentucky."...W. C. Fields charged $50,000 to look over a script and fix it up...Perry Como, once a barber, made his nightclub debut at New York's Copacabana in 1944, and in 1945 had the hit record of the year for Victor with "Til the End of Time."...Orson Welles said of the movies, "The cinema has no boundary. It is a ribbon of dreams."...Fred Astaire insisted that the camera remain still and he do the movements, and always a full shot...Spencer Tracy roomed with Pat O'Brien in their early days in the theatre in New York...Clark Gable caused Jack Warner to scream, "His ears are too big!" At his death, the *New York Times* said, "Gable was all man. He was as certain as the sunrise."...During World War II the father of Elizabeth Taylor got in a conversation with a producer in an air raid shelter and found out they were looking for somebody to star in *Lassie Come Home*...Marilyn Monroe, from a memorial poem to Yeats, "Your gift survived it all."...It is strange that Grace Kelly had the same last name as I, the father who was also John Kelly, the brother was also J. B. Kelly, and when I walked into the Monte Carlo casino at Monaco, one of the administrators there called me into his office and asked if I were the "Princess Grace." He must have needed his trifocals changed...Even FDR said to get this picture out fast after seeing Greer Garson in *Mrs. Miniver*...When John Wayne died, the banner headline on an Argentina newspaper read, "Good-bye, Cowboy!" and on a Tokyo paper, "Mr. America Is Dead."...Katharine Hepburn insisted that the cameraman photograph her mind and her mood as well as her face...If you drove a new car anywhere near the Laurel & Hardy Hal Roach lot, it would be confiscated as a gag and painted some ridiculous color...

The look on Ed Sullivan's face on camera when he thought comedian Jackie Mason was making an obscene gesture in his act on the show...Lucille Ball was awakened with Jack Benny playing the violin next door after she had just moved into her home, so I thought I'd do the same. When I was in Beverly Hills I walked over to Lucille's house and stood listening for Jack Benny to start playing his violin next door, but the police stopped me and told me to move on! I didn't know they investigated strangers walking alone in Beverly Hills...One of the funniest scenes on television was the time Carol Burnett portrayed Scarlett O'Hara in the famous drapery-made-into-a-dress scene. She left the drapery rods protruding out the shoulders and proudly announced, "It's just something I

297

saw in the window!"...When in Hollywood a few years ago, I went down to the Vine Street studio and saw Orson Welles as a guest on Merv Griffin's show. From *Citizen Kane,* which many believe is the greatest motion picture ever made, to Commander of the French Legion of Honor — Orson Welles accomplished it all. When Steven Spielberg paid $65,000 for the little sled used in the Kane movie, it was the highest price ever paid for one "Rosebud."...I never saw an audience enjoy a show as much as *The Tonight Show* and the star as much as Johnny Carson. He has that audience in the palm of his hand right up to the last row and never lets go. A row of young fellows was sitting in front of me and called out, "Hey, Johnny, we were out at your house this afternoon and couldn't get in." To which Johnny quickly retorted, "Oh, that's too bad. Come out again tomorrow and you won't get in either!"...I saw Mary Martin in New York in *Peter Pan*; and when they started to fly off to Never-never Land, I haven't come back down to earth since...likewise Julie Andrews in *Camelot*, and Richard Burton saying, "We shall all live through this together — they, you and I — and God gave mercy on us all."

And the list of this cross-section of unforgettable people in the communication arts, performing arts, and creative arts goes on and on. It is as endless as the arts themselves.

(Photo courtesy Ludlow, Kentucky, City Building)

ELMWOOD HALL, historic old mansion in Ludlow, Kentucky, built in 1818 by Thomas Carneal, wealthy Virginia land trader, legislator and military campaigner. Carneal sold- the home to world-traveller, William Bullock, who owned a museum in London's Picadilly, which included Napoleon's carriage. He planned to make Ludlow the dream city of the world. But he gave up the idea and sold Elmwood Hall to Isreal Ludlow, Jr., son of one of the founders of Cincinnati.

(Photo courtesy Walter Closson's daughter, Martha Closson)

"CLOSSON'S" of Closson's elegant store in Cincinnati. Somerset Hall, Closson's old home, is on Closson Court in Ludlow, Kentucky, where the family lived from 1875 to 1925 It was built in 1832 as a summer home by George Kenner, wealthy Louisiana plantation owner and brother-in-law of Isreal Ludlow, Jr., whose family was one of the founders of Cincinnati. It was later sold to Henry Jenkins, wealthy Cincinnati jeweler. It was a vital link in the Underground Railroad, the escape route for slaves from Kentucky. Now it is a Masonic Lodge. Its appearance surely recalls the deep South and bayou atmosphere.

(Photos by David Ziser)

A FIVE ALARMER! - This beautiful home on Latta Avenue in Ludlow, Kentucky, was designed by Alexander Latta, inventor of the first steam-powered fire engine. Hidden away among the tree-shaded streets leading to the river, it stands as the only 12-sided home in America. It is richly furnished and preserved by its present owners, Bob and Mona Stroup Tritsch. Mrs. Tritsch was an accomplished dancer, as is one of her daughters who has performed at the Cincinnati Summer Opera. Her Broadway and varied fine international career includes the Royal and Bolshoi Ballets, the DeCuevas Ballet in Europe, the New York City Opera, and Broadway hits from Carousel to Brigadoon, plus the command performance for President Kennedy of the Agnes DeMille Dancers in honor of the prince of Morocco. A son signed to play with the Chicago White Sox.

301

GONE WITH THE WIND program for that premier night in Atlanta back in 1939. It sold for 25¢. The title of this famous work came from an old poem, long forgotten, now forever remembered: "I loved you Cynara, gone with the wind..."

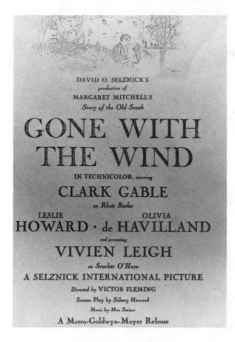

Chapter 15

It Was the Image Orthicon Tube for Sure

Say...have you ever been half-sick? It's quite an experience. So take my advice...if you're going to be sick, be all the way sick. Or else be all the way well. Because they can cure you from being all the way sick or all the way well. But they can't cure you from being half-sick. Maybe you know the routine. You feel "icky"...been feeling that way for some time. You drive the doctors crazy and the druggists, and they drive you crazy. Half a dozen different doctors and half a dozen different druggists say there's half a dozen different things wrong with you. Maybe it's just the forties' fatigue. Or is it something more that's causing that groin groan? Something really wrong to make my breadbasket feel so crumby. Maybe I just need an internal core redevelopment. An intestinal urban renewal project.

Oh, I have it! I have it! I know what it is! I've simply blown my image orthicon tube! After all those years with television it was bound to give out!

So I started going to M.D. repairmen. They won't make housecalls anymore, so you have to take your wobbly antenna into them. I started with the internal medicine specialists, the gizzards wizzards. I tried to convince them that I wasn't feeling well. Something was wrong with me. It was either a liver quiver. Or the bile was in a pile. Or my gut was in a rut. Or there was a sheen on my spleen. Or the lymps were limp. Or all the gall was divided into three parts in my gallbladder. Or I had 20th century smog disease known as dung-lung. Or just plain old television telakucha, creeping vine-like numbness of the nymph glands.

Then I began to get all the advice. No help, but plenty of advice from everybody — doctors, druggists, family, friends. One doctor actually told me to go to the planetarium. It must have been his way of telling me to get lost or catch the next sky lab that came through. Another told me to take a trip down through Kentucky. Now what Daniel Boone's trail or Lincoln's boyhood log cabin had to do with my intestines, I'll never know. Then a doctor-friend told me he knew a woman who was helped by taking in a four-year-old. "What kind of a dog was it?" I asked. "It wasn't a dog," he barked. "It was a child."

303

A Capella Gastroenteritis

But the classic of advice was for me to join a choir. Only trouble was if we hit a high note in a hymn, with my intestinal condition, I'd ruin the whole choir loft.

Now what started me feeling bad was my office lunch hour. You see, a little old lady used to insist on sitting with me in a cafeteria where I frequently ate. One day I asked her why she always picked me to sit with. She smilingly replied, "Because you remind me so much of my daughter." Well, that made me very happy...I was being of some service, some cheer to somebody. Then one day I asked her where her daughter was. "Oh!" she said, "she wasted away to nothing and died."

Of course, having medical people in the family doesn't help. It's actually a hindrance when you get sick. Like the cobbler's children who never have any shoes or the silkworm's off-spring who wear cotton pajamas. With two doctors, three nurses and six pharmacists among my relatives, the most help they could muster for me was a sample bottle of old vitamins. No matter what's wrong with you in this family, you have to take whatever is hanging around among the drug samples. If the sample on hand is a cure for dandruff, you have to take it even though your ailment might be of the bunion extremity. And no matter how old the drug sample is. I didn't mind the label reading San Juan Hill malaria tablets, but I did mind Valley Forge rheumatic capsules.

Then after a while you are graduated to the top banana of the illness routine — the hospital act. There have been many classic descriptions of this experience. My favorite hospital employee is the one who fills your water pitcher with ice at 2:00 o'clock in the morning. Who needs ice at that time of the night? And in bed in a hospital room? Where's the party? And they usually select the 200-pound woman aide for this owl shift. So she comes into your darkened sleeping room with all the quietude of an octopus going through a revolving door. Then she dumps the already-full ice pitcher down the drain in the sink by your head like the coming of the second Niagara. And fills it up again like the coming of the third Niagara.

Between visits of aides ice-pitchering, emptying wastebaskets, running dustmops, selling bedsocks and whistling "Dixie" — some strange character keeps coming in all day wanting to know if you don't wish the television set turned on. And you have to keep telling her that is precisely what you do not want. Because that might be what made you sick in the first place. Too many wavy lines...in life. Then she looks at you with a sad look and suggests a back rub as an alternative. And she leaves very disappointed, with your morning paper, and an extra package of sugar from your tray. And last bonbon.

Nothing in the hospital room ever works properly. The window kept falling down. And on the hottest night of the year. After getting up to raise it again for the tenth time, I used the only thing available in the room to prop it up. My head. And sat in this position the rest of the night. From the street, it must have looked like the headless horsemen had been admitted to the Sleepy Hollow Hospital for a cranium transplant.

Everybody loves the music they play down in the x-ray department. "Casey would waltz with the strawberry barium..." But the hospital masterpiece takes place in the basal metabolism room when they stick a clothes pin on your nose, a hose in your mouth, a cold hand on your pulse...and calmly say, "Now breathe normally."

Then when I went home something happened to the bathroom plumbing. So I called the local pipe-fixers, who promptly announced that the bathroom needed a major overall overhaul. No more than I did, I moaned. So as I lay under the covers in my bedroom trying to recuperate from the hospital where I went to try to recuperate from my illness, I opened my half-sick eyes to behold the bathtub being shoved through the wall...followed by plumbers on sleds.

"I just saw Edgar Bergen go by...."

So to recuperate from the plumbers and the hospital and my illness in color and black and white, I blissfully went to my pediatrician-brother's home. Now this dwelling housed eight children, 298 socks without mates, plus a pre-school Irish setter who darted like a rust streak over the surrounding countryside. And after each dart, this jovial fellow comes in and sits at the bottom of my bed and pants. If there is anything not inducive to recovery from anything, it's a panting Irish setter sitting at the foot of your bed. Unless you are another Irish setter. Even then, it's a drooling experience.

After a while, I decided I had better get well in a hurry because my mysterious illness, my forties' fatigue, my iconoscope iconoclasm...was beginning to have a strange effect on everybody else. I came down to breakfast in my brother's home one morning and my sister-in-law casually remarked, "I just saw Edgar Bergen go by." After I dropped the pot holders in the toaster, I regained my composure and masterfully replied, "You did?" And brilliantly followed through with, "What did he go by in?" Still gazing out the window, she answered, "He was walking."

305

"Good heavens!" I thought as I buttered the toasted pot holders, we must all be cracking up. I've heard of people seeing pink elephants, flying saucers, strange creatures in the DT's...but I've never heard of anybody seeing Edgar Bergen go by. That does it. Then, in the depths of my despair, the phone rang. It was my other sister-in-law calling. In a long, thoughtful, philosophical tone she said, "You know...I've been thinking and thinking about you. Yes, I've given your illness a lot of thought. And I've decided what's wrong with you. I know what's making you sick."

Ah! At last somebody is going to hit on the right diagnosis.

"Yes! Yes!" I pleaded. "What is it!?"

"You have the same thing wrong with you as King Tut."

"King Tut! A royal disease common only to uncommnoners. That's it!"

"Yes, he had the same thing you have. Digestive disturbance, loss of weight...even lost his hair prematurely..."

"Probably from working too hard on some dynasty. Wound up in King Tut's tomb," I sympathetically sympathized.

"So what you should do is find out what they gave him to help him," my sister-in-law advised.

"I'll do just that!" Then I thought, but how will I do just that? Probably have to make a trip to the Valley of the Kings by way of the Thebes subway. Surely there's some old papyrus prescription there from a Ramses pharmacy open on Sunday. So I set to work in the depths of the public library, doing research on King Tut, and driving all the librarians to despair trying to find out what caused his "acid" indigestion. Finally, I gave up after going through the final blueprints for the Aswan Dam. So I called my sister-in-law and told her I couldn't find a thing on King Tut.

"That's too bad," she replied. "But here, call this number and they'll tell you. 281-4700."

"Gee thanks," I said. Then I dialed the number and a voice answered, "Cincinnati Zoo!"

"Oh, I'm so sorry!" I apologized. "I must have the wrong number."

"Whom did you want?" she asked.

"You'll never believe this," I laughed. "I wanted King Tut!"

"Just a moment, I'll connect you."

Holding onto the phone receiver in a state of stupid stupor, I dumbfoundedly waited to see who answered next.

"Yes?" a voice came on the line.

So I started to apologize again. "I'm sorry," I stumbled. "You see, I've got the wrong number. The operator connected me with you.

As I told her, you'll never believe this, but I'm looking for King Tut or something about him because..."

"He's here," she interrupted.

"He is!?" I exclaimed. Then thinking I might as well pursue this to its weird end, I mumbled, "Can I speak with him?"

"I hardly think so. He's the gorilla."

"The gorilla!?" I managed to whisper..and hung up.

Now this really gave me pause for thought. I have the same thing wrong with me as a gorilla? How could that be? He never watches television. How could he have blown his image orthicon tube? And not be able to adjust his lightness/brightness anymore? But, nevertheless, this was a startling new approach to my illness and diagnosis. Yes, a real cause for pause. A time for deep introspection and soul searching. Was I beginning to walk with my arms dangling under me? And did I kind of swing into bed last night? And how long has it been since I shaved my legs? Maybe I needed a veterinarian and that famous prescription they give an elephant with the "G.I.'s" — just plenty of room.

P.S. Edgar Bergen really did go by. He was appearing at a nearby nightclub!

A Gastrectomy!"

Or as they would ask on *Jeopardy*, "What beats the Wildcat ride at Coney Island?"

Now I have had thrills in my life, but never have I experienced anything like having my gut cut out! It's enough to decalcify one's molars and send you to the stockyard to experience the electric steel cattle prod.

What will become of me? What will become of my work? What will become of my becoming? I took my precious manuscripts to the hospital with me and hid them under my bed. "You can't take whatever is in that shopping bag up to the operating room," the nurse sergeant-at-arms shouted at me. So she quickly confiscated the bag as I went pleading after her down the hall in one of those southern exposure hospital gowns, much to the amusement of electricians repairing a light fixture. But to no avail. My two book manuscripts were gone for good wherever things go for good in a hospital. To the elephants' graveyard. Never to be seen or heard from again!

Every writer has written about what happens to them in a hospital. My favorite of all is the preparation for an operation. Everything to make the charming experience more charming, like the Zulu who comes in mysteriously at the crack of dawn and whispers in a mystic voice, "I've come to prepare you for your operation." And you feel like answering, "Oh, you can skip that, honey. Haven't you got anything better to do than hover over me with that razor!" Meanwhile, she goes spookily on her way with the flashing blade and turbaned headpiece as if performing some circumcision rite in a far Eastern religion.

Next comes the orderly who is to wheel you to the operating room. The orderly for whom the disorderly orderly was named. Why do such creatures pick out the most wrinkled outfits in the hospital laundry? And why do they always wear a headpiece that looks like a John McEnroe discard? Or better still, a salami slicer at Izzy Kadetz?

Then when you get up to the operating room, two kindly robust black women approach you with the salutation, "Ain't she the skinniest little white thing you've ever seen!" And they put a dust cap on your head immediately as if you were going to start spraying Pledge or Endust all over the room, including the nice lineup of carving knives waiting to greet you. Won't that fog up the surgeon's glasses, I thought, who, by the way, was nowhere to be seen.

At about that time they rolled in the TV cameras! "What in the world is that for?" I yelled. Am I going to be on *Let's Make a Deal*? Or an old episode of *Gunsmoke*? Or probably on *Wall Street Week*? That's it. Of course, PBS. Or better still, an episode of *Wild Kingdom*, roving overland in the landrover with Marlin Perkins in the bush!

The grand result was that I wound up in a nursing home and had lost everything. My stomach, my brother, my job, my home, my furnishings, my belongings, my health, my "wealth," my dog, in one turn of the dial. Woe is me! I thought of committing you know what. I pondered it for a long time. About two seconds. First, I thought of using the light fixture in the lavatory for a hanging tree. But I discovered it would not hold and would probably propel me feet first into the toilet. Then I toyed with the plastic bag approach. But I was afraid someone would mistake my head for a cabbage and would grate it for supper. Then there was the overdose. I could never stand the underdose, so I discarded that idea. Finally, I contemplated shooting myself, but my aim with a gun would be so poor that I might hit a barn in Boone County, ten miles away. Besides, I'd miss Johnny Carson that night.

So I decided the best thing to do was to do nothing...on my work which had been interrupted when I got sick. But every time I opened the bottom drawer where the manuscript of *My Old Kentucky Home, Good-Night,* was stored, the song "My Old Kentucky Home" came pouring out! No kidding! A capella at that! I would quickly shut the drawer and pretend nothing had happened. And when I opened the next drawer, "The Marseillaise" came pouring out! Why the French national anthem for a book manuscript entitled *The Trouble is Not in Your Set* and filled with information and anecdotes on the communications business? Maybe secretly everybody in the advertising or television or newspaper business wants to tell off his or her boss and go out in a blaze of glory, waving the French flag.

Well, I thought, I can at least get my songs out. So I proceeded to editing my songs, but realized that I needed to put them on tape. No song publishing company or recording company or performer would be impressed with a song sheet on paper, only if they're at least semi-produced on tape. So I corralled a friend to bring me in a tape recorder and some records for background music. Ah! I was in business, running a song-writing company from my little nursing home room! Or rather from my little nursing home room's little nursing home lavatory. It already had my typewriter open on a rickety chair in there. Now it was to be joined by a record player, a stack of records, a stack of blank tapes and a tape recorder. It was getting pretty crowded! When I wanted to go to the bathroom, I had to wedge my way between Barbra Streisand's "People Who Need People" and Barry Manilow's "I Write the Songs." The result was often catastrophic, like Snoopy with the tape recorder at Peppermint Patty's ice skating competition. But I had no Woodstock to whistle me home. I was on my own and hoped that my aim was correct.

One time, when in the middle of a commode recording session, I overheard two of the nurses in my room wondering what those strange sounds were coming out of the lavatory. Just when Streisand hit a high C, I fell into the toilet and staggered out with my lower clothing wringing wet and the tape recorder running wild, playing the bell-ringing at St. Peter's Square.

That night as I was listening to my productivity for the day, I thought of the recordings I had seen in back of the chapel. So in my pajamas and robe I tiptoed into the holy of holies. Just as I was looking through the records, a nun entered the chapel. So I hid behind the folding doors with the hymn books. Then another nun came in and then another and another. I had accidentally come in at their evening prayer hour. All I could do was remain absolutely motionless while they finished their prayers. When I heard them say out loud, "We pray for all our patients..:" I added, "especially the one behind the folding doors." Then I peeked out and they were gone, so I shuffled out of the chapel in my bedroom slippers and hair rollers and purloined records. When I got back to my room, I looked over my loot and found that the first one was Cab Caloway singing "I'll be glad when you're dead, you rascal you."

So I carried on and when the going got tough I wasn't tough enough to get going. I collapsed in bed and cried myself to sleep, only to be awakened by the glorious thought that Johnny Carson was on again.

One day a friend agreed to take my book manuscript for *My Old Kentucky Home, Good-Night* out of the bottom drawer and get it published. What a thrill to see the line awaiting my autograph at the local bank and book departments of the stores! Even the mailman told me, "They were all out waiting for the book this morning." The people in the old hometown were waiting for it to arrive when they heard the book had been delivered to the local post office. Some were even out in their nightclothes with umbrellas in the rain. *The Umbrellas of Cherbourg.*

The stories behind the story are always as good as the story itself. And my book was no exception. The person who was supposed to have copies made of the original manuscript left it overnight in his car. And it would happen that night his car caught on fire with manuscript in the back seat! Luckily they rescued it. But when the publisher opened the box, the strangest odor of burning automobile upholstery came pouring out. Publishers are used to manuscripts smelling like copying machines, or carbon paper, or typewriter cleaner. But never in the history of publishing did a manuscript arrive smelling like a bonfire!

I often thought of leaving my secure surroundings of that lovely nursing home. But how could I leave Millie, across the hall? We were probably the two youngest patients there. And how could I leave Dorothy McKinney of the housekeeping staff? We talked over the daily news and old family railroading days together. Who would answer the hall phone if I didn't run out and get it? One day somebody called and wanted to know if this was the End of the Line. "Yes, I guess you'd call it that," I replied. Then, when he said, "How is good Old Grand Dad today?" I said, "Full of the old nip!" To which he replied, I mean how much is it? Isn't this the End of the Line Liquor Store?"

I will never forget what the candystripers meant to me in that nursing home. Always bringing me things and little notes of encouragement. Especially Susie Freihoffer and Jeni Cleves, two of my favorites. How could they have known I wanted Snoopy dressed as Abraham Lincoln?

And how could I ever forget little Sister Bridget? She was from the old country, from Germany, spoke with an accent, and couldn't understand that I was a career girl and so undomesticated. "Didn't your Mama ever teach you to sew?" I replied that "My Mama never did sew herself." And she would continue, "Didn't your Mama ever teach you to knit?"..."Didn't your Mama ever teach you to crochet?"..."Didn't your Mama ever teach you to cook?"..."You don't know anything," she would sigh and shake her head. But one thing I did know — I'll never forget the sight of her looking like a Hummel figurine, bent over, going through the

310

darkened halls on Christmas Eve with a lantern, singing in German, "Silent Night, Holy Night..."

Then one day I thought if I'm not going to die as they thought I would, if I'm going to live on, why not live on in Hollywood! That's it! I'll go to what they call in Los Angeles, a board and care home. So I packed up all my belongings, including what was in the bathroom, my do--it-yourself communications center. When I told them I was going, they thought somebody has spiked the Maalox or put cocaine in the prune juice...or angel dust in the powdered sugar on the brownies.

So at 6:00 A.M. one morning I piled all my things on a body-cart, for want of a better name for it, and wheeled them out the front door. Only trouble was, it had wobbly-noisy wheels as all things do in hospitals. It kept running out of control into the wall as I tried to make my "escape" without waking everybody up. When I finally made it to the front door, I thought, "I'm free at last! Thank God I'm free at last!" But then when I got to the airport I wanted to come back! How could I have left the security and tranquility of that beautiful nursing home? Then they announced, "The plane for Los Angeles is now boarding at Gate 2."

To go from a nursing home to the jungle of Hollywood and trying to sell my books and other writing projects for TV, was like having static in the attic or both oars not in the water. I would have given anything if I still had that fortune cookie someone once brought me that read, "Help! I'm a prisoner in a nursing home!" Oh, to be such a prisoner now that spring is here. What have I done? Where am I going? But it all worked out all right. The board and care home was right around the corner from Hollywood and Vine — the beginning of the great adventure!

Chapter 16

The Man Who Went to the Milky Way
Long Before the Astronauts

Haven Gillespie told it like this: "I just came back from a lovely trip. Along the Milky Way..I stopped off at the North Pole...To spend a holiday...I called on dear Old Santa Claus...To see what I could see...He took me to his workshop...and told his plans to me...So, you better watch out, you better not cry..Better not pout, I'm telling you why...Santa Claus is comin' to town...."

Yes, Haven Gillespie, the songwriter from Covington, Kentucky, who wrote these words of his famous song, "Santa Claus Is Comin' to Town," will forever be a part of this city, its history, its heart, its soul, its music, and above all, its dreams. As I write this, I can see his old house from my window. Recently when passing this old home, I wondered if the present occupants knew that forty years ago the man who lived there wrote that well-known Christmas song. "He's making a list and checking it twice...Gonna find out who's naughty and nice...Santa Claus is comin' to town."

One day I saw a woman in the yard, so I went over and asked her the big question. "Indeed, I do know," she smiled. "There are still some of his things in the basement." To which I immediately replied, "Lead me to them!" I found there wasn't much, about a hatbox-full of old blank letterheads, business cards, copies of printed sheet music, etc. But the most important thing was a file-box of index cards on which he had typed all the theaters, the organists, the pianists, his contacts throughout the United States, and a few in Mexico, Canada, Australia! With the permission of the present owner, I turned these over to the Kenton County Library and Kentucky Historical Society here, who contacted his only son in Encino, California, about the findings.

Haven Gillespie grew up with his nine brothers and sisters in a basement apartment near Third Street in the riverbottoms of Covington. Little did the world know the sounds that would eventually come out of that basement...out of those humble beginnings...out of that harmonica-playing child...the hopes and dreams of children everywhere..."The Kids in Girl-and-Boyland will have a jubilee...They're going to build a toyland all around the Christmas tree..."

313

HAVEN GILLESPIE - Kentucky's greatest song writer, who wrote the words to" Santa Claus Is Coming to Town," shakes hands with his old buddy and fellow music man from Covington, Kern Aylward. Kern was a former song plugger for Leo Feist Music Publishers and later owner of the famous old Irish Pub at Sixth and Main Streets in downtown Covington. Gillespie's many famous songs include: "Up a Lazy River," "You Go to My Head," "That Lucky Old Sun," "The Old Master Painter," and several hundred more.

A WARM WELCOME greeted everybody who came to Kern Aylward's Old Irish pub in downtown Covington. Star performers and celebrities from all walks of life ended up at Kern's place, even from the famous Beverly Hills Supper Club. And the people came from miles around to see and hear them as each put on a show on the house. (l to r) Bandleader Wally Johnson, Kern Aylward, singer Beatrice Kay, Irene Rohan Aylward, Sylvan Greene, Beatrice's husband and piano player.

CHRISTMAS CARDS from every state in the Union hung over the bar, 516 that year, some from celebrities Kern had known since his entertaining song-plugging days including Irving Berlin, Myron Cohen, Little Jack Little, Eddie Peabody, Haven Gillespie and many more. About Kern and Haven and all the rest, Berlin himself said it best, "The song is ended but the melody lingers on."

315

It was inevitable that when he grew up he would become a songwriter, and for one of the biggest firms of the day, Leo Feist Music Publishers in New York. But first he was printer's devil and typesetter for the *Cincinnati Times Star* and *New York Times*. At the *Times Star* he met his future partner, Paul Mathauer. It was Charles Phelps Taft, half-brother of President William Howard Taft and publisher of the *Times Star*, who suggested he see columnist Joe Garretson about his work. Joe put him in touch with Tin Pan Alley in New York.

It was on a business trip to New York that Haven Gillespie wrote the words to "Santa Claus Is Comin' to Town." And it was on the back of an envelope while riding on the subway! Based on his boyhood memory of his mother's admonition that Santa was coming. The song was introduced on the old Eddie Cantor radio show at Christmastime in 1933. And the world listened. And never stopped playing it or singing it at Christmastime ever since. Especially after Bing Crosby and the Andrews Sisters recorded it. "He sees you when you're sleeping'...He knows when you're awake...He knows if you've been bad or good...So be good for goodness sake!"

The other musicians who recorded Haven's songs included Nat King Cole, Frank Sinatra, Louie Armstrong, Dean Martin, Rudy Vallee, Guy Lombardo, Fred Waring and many more.

An Irish sentimentalist, a brilliant composer and lyricist, a storyteller, a man with a heart, a lonely lover, a creative dreamer, a Christmastime Pied Piper, he was them all and put it all down on paper in song. A handful of his other famous songs included "You're in Kentucky, Sure As You're Born"..."The Old Master Painter"..."Breezin' along with the Breeze"..."You Go to My Head"..."Drifting and Dreaming"...which were way up there on the charts for a long time.

One day while driving through a cottonfield in Arkansas, he was moved by the sight of the black men picking cotton, bending over and slaving in the hot sun. And so he wrote one of his most famous songs, "That Lucky Old Sun." In 1950, he received the Freedom Foundation Award of Valley Forge for "God's Country."

One song even figured in a murder trial! In 1923, police entered the apartment of a woman who had just murdered her sweetheart and found Haven Gillespie's blues song still spinning around on the old phonograph, "Just a Little Bit Blue for You."

So as I write this at Christmastime, the city outside my window covered by a light blanket of freshly fallen snow, I think of Haven Gillespie and his tombstone which bears at his request his only epitaph, short and sweet, the title of one of his songs, "Drifting and Dreaming."

And I think, too, of the millions of children around the earth who

316

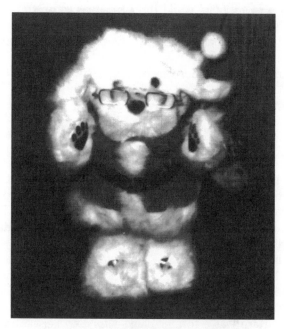

(Stuffed toy created for APPLAUSE by the author.)

ALL THE WAY FROM THE SOUTH POLE - SANTA PAWS (c)
So when you awake on this Christmas day nigh
Right there 'neath the tree your dog will lie
With the toys and the dolls and the games and the clown...
Because Santa Paws was coming to town!

317

will wake to a more joyful world this Christmas morning..."With little tin horns and little toy drums...Rooty-toot-toots and rummy-tum-tums...And curly-head dolls that toddle and coo...Elephants, boats and kiddie cars too..."

Because...Santa Claus was coming to town.

The Creation of Santa Paws
Hollywood, Here I Come!

Yes, Santa Paws is coming to town! In fact, he has already come! And was to be one of the toy highlights that Christmas. With a puppy in his sack from the pack on his back. Some even with a dog collar that reads, "Santa Paws, Bark-a-lark Lane, Bow-wow-Ville, South Pole."

He was made by Applause, division of Wallace Berrie Company, Woodland Hills, California.

It all started a long time ago with Haven Gillespie and Kern Aylward. Haven was Kentucky's great song writer. He wrote "Santa Claus Is Comin' To Town," (lyrics), "Up a Lazy River," "You Go to My Head," "That Lucky Old Sun," "The Old Master Painter," and many more songs. Kern was a former plugger for Leo Feist Music Publishers; and when he retired he operated an old Irish pub at Sixth & Main Streets in Covington, Kentucky.

Haven, who formerly lived in Covington, used to come in Kern's pub when he was back in town, as did many celebrities, even from the famous Beverly Hills Supper Club which burned down killing over 150 people. Haven would sit down at the piano and play his famous songs. One night when he came in, I happened to be there and remarked to him that some day I was going to write a song like his "Santa Claus Is Comin' to Town," but it was going to be all dogs "Go to it, Kid!" was his good-natured reply. And so I did.

"Santa Paws Is Coming To Town"©

We know that you've heard about Santa Claus
But, say, have you heard about Santa Paws?!
He's coming to town, yes, he is for sure, too,
And bringing a puppy for me and for you.

Yes, Santa Paws — he's the one brings the new dogs,
You can't pick them out from the gift catalogues;

318

He says that they come from Animal Land,
It must be a place that is surely so grand!

With collies and setters and huskies so tall,
Toy breeds that are ever and ever so small,
And cockers and beagles and terriers — My!
Great Danes that are ever and ever so high!

A sleigh full of poodles and poodles and poodles,
All kinds of dog breeds by the oodles and oodles;
Some spaniels and dachshunds and bird-dog-dog-dogs
To point all the way through the South Pole fog-fogs.

And what will we call the new pup — her or him?
The dog for this Christmas — "Here, Tiny!" or "Tim!"
Or Peppy or Barkley or Lassie or Dolly
Or Benji or Snoopy or how about Holly?!

So when we awake on this Christmas day nigh,
Right there neath the tree the new dog will lie
With the toys and the dolls and the games and the clown
Because...Santa Paws...was coming to town!

    I happily spent some time in Hollywood on my work, including Santa Paws. At first I created Santa Paws for Snoopy, but the producers of Charles Schulz work said he wouldn't use anybody else's ideas, and why should he! Since Snoopy wouldn't be Santa Paws, I tried to get Benji, but that failed, too. Then I thought, he is a character in himself. Let him be himself.

    I'll never forget that year in Hollywood! What a happy year, which included a visit to Earl Hamner at Warner Brothers. Earl created and narrated *The Waltons* and used to work with me in Cincinnati years ago at WLW-T. He gave me a complete pass to the Warner brothers lot, which included a visit to the old Walton house where the episodes were filmed. I took a piece of the porch for a souvenir! Much to the bewilderment of the guards as I left.

    On the *Little House* on the Prairie set I helped myself to the daisies in the window box and put them in the lapel of my jacket. Again, here the guard — all sets are heavily guarded — looked at me and my ragweed boutonniere very strangely.

    After my purloining day, I was so tired that I fell asleep on a set at Warner, only to wake up to Robert Wagner using the phone beside the

SHIRLEY TEMPLE - the bright little star in long dark night. As children we had the same doctor in Pasadena, Calif., my only claim to fame!

bed and his co-star sitting at the bottom. I had no idea it was the *Hart to Hart* set and they were about to begin shooting.

One day I decided to go see George Burns to narrate my Santa Paws script, but how will I get into his office on the studio grounds? When I arrived the guards were changing shifts, luckily for me. So I said to one that just came on duty, "I left my umbrella in George Burns' office." He replied, "Sure, you can go and get it." After all this subterfuge, though, I didn't have any luck with Burns. He wasn't in and his staff told me he had his own writers and didn't do outside work. But it was worth it to see that they all looked like George Burns!

So I finally got in a cab and the elderly cab driver told me that I was going about it all wrong. "You gotta be creative in this, too," he said. "Tell you what I'm gonna do. I'm gonna take you to a restaurant in Beverly Hills. Go in there and eat lunch and ask for the owner. I won't tell you who it is, except it's the mother of a famous person. I'll be back to get you in an hour."

I did as he told me, ate lunch in the restaurant, waited for the owner to come in, waited and waited and waited. Finally, I said to the waiter, "Pardon me, sir, but did the owner ever come in, and is she the mother of a famous person?" He scowled at me, "No and no!" And went off muttering to himself, "One more nut to add to the collection in California."

Then I hurried out and waved down the cab driver and related my ill-fated luncheon encounter. "You dummy," he shouted. "You went in the wrong restaurant! Go in the one next door! I'll be back in another hour."

Oh, my goodness, I groaned. How was I going to force down another lunch? And kosher, at that. And kosher prices, at that. But I did and finally got to talk to the owner. She came over and sat down at my table and I laid it all on her! Scripts, books, etc. "Now who are you?" I blurted out between burps. "I'm Steven Spielberg's mother," she replied. When they swept me up off the floor, I said "I think I'm going to be sick."

Next, I think I'll go to see Shirley Temple, since we had the same doctor some humpteen years ago in Pasadena where I was born. But she was not as impressed with this astounding fact as I was and immediately disowned any acquaintance due to a gynecological or obstetrical accident.

Next, I put Frank Sinatra's attorney on the list. He would surely put up the money to produce some of my work. One look at his attorney's office and I decided to return to the poorhouse.

Meanwhile, back at the ranch or where I was staying, my horde of hungry stray cats waited for me to feed them. They made their home in the underbrush along the Hollywood Freeway in back of the hotel. That is, during the day. At night, they made their bed among the multi-million

321

dollar collection of antique cars in the hotel basement garage! I couldn't believe it the first time I saw them sitting there in a 1905 Duryea, and a 1925 Buick, and a 1935 roadster, and about fifteen other antique cars. What a story, I thought. "The Cats and the Cars in California!" What a time I had with them, including hiding under a quilt trying to catch them.

I called many groups to find homes for the cats. Finally, one woman came out. She said she'd meet me in the lobby. I asked her how I would know her, and she replied I'd know her. Still trying to figure out how I'd know her, I suddenly spied a woman who looked just like Bette Davis. "My! You look like Bette Davis," I ventured. "I should, I'm her double!" she proudly said. It was the cat lady of California.

I thought of calling Goldie Clough, who had been Florenz Ziegfeld's secretary. And his daughter by Billie Burke, Patricia Ziegfeld Stephenson. They advised me to get with a large agency. Ah, ha — things are finally coming together! That's it, I thought. Finally, my big chance would come the next day at ICM!

Did I say the next day at ICM (International Creative Management)? I approached the building cautiously — and was immediately thrown out. Then I thought I would approach the building uncautiously — and was immediately thrown out. Then I thought I would just plain approach the building. Success! No one stopped me this time! No stuffy guard. No little receptionist. No know-it-all secretary. I had made it up to the fourth floor by the back stairs and was still going! How lucky, I jubilated. They'll not turn me back now. Suddenly the police standing down on the lawn yelled up to me, "Get out of there, you idiot! There's a bomb planted in the building!" So I olympic bounded to the first floor and out the front door, only to be met by the scowling police department of Los Angeles, who had cordoned off the building by now, and a group of spectators who cheered as I was ushered out the door by one LAPD. I bowed gratefully to the cheering section, thinking that was all I would get in my stay in LA, yet feeling like Norma Desmond in her great scene as she came down the stairs. "Did you get it, Mr. DeMille?" But then, I thought, how would I approach the building with dignity the next day after I had been evicted as the "mad bomber" the day before?

How about Gene Autry, I thought. He had made a hit out of "Rudolph, the Red Nosed Reindeer." The closest I could get to him was in the big annual Hollywood Parade. He was the grand marshall that year. So, as he went by, I shouted to him about my idea of Santa Paws. He yelled back, "Sorry! I'm not singing anymore! But I persisted, running after his car in the parade, yelling out the Santa Paws song I had written. Finally, the Los Angeles police broke up my act and ushered me to the sidelines.

322

And I made it onto a quiz show. I did. I did. It was produced by John Barbour, one of the talent on *Real People*, and televised to about fifteen cities. Won $500, but went down on a question about the definition of a "one-night stand!" I thought it was the single appearance in a city made by performers on a whirlwind tour. My partner on the quiz show scowled at me for not giving the correct answer. Now if only they had asked me a question about dogs!

One has not lived until one has taken the Universal Tour. People enter the studio gate, never to be seen or heard from again! They ought to get *Mr. Keen, Tracer of Missing Persons*, the old radio show, or somebody, to find out where they hide all those bodies that go in one gate and not out another.

I thought one day I would go out to 20th Century Fox and see Jane Fonda about starring in my book, *My Old Kentucky Home, Goodnight*. But I found out that she was back in Tennessee filming her work in *The Dollmaker*, which was set in Kentucky.

Incidentally, we couldn't get near the Dallas set the day we were there at MGM because they were filming some "sensitive" material, as they called it. I never saw a set so heavily guarded, three levels of guards you have to go through, even with the professional passes we had. The "sensitive" material must have been Bobby coming out of the shower.

Motown, yes, Motown. That would be my victim today. I'll try the great music producers to do some of my songs. The Supremes, Smokey Robinson, Barry Gordy, all the greats on the famous Motown label, Stand back! You haven't seen anything yet! Here I come! But I only got as far as the receptionist. "Who do you want to see, girl?" Well, just anybody who would be interested in good music, I thought. "You haven't got an appointment with anybody, you can't come in here!" she kept insisting. "And what's this?" she continued. "Stephen Foster and his Ethiopian Melodys. Who are you calling an Ethiopian? There isn't anybody here by that name!" as she raved on and on. Oh, me, I thought. And to think that I once had a black and white television.

You haven't seen the world until you've seen the Rose Bowl Parade and the Rose Bowl game in person. The first coast-to-coast colorcast on television in 1954, both on NBC. I picked up some rose petals from the street to save for a souvenir as the parade went past where I was born. And I cried a little at the memory of it all.

One Sunday morning we went to an ecumenical Mass they were having for people in show business. Ted Baxter, (Fibber McGee) Jim Jordan, Greer Garson, Jane Wyatt, Penny Singleton, Virginia Mayo, Les Tremayne, Mae Clark and many more celebrities were there. I asked Mae Clark if the grapefruit Jimmy Cagney smashed in her face were real. She replied, "Seeds and all!" And you should have seen the look on Ted Baxter's face when I told him that I needed $1,000,000 to get my work started. He did one of those spurting doubletakes for which he became famous on *The Mary Tyler Moore Show*.

When I got to my hotel one day, there was a message for me that Schwab's Drug Store had called. I've been discovered! I thought. Like the legend of Lana Turner discovered sitting on a stool at Schwab's. When I picked up the phone, a voice said, "You left your glasses on the counter at Schwab's." I excitedly replied, "Wait a minute! Was there anyone in there looking for me? Like a talent scout, for instance? Let me speak to Mr. Schwab! Hello...hello...hello." At that, they hung up, missing for all time my fleeting chance for stardom!

My friend and colleague in the television business was Helen McCrea at CBS, Los Angeles. She kept urging me on to greater heights. I don't know what I would have done without her. She was from Philadelphia and was one of Grace Kelly's best friends. "Keep trying," she said. "You'll make it." So I thought I'd drown myself in a treat at the Brown Derby, followed by a nip at The Ginger Man, which was Carroll O'Connor's place. The famous Brown Derby was, of course, the place where many memorable things happened, including Clark Gable's proposal to Carole Lombard. They even have the booth set aside where he popped the question. When I asked if I could take my chicken sandwich home in a doggie bag, the waiter looked at me as if the stars on the Hollywood Walk of Fame, which were just outside, had all fallen on him at the same time.

When I'd get back to the hotel board and care facility (incidentally, right under the famous "Hollywood" sign on the hillside) where I was staying, the doctor would be waiting for me. Screaming, "I told you that you could go out once a week on your work, and here you are running out all the time. I'm not going to be responsible if you're sent back to the University of Cincinnati Medical Center with a tag around your big toe some day soon." To which I replied, "Would you be responsible if the tag were around the little toe?"

324

'"THE OLD LAGOON"
BEFORE TV - Before radio, before other forms of entertainment and communications, there was the "Old Lagoon" in Ludlow, Kentucky. Billed as one of the largest and mostbeautiful amusement parks, it drew crowds from all around, 1890 to 1920, when Prohibition and a tragic accident at the park's Motordrome ended it forever. Only the clubhouse now stands in silent memory and tribute to its days of glory.

ROMANTIC SCENE—our father in his world War I uniform with our mother's hat beside him, on their last date at old Lagoon Park, celebrating their engagement, before he was sent "Over There."

"SMILE THE WHILE you kiss me sad adieu ... When the clouds roll by I'll come to you...Then the skies will seem more blue...Down in lovers lane with you... Wedding bells will ring so merrily... Every tear will be a memory... So wait and pray each night for me... Til we meet again..."
*Raymond B. Egan, Richard A. Whiting, Remick Music Corp., New York,1918.

325

Even a flying machine was tried at the Lagoon!

The world-famous Motordrome, which ended tragically.

The Balloon Ascension always attracted a crowd. So did train crossing trestle.

Scenic ride around the lake. Aren't those the Brady girls?

(Photos courtesy Jack Hellebush, Ludlow, Kentucky, and Don Thomas, Ft. Mitchell, Kentucky)

Even its delivery wagon called it "beautiful."

Kaiser sent boats to St. Louis World's Fair as German exhibition.

Pony Track and everyone going in a different direction!

Around the Lagoon world in 80 minutes!

Electric launch to launch your day at the park.

327

THE OLD QUEEN CITY TRACK - In Ludlow, Kentucky, in an indistinct rare photo of the past, showing stands and clubhouse, which ran before and after the Civil War. It is thought by many to be the track on which Stephen Foster based his song, "Camptown Races," partly written while he worked for his brother's steamboat agency at Second and Broadway in Cincinnati. Our great-grandfather had an interest in the track. (Cincinnati Enquirer. 1920 edition)

Chapter 17

I'll See You in the Funny Papers

Harking back to my college days as a journalism major, before there was a communication arts major, I recall H. L. Mencken. He was the great writer, reporter and editor of an earlier day. He said of writers that theirs is a desperate business and they often suffer from severe depressions, Mighty men as Lincoln, as Bismarck, as Churchill had them. He called them "Black Dog."

That's why there are the funny papers! Who doesn't love the comic strips? The greatest comic strip of all time was *Krazy Kat*. And Inatz Mouse in the strip had one single purpose in life. And that was to "krease that Kat's bean with a brick?" They said President Wilson never missed a day of the funny papers. I remember when Snoopy went out to look for his mother. Finally he found her, but it didn't show who she was from Friday until Monday. The last panel in the strip simply showed Snoopy yelling, "Mom!" that Friday evening. Then, on Monday, when the papers were thrown from the truck, many people were waiting to see who Snoopy's mother was. Doctors, lawyers, merchants, chiefs had come down to the street from our building to a busy corner to get a paper. Incidentally, she was a cow! Or so he thought.

During the newspaper strike in New York, Mayor La Guardia went on the radio reading the comic strips so New Yorkers wouldn't miss them. Even St. Patrick's Cathedral was asked if they could reschedule their Masses so the parishioners wouldn't miss La Guardia reading the funny papers. My favorites were "Barney Google," "Snuffy Smith," "Little Orphan Annie," "Popeye," "Prince Valiant," "Gasoline Alley," "Li'l Abner," "The Katzenjammer Kids," "Blondie." But my favorite of all was Walt Kelly's "Pogo," that wonderful cast of characters that lived in the Okefenokee Swamp. If only television could capture such creatures, such imagination, such fine art, such fine writing. It does, with Snoopy and Garfield and a few others. But why isn't there enough lasagna to go around?

329

KRAZY KAT - Considered by many to be the most famous comic strip ever written. Today's "The Far Side" by Larson is the only one that approaches it in merit, humor and artistry. Forever playing the cat-and-mouse games that endeared its place in the funny papers. See what you've been missing all these years by not carrying a comic section...*New York Times!*

(Illustration courtesy Chicago Tribune New York News Syndicate.)
ANNIE - Leapin' Lizzards! I'd know those no-eyes anywhere. And with Sandy, too! Arf!
Daddy Warbucks will be home soon, so says the decoder ring. Until then, Punjab will
protect Little Orphan Annie from everything. Until tomorrow...tomorrow...it's just a
day away.

After Germany Surrendered
Gremlin Got in Works

The subjects in communication arts were interesting ones —
broadcasting, journalism, advertising, literature and creative writing, at
Mount St. Joseph College, Cincinnati. A man from Procter and Gamble
taught advertising. Miss Irene Daly, the dedicated teacher who must have
read everything ever written, was one of our literature and creative writing
professors. Sister Ruth Adelaide, who recently spent two years living
among the natives in French Equatorial Africa, was our French and literary
professor. Peg Whitehead Gokay, who had worked for the Associated
Press, taught broadcast news writing. Journalism was the specialty of
Sister Margaret Agnes, who will be forever enshrined in the memory of
the Printers' Union. It seems that a printer was going to refer to a
printing type by its actual name, but hesitated to do so in the presence of
a nun. She did it for him, and calmly commented, "That's called 'bastard.'"

In the journalism room there was an Associated Press news wire
service machine. One day in class its bell rang like crazy, signifying an
important news flash. We all ran to the machine to see what the big news
was. The teletype message read: "REIMS, FRANCE, May 7 (AP) —
Germany surrendered unconditionally to the Western Allies and Russia at
2:41 a.m. French time today. (This was 8:41 p.m. Eastern War Time,
Sunday). The surrender took place at a little red school house which was
the headquarters of Gen. Eisenhower.

"The surrender which brought the war in Europe to a formal end
after five years, eight months and six days of bloodshed and destruction,
was signed for Germany by Col. Gen. Gustav Jodl, the new chief of staff
of the German army.

"It was signed for the Supreme Allied Command by Lt. Gen.
Walter Bedell Smith, Chief of Staff for Gen. Eisenhower. It was signed by
Gen. Ivan Susloparoff for Russia and by Gen. Francois Sevez for France.

"General Eisenhower was not present at the signing, but
immediately afterward Jodl and his fellow delegate, Gen. Adm. Hans
Georg Friedeburg, were received by the Supreme Commander.

"They were asked sternly if they understood the surrender terms
imposed upon Germany and if they would be carried out by Germany.

"They answered yes."

When the school term ended in June, we thought we'd play a
trick and "kidnap" the mascot kept in the journalism room, a happy
stuffed gremlin. We hid him with an oil can in his hand inside the AP
teletype news machine. But in the rush of school closing, we forgot about

MARY ANN KELLY and Carol Bueker Cooper way back when. Winner of the America's Cup? Well, not quite. It's the trophy from the Ohio College Newspaper Convention. The editors of the small College of Mount St. Joseph, Cincinnati, beat out even the giant Ohio State. Little did anybody know they forgot they hid the journalism department gremlin in the AP teletype machine...with world-wide results!

him. When it was time to turn on the teletype again in September, it wouldn't work. So the college called the local AP office to send a man out to look at it. He opened the machine and there sat the gremlin with the oil can in his hand! The Associated Press representative got such a kick out of it, he had the story sent out on the AP teletype news wire to cities around the world! "Gremlin in AP works..."

The wonderful crowd of girls at the college then were really something special. Marianne O'Regan, an editor of the *Cincinnati Post*; Anne Murphy, our Ogden Nash; Ruth Brookbank, Pat Burns, Flo Gibb, three other wonderful writers; Estelle Topmoeller, the talented musician, and also Patti Thompson from Chillicothe; Eileen Conway, the artist; Vivian Richter, the elegant prom queen and voice major; Elizabeth Schlichte, the dietitian who went on to Mayo Clinic; Eileen Bartunek, our speech major from Cleveland; Faye McGraw, the girl who had read every book ever written; Julie Crotty, my Kentucky colleague from Falmouth; Ginny Barry, who became a nun; and Rae Hartman, who became a doctor; Ann Rasche, the math whiz; Pat Carroll, Martha Lee Heimbrock, Catherine Grothaus...and the rest.

One of my best friends, and an extremely talented writer in the journalism gang, was Carol Bueker. A printer once misspelled her name in a byline in our college paper so it read, "Barol Cueker." The misprint stuck as her name from then on. We went to the Ohio newspaper convention and won first place for our college paper, beating out the large universities. Barol's room in the dorm always looked as if a whirling dervish marathon was taking place there. One Christmas, I pinned a note on her desk lamp. It was still there when the flowers bloomed in May. So were 29,000 others.

Was There a Golden Age of Television?

Yes, there definitely was a Golden Age. It's no myth, but truly a golden memory for us who were such a vital part of it.

Yes, a fact, as surely as the Golden Age of Assyria up to the fall of Nineveh...of Babylonian Empire a hundred years later...of China in the Tae-tsong and Tang dynasties...of Egypt with Ramses II...of Persia five hundred years later...of England in the Elizabethan period..of Germany in the reign of Charles V and in the 16th century...of France in part of the reign of louis XIV and XV...of Prussia and Frederick the Great...of Russia and Peter the Great...of Spain with Ferdinand and Isabella combining the crowns of Castile and Aragon...and of the Golden Age of Greece with its Golden Verses of rule, whereby a person must make a critical review, an examination of conscience, each night regarding the actions of the day.

This was either the forerunner of the first TV critic or an early admonition to the NBC peacock, the CBS eye and the ABC alphabet.

To the ancient alchemists, gold represented the sun. And in heraldry, it was depicted by dots. A strange prophetic sign, perhaps of the coming of television centuries later, transmitting its magic dots through the airwaves to form a picture, greatest under the sun. But was the picture to be an image of the golden calf? Or an image of excellence? Was it to be merely an idol beckoning to everybody to cross over to the sunny side of the street, to have gold dust at their feet?

Remember what Shakespeare said in *The Merchant of Venice*: "All that glitters is not gold."

And Chaucer in *Canon's Yeoman's Tale*:
"All things that shineth as the gold
Is not gold as that I have heard it told."

And Gray in his "Ode on Death of a Favorite Cat":
"Not all that tempts your wandering eyes
And heedless hearts, is lawful prize;
Nor all that glitters gold."

We agree that even Morris would have known better and have finer taste in all of his nine lives on the TV screen. We're all in favor of Jason's search for the golden fleece as long as it isn't the TV audience who are being fleeced with trashy and poor programs, being fleeced of TV's great potential in the greatest miracle of communications ever known to and invented by man.

Will "the golden bowl be finally broken"...the TV picture tube...like the golden bowl of biblical illusion to death? The golden TV tube finally broken and dying from idiot ratings and idiot programs? The technical progress of television has been tremendous — to a 24 carat perfection. But too much of today's programming is diluted with an alloy of metal for television really to show its mettle.

There's no doubt about it, the golden rule everybody worked by and wrote by in the early days of TV is what made it the Golden Age of Television. In ancient Egypt the highest position was held by the scribes, the writers. It's time to start another oldtime Gold Rush back to those days and let a breath of fresh air from the Klondike and Yukon blow across TV-land. We hope cable and the satellites and all the other advances in the medium will bring in a better lode than the recent batch of "Fool's Gold." Surely, we can grind out something better than most of that in the Sutter's Mill of TV.

Chapter 18

Summing It All Up

The old sounds and sights come rushing back: the Shadow, who vanished with the coal furnace, "Who knows what evil lurks in the hearts of men? The Shadow knows!."...Jack Armstrong, the All-American Boy for the breakfast of champions, "Won't you try Wheaties?:"..Tom Mix and Gene Autry, "Back in the saddle again."...The Lone Ranger and "The William Tell Overture" and Tonto...the Green Hornet and the "Flight of the Bumble Bee"...Little Orphan Annie with the decoding rings and secret messages...Grand Central Station — "crossroads of a million private lives"...Fibber McGee and Molly (I sat with Jim Jordan at a broadcasting breakfast in Los Angeles and recognized him by his voice!)...Orson Welles' *Mercury Theater's* broadcast of H.G. Wells' *The War of the Worlds*, forerunner of E.T.!...Ed Wynn, the Texaco Fire Chief...The Singin' Lady...Rudy Valley's *Fleischmann's Hour* and "My time is your time"... Lowell Thomas' "So long until tomorrow"...Lanny Ross and *Showboat*...Jack Benny, Fred Allen feud on radio...Arthur Godfrey...Edgar Bergen and Charlie McCarthy, one of the classics...George Burns and Gracie Allen...Boake Carter and Floyd Gibbons' report of the Lindbergh case..Guy Lombardo and his Royal Canadians...Graham McNamee...Amos 'n Andy..Paul Whiteman playing George Gershwin's "Rhapsody in Blue."

Yes, the old sights and sounds flash upon that inward eye. Everybody thought that the word "television" on a push-button radio was about as ridiculous as the old words of "weather," "aircraft," "ships at sea," "amateur receivers," "police." The Shadow was really in the shadows of firelight and the mind. And Sandy barking was your own dog. One Man's Family was your own family. Early communications by relay runners, sails on ships, signal flags, smoke signals, even fires, were things of the past when radio's early pioneers took over with their "black magic" of radio to send a message.

But radio was blind. Television gave it sight. In its early days it had come out of the darkened attic, the garage, the storeroom, the basement. Now that television was here, radio had come into light. Do you remember that first baseball game under the lights, broadcast way back in 1935? Have you heard about the first experimental TV camera,

337

back in 1933? Or the first TV set in a home, back in 1928? When Bell invented the telephone, he had to engage a visiting prince from Brazil to stop at his booth at a World's Fair to try to attract attention to his invention. "Hear a voice over a wire." And nobody stopped to listen. And nobody stopped to look when the *London Times* ran an ad, "Need help in transmitting pictures in my attic." But as The Little Prince said, "It's only with the heart that one can see clearly. What is essential is invisible to the eye."

"A kind farewell...tune in again..."

Allen Thrasher was the only account executive we knew who could write poetry. One of his great poetic endeavors was so great, that the big *Advertising Age* ran it to cover half a page. And its front page, at that. When Allen, who handled our brewing account, left the advertising agency to join a conservative bank advertising department, we were sorry to see him go. So they asked me to write him a poem as a farewell. And it turned out that the piece, based on the well-known lines so often put to parody in this business, became a kind of symbol for the whole business of the communication and performing arts, especially now, looking back as over forty years of television says good-bye.

ALLEN THRASHER

Tell us it ain't so, Allen,
It ain't true we all implore
That an ad account exec
Leaves to "ad" a banking corps.

Allen in the bank-note field
Advertising banking trade?
Far from show biz and the Hayride
All the old pink lemonade?

Allen, let us have the low-down
When you hear a brass band swell
Can you love bank advertising
Like the old street barker's sell?

You can't say a bank's "amazing"
"Shop here for your money's worth!"
You can't say a bank's "colossal"
It has the crisp-est bills "on earth!"

338

Though banking's now the line you've chosen
Every springtime you will hear
The crocus and the daffodils
Whispering that "Bock's now here!"

And what of beer ads for next time?
Is it pint or quart or gallon?
And who's to be the poet laureate
Now that there's no Allen?

Yes, who's to be our Christmas bard?
What can rhyme with "Dasher?"
We'll just have to stick to "Rudolph"
Now that there's no Thrasher.

You've sold shows from jazz to sports
Even the Grand National
But, Allen, they won't bet that much
Over at First National.

Is that really "greener" pastures
Even though you fill the bill?
'Cause nothing comes from here to there
'Till it comes from TV's till.

Tell us it ain't so, Allen,
Say it's just a gag instead
And that for those TV luncheons
More great plans are just ahead.

But if you say that it is so
Then we hope that this thought brings
A kind farewell...tune in again....
A summary of by-gone things.

"The moving finger writes; and having writ, moves on..."

But any way you look at television, it has made a difference in our lives...taking its place along with radio, newspapers, magazines and the other forms of communication — man's gift to man. Climaxing that unforgettable summer night in 1969 when mankind communicated the farthest and the fastest in its history, taking only one single second to send a television picture over two hundred thousand miles from the moon to the earth. And proving to be more than a William Butler Yeats character once observed: "the dreams the drowsy gods breathe on the burnished mirror of the world."

Television, and radio, read like a legend in every way with the cast of characters behind the scenes, some of whom you have met here. And the cast of characters in the scenes, some of whom you will never forget. Brought into our homes and hearts and hopes.

Looking back at all these years in this most glorious profession of the communication arts, the performing arts, the creative arts — the words of Omar Khayyam sum it up best in the Rubaiyat:

"The Moving Finger writes; and, having writ,
Moves on: nor all your Piety nor Wit
Shall lure it back to cancel half a Line
Nor all your Tears wash out a Word of it."

TAKE ONE MORE BOW—You know them! You name them!

344

346

INDEX

Williams, Billy Quartet, 37
Williams, Carol, 231
Williams, William B., 183
Williams, Hank, Sr., 294, 349
Williams, Andy, 6, 12
Willer, Stan, 81, 83, 85, 89
Wizzard of Oz, 351
Wilson, Ron, 72
Wilson, Lee, 150
WJAR, Providence, 16
WKY, Oklahoma City, 15
WKRC Radio & TV, 16, 28, 199, 202
WLW Radio, 16, 36, 43, etc.
WLW-T, 7, 16, 47, 49, etc.
WLW-I, 213
WLW-A, 213
WLW-C, 212
WLW-D, 216
WLS, Chicago, 164
Wood, Mary, 157, 158
WRR, Dallas, 15
World's Fair, 1939, 1, 25
Wright, Ruby, 154, 155
WLWJ, Detroit, 15, 37
Wynn, Ed, 337, 346

Y

Young & Rubicam Adv. Agency, 75, 100

Z

Zink, Larry, 212-217
Ziv, Frederic, 119, 131
Zworykin, Vladimir, 7, 10
Ziegfeld, Florence, 322